THE FAITH
of
SECULAR JEWS

THE LIBRARY OF JUDAIC LEARNING

EDITED BY

JACOB NEUSNER

University Professor
Professor of Religious Studies
The Ungerleider Distinguished Scholar of Judaic Studies

BROWN UNIVERSITY

THE FAITH
of
SECULAR JEWS

Edited with an Introduction

by

SAUL L. GOODMAN

KTAV PUBLISHING HOUSE, INC.
New York
1976

Library of Congress Cataloging in Publication Data
Main entry under title:
The Faith of secular Jews.
  (The Library of Judaic learning)
  Bibliography: p.
  Includes index.
  1. Judaism—20th century—Addresses, essays, lectures.
2. Judaism—United States—Addresses, essays, lectures.
3. Haskalah—United States—Addresses, essays, lectures.
I. Goodman, Saul Lederman
BM565.F34   296.3   76-39982
ISBN 0-87068-489-2

MANUFACTURED IN THE UNITED STATES OF AMERICA

TABLE OF CONTENTS

The preparation of this book was made possible by a grant from the National Foundation for Jewish Culture, New York, N.Y.

To my son

Jacob Eli

ACKNOWLEDGMENTS

The editor thanks the following publishers for permission to reprint: YIVO Institute for Jewish Research, for the excerpt from *Peretz,* translated and edited by Sol Liptzin (New York, 1947); Jewish Frontier Association, for the excerpts from *The Inner Eye,* by Hayim Greenberg, edited by Shlomo Katz (New York, 1964); the Jewish Publication Society of America, for the excerpts from *Nationalism and History,* by Simon Dubnow, edited by Koppel S. Pinson (Philadelphia, 1958), and the excerpt from *Selected Essays of Ahad Ha-Am,* translated by Leon Simon; Congress for Jewish Culture, for the excerpt from *H. Leivick: Essays* (New York, 1963); *Congress Bi-Weekly,* for the excerpt from *The Long Way Round* by Maurice Samuel, June 14, 1954; Bloch Publishing Company, for the excerpts from *Judaism at Bay* and *Of Them Which Say They Are Jews* by Horace M. Kallen; Dr. William Charney and Elizabeth Shub for the excerpt from their father's *Israel: Folk un Land,* by Sh. Niger (Chicago, 1952). MacMillan Publishing Co. for excerpts from: A Dreamer's Journey by Morris Raphael Cohen, The Free Press, Glencoe, Ill. 1949; Europa Verlag, A. G. Zurich for: Jewish Ideals, and: Is There a Jewish World-Outlook by Albert Einstein; "Midstream", March, 1972, for Maurice Samuel: My Three Mother-Tongues.

PREFACE

It is usually taken for granted that the American Jewish community comprises but three denominations: Orthodox, Conservative, and Reform. Many people are hardly aware that there exists a fourth current—the Secularists, or Humanists—which refuses to dry up. This intellectual current may be relevant for a considerable number of the Jewish community.

Many American Jews, especially of the younger generation, are ignorant of this current, and because they cannot accept normative Judaism in its three variations, become alienated from their heritage and lose their moorings. For this reason I felt that Jewish secularism, in all its nuances—a lineal descendant of the Haskalah (Jewish Enlightenment)—should be brought to their attention.

In the introduction highlighting the evolution and the problems of Jewish secularism, I have tried to place it in historical perspective, not as an aberration but as integral to the development of Jewish thought and culture. As illustrations of the diverse approaches to Jewishness on the part of Secularists, I have included writings of various secularist thinkers—Yiddishists and Hebraists, Zionists and Diaspora Survivalists—both European and American, all of whom are instructive and pertinent for our perplexed generation. For each I have also provided a brief biography, with one for myself at the publisher's request.

I acknowledge with gratitude my indebtedness to Dr. Percy Matenko for a number of translations from Yiddish, and for his advice and help in obtaining permission to reprint some material; to the philologist and educator Yudel Mark, who goaded and encouraged me and offered many suggestions; to Dr. Meir Ben-Horin for his constructive suggestions, and to Dr. Judah Shapiro for his encouragement.

Finally, my appreciation and thanks to my wife, Sarah, who has helped with the translations, with many excellent suggestions, and with the typing.

S. L. G.

I

The Faith of Secular Jews

INTRODUCTION

The Origin of Secular Jewishness

In trying to assess Jewish secularism in America and to evaluate its relevance for our generation, we must bear in mind that Jewish secularism, like Judaism and Jewish nationalism, is a complex phenomenon that has undergone many changes in the course of its development as a result of the vicissitudes in the non-Jewish environment and in internal Jewish life.

The roots of Jewish secularism are to be found in the beginning of Jewish history, starting with the ancient kings of Israel and Judah, with the socio-ethical ideals of the Prophets, and continuing with the philosophical disputations of the creators of the Talmud,[1] and with the Spanish, Dutch, German, and East European cultural movements in Jewish history. We may refer to Philo, Maimonides, the Ibn Ezras, Elijah Levita (1469–1549), Uriel DaCosta (1585–1640), Solomon Maimon (1753–1800), and their followers, who even before the Haskalah (Jewish Enlightenment) tried to bring Jewish culture and world culture closer to each other.[2]

Until the seventeenth century Jews maintained cultural contacts with other nations.

> It was Jewish and Arabian mediation that conveyed to the Occidental world that stream of ancient tradition which led to the flourishing of scholasticism and, later on, to the awakening of the early Renaissance. The circles of Jewish culture had reflected the general movement of their times, Arabic philosophy, the transmission of natural science, medieval Aristotelianism, Neo-Platonism, scholasticism, and Renaissance.[3]

All these influences were adopted into the core of Jewish culture and fused into a dynamic force, not to negate Jewish traditions, but rather to bring into the Jewish world the most worthwhile and prevalent elements of world culture. By the beginning of the seventeenth century, however, this free cultural current manifested symptoms of stagnation; there was an increase of conservatism and narrow-mindedness; the secular ingredients in Jewish culture became inert—until the Haskalah.

3

The Rebirth of Secular Jewishness at the Time of the Haskalah

Jewish secularism, then, has been a central motif in Jewish history from its beginnings. But during the period of the Jewish Enlightenment, secular Jewishness was *reborn,* together with the modern Hebrew and Yiddish literatures and with Jewish nationalism and socialism in their various shadings.[4]

The Jewish Enlightenment in Western Europe, which was inaugurated in the middle of the eighteenth century—about a hundred years earlier than in Eastern Europe—culminated in the disintegration of Jewish culture, with the relinquishment of the Yiddish language and way of life, and in assimilation with non-Jewish culture. The Haskalah in Eastern Europe, on the other hand, produced a rich, vibrant, authentic Jewish culture, with indigenous ideologies, movements, and literary creativity.

This is not the place to analyze the causes of the contrasting results of the Eastern and the Western Haskalah. For the Jews in Germany it was logical to repudiate separatism and seclusion and publicly acknowledge that they were not a distinct people but a purely religious community. For nationalism, which was later to become such a mighty factor in the social and political life of Europe, was then still in its infancy. Jews therefore readily acquiesced in the doctrine that they were members of a religious group, not only because they were eager for Emancipation—and assimilation was a precondition for Emancipation—but also because of their conviction. In the prevalent notion of man as citizen of the world, or citizen of a particular country, the Jew thought he could fit into either category and thus rid himself of the dilemma: Jews as a nation or Jews as human beings.

In Eastern Europe, on the other hand, where Jews formed concentrated settlements and led an isolated and intensive life of their own, Misnagdim and Hasidim were powerful voices for traditional Judaism. Russia and Poland were hardly touched by industrialism, and their despotic regimes would not permit any free thought to emerge. Aside from these main obstacles to assimilation, Russia and Austria, the two countries with large Jewish populations, were multinational states, where oppressed minorities strove to establish an autonomous national life. These minority populations, in order to strengthen their position, insisted that the Jews in their midst be counted as their own nationals. In such a densely charged nationalistic atmosphere, Jews were compelled to proclaim themselves a separate nationality. Because of all these factors there occurred a major crisis in the 1870s, which culminated, at the beginning of the eighties, in the horrors of the pogroms that swept over the Jewish communities in Russia.[5]

But this turn from cosmopolitanism toward Jewish nationalism affected only the second generation of the Jewish Maskilim (Enlighteners). With the exception of the Galician group of Maskilim, the first generation in the Jewish Enlightenment in Eastern Europe aimed at Russification and assimilation. Notwithstanding their initial assimilationist program, the pioneers of the Jewish Enlightenment in Russia prepared the ground for Jewish secularism, which sprouted forth in various manifestations and shadings. In the field of Jewish education the Maskilim laid the foundation for the modern Jewish school with its secular curriculum. They tried to secularize, to modernize the Jewish education of their day in the spirit of liberalism and Europeanism.[6] Thus, I. B. Levinsohn (1788–1860), the literary father of the Haskalah in Russia, and his disciples attempted to reconstruct the Jewish school system to include religion and secular subjects, science and languages.[7]

The Haskalah also gave impetus to another aspect of Jewish secularism. As the noted philologist and literary critic Nokhum Shtif (Baal Dimyon) has pointed out, the Jewish Enlightenment freed the individual from his subjugation to the group, and stirred him to fight for his rights as an individual. "The Jewish community held itself responsible for the individual and considered itself the guardian of the individual. . . . The awakened individual tore himself loose from the group which smothered and stifled each and everyone." [8] When, in the first stages of the Enlightenment, the control of the group was loosened, the individual became attracted to the great world beyond the ghetto. He felt that there should be no barrier between Jew and non-Jew, between one nation and another. Moreover, the new world-outlook of the Haskalah emphasized the affairs of *this world,* and created an atmosphere for literature as an esthetic experience, not only as edification. "Jewish literature became the fulcrum of ideas, and an object of adoration on the part of the masses. . . . For it was the only secular and modern asset that we possessed in Yiddish." [9]

The first generation of the Maskilim secularized Jewish life and thought, and when the opportune moment arrived—at the end of the nineteenth century—the new generation of Maskilim only altered the emphasis, the direction, and the methods; it built the secular structure upon the foundation which had been laid by the pioneer generation.

The aspiration to blend secularity and religious Jewishness which was characteristic of the first period of the Haskalah movement, was superseded during the second period by the struggle to create a synthesis of secularity and national Jewishness. There was no more a question, as there had been formerly, of education for the sake of the individual alone. The ideal was now *people's* education, *national* education. One shed the early Haskalah illusion that the survival of a people can be assured by the enlightenment of individuals; one realized, on the contrary, that the individual must go to the historic treasures of the people. The individual Jew was now to seek for personal salvation in the salvation of the group, and not the other way around—the group through the emancipation of the individual.[10]

This crisis in the ideology and psychology of Jewish intellectuals at the end of the nineteenth century was, as is now commonly recognized, the result of a series of factors and processes—economic, intellectual, political—external and internal—that matured in the Russian-Jewish life of that period, and culminated in Zionism, in Diaspora Nationalism (Dubnowism), and in several varieties of Jewish socialism.

We are not concerned here with the causes which led to the disillusionment with Emancipation and assimilation as a solution to the Jewish problem. But we should emphasize that the ideological crisis of the Jewish intelligentsia could be observed *before* the pogroms of 1881–82, and that a segment of the Jewish intelligentsia yearned to link its fate with the Jewish masses in order to serve them; it was a sort of Jewish populist movement similar to the Russian "Narodniki." This resulted from the economic depression in Russia, from the rise of anti-Semitism in Western Europe, from the Russian pogroms, and even more from the attitude of the educated class of Russian society. Jewish socialists, who had accepted the proposition that the Jews were not a nationality, now suddenly realized that Russian society considered the Jews a separate nation, and what is much worse, that some of the Russian revolutionaries sympathized with the perpetrators of the pogroms.[11]

The Transplantation of Secular Jewishness to America

Peretz Smolenskin was among the very first harbingers of the new state of mind. As early as 1872 he published in his magazine *Hashachar* ("Dawn") the famous editorial "The Eternal People," wherein he criticized the "emancipated" Western European Jewish assimilationists. In 1882 Nachum Sokolov and Leon Pinsker, in the brochures *Eternal Hatred of the Eternal People* and *Auto-Emancipation,* gave dramatic expression to the new turning point for Jewish intellectuals. It was during this time that the great debate among Russian Jews began to shape up: Emigration —to America or Eretz-Israel? As a result of this debate two vanguards were formed: the "Bilu"—the vanguard of Zionism—and "Am Olam," —the vanguard of American Jewish radicalism—both of them disillusioned with Russia. In addition to their divergence of opinion about the country of destination, there was a basic difference in their goals; the leaders of Am Olam were concerned mainly with the improvement of the Jewish socioeconomic position, while the Bilu emphasized national cultural matters. That is why Jewish radicals in America remained, for a long time, Russianized intellectuals, as if they had been living in Eastern Europe.[12]

As late as 1890, the beginning of the Russian "pre-Bund" and "pre-Zionism" period, the Jewish radical newspaper in New York, *Arbeiter Zeitung,* published a declaration regarding a forthcoming conference to organize a federation of Jewish workers in the United States, wherein we read:

> We have no Jewish problem in America. The only Jewish question that we recognize is the question of how to prevent such "Jewish problems" from arising; and only because we alone, the Yiddish-speaking citizens, can influence Jewish immigrants, only because we speak their language and are familiar with their life, are we creating this special Jewish body.[13]

Parallel to the main current of cosmopolitanism among Jewish radicals in America, we discern, as early as 1888, the beginning of another current, directed toward blending nationalism and socialism. The *New Yorker Yiddishe Folkszeitung,* which appeared only during the two years of 1888–89, was the first sign of the arrival of ethnic Jewishness in America. Outlining its program, the newspaper promised to devote its columns to the interests of the Jewish workers in America and in the rest of the world, to the Jewish problem as it related to world culture, and to the highlights of Jewish history[14]—Jewishness stressed for the first time among radical Jews in America.

This nationalist current broadened and deepened at the end of the nineties both in Russia and America. In the old country, where Zionism and Jewish socialism assumed a mass character, the Zionists began establishing the modern school (Cheder-Mesukan), which, according to the historian Simon Dubnow, represented the first attempt to secularize Jewish education. Ahad Ha'Am then came out in support of secularization and declared that "the goal of the Jewish school should be to educate, in the student, both the human being and the Jew as an entity, because they are inseparable."[15] Similarly, the socialist movement, the more it penetrated the Jewish masses, the more it reckoned with their cultural needs, and gradually, Yiddish, the language spoken by the people, became a value for its own sake, not only a means of propaganda. Thus the ground was prepared for the program of Jewish autonomy by the Bund and for the Czernowitz Conference[16] in the first decade of the twentieth century—two manifestations of a crystallized concept of secularity.

In the old country, Ahad Ha'Am, the exponent of Spiritual Zionism, and Simon Dubnow, the exponent of Spiritual Nationalism, were the theoreticians of secular Jewishness. In the United States where the main body of secularists was recruited from among Socialists and Folkists, we find that Dr. Chaim Zhitlowsky and Simon Dubnow were the most influential formulators of Jewish secularist thought. Due to his articles and correspondence, which appeared in American newspapers and magazines even before he had arrived in the United States in 1904, Zhitlowsky's influence was enormous. From 1904 on, living mainly in America, Zhitlowsky became the mentor and recognized leader of the secularists. It was he who gave a precise formulation of Jewish secularism.

Simon Dubnow also exerted a significant influence over the radical element in the American Jewish community. Most of the immigrants after 1905 among the younger, national-minded Jews—teachers, writers, intellectuals—had read Dubnow's writings; they were people of broader outlook and more sophisticated ideas than the earlier immigrants. Following are the main tenets of the secularist ideologies of Zhitlowsky and Dubnow.

Stages of Jewish Secularism in America

Dr. Chaim Zhitlowsky (1865–1943)—notwithstanding the inconsistencies in his world-view, and his tendency to simplify complex matters and to build ideological constructs foreign to the environment which they aim at modifying—was undoubtedly the ideologue of two generations of Jewish radicals, whom he dissuaded from cosmopolitanism (assimilationism) and turned toward a humanist Jewishness adapted to liberalism and

Western culture. And if we discern today some fallacies in his philosophy, it is because we live in a completely changed world which confronts us with many new dilemmas; and it is because we stand upon his shoulders that we see farther.

The main tenet of his credo was that Jews are a nationality with a historic culture, whose central characteristic is the Yiddish language. A descendant of the Haskalah he strove to "normalize"; Jews must become like Gentiles. And as a disciple of the Russian Folk Socialists (Narodniks), who extolled the Russian peasant and saw in him the conscience of the people, Zhitlowsky advocated that Jews turn to agriculture. In accordance with the ideas of that epoch, he believed that with too many middle-class and professional groups the Jews would remain an abnormal, unproductive people. His idea was not original; it stems from the Physiocrats of the eighteenth century, and all Jewish socialist parties had adopted it in varying degrees. From this central tenet, which emphasizes the idea that the Jews constitute a nationality whose fundamental cohesive force is Yiddish and possibly their own land, flows the corollary that there is no anational man as the Jewish cosmopolitans had claimed. Genuine or progressive nationalism is not exclusive of internationalism. On the contrary, Zhitlowsky believed, true internationalism implies the brotherhood of man as well as the love and cultivation of one's native culture.

In Yiddish and Yiddish literature he perceived the center of nationality in the present period. Yiddish is, according to him, a substitute for religion, which it surpasses, for it does not thwart the free advancement of the individual. Furthermore, while religion, if imposed upon the Jews, would construct a barrier between the intellectuals and the people, Yiddish, on the other hand, would unite all segments of the people and at the same time allow the individual freedom to accept or reject any belief. And because the ethos of the people is identical with its culture, and the national language is the clearest expression of the cultural heritage,[17] Zhitlowsky argued that "the struggle for the advancement of Yiddish is the struggle for a normal, free, comprehensive, rich, and fruitful culture of the Jewish people; the struggle for its life, development, honor, and worth."[18]

Normalization, Zhitlowsky held, should apply to all phases of Jewish life, including religion. Jews should emulate the *normal* nations, where religion is not obligatory but a matter of personal choice. Otherwise the individual would be imprisoned by chains of dogma which would not permit him to live according to principles of freedom of conscience and tolerance.

An obligatory world-view would perpetuate and preserve the antagonism between the official views of the group and the freedom-loving
yearnings of the individual—an antagonism that prevailed in Jewish
history and which represents its most tragic and least admirable
aspect. An obligatory world-view would lead to regression.[19]

Zhitlowsky differentiated between two contrasting connotations of the
concept of secularism, indicating both a culture-concept pertaining to content, and the separation of church and state among non-Jews; i.e., secularism in the world at large versus secularism in internal Jewish life. He
made clear that for him secularism is not synonymous with anti-religion,
that it has two meanings: one pertaining to public life in general, and the
other regarding the educational system and cultural activities.

In public life secularism suggests that both religion and anti-religion
are private matters. In the educational system, and in general cultural activities, secularism connotes the exclusion of everything pronounced in the name of any revealed, superhuman, supernatural authority, any divinity. . . . Atheistic materialism, which is often thought
of as the essence of secularism, is only one of its variants.[20]

It is thus not out of hostility to religion that Zhitlowsky favors the secularization of Jewish life, but rather to make it possible for every Jew, believer or nonbeliever, to belong to the Jewish community. It must be left to
the choice of the individual to be religious or nonreligious. For otherwise
Jews would have to exclude the most intellectually advanced Jews of our
time, such as an Einstein, a Freud, a Brandeis, a Morris Cohen. And
Zhitlowsky maintained that the past failure to separate the two concepts of
people and religion had lost the Spinozas, the DaCostas, the Solomon
Maimons.

As an adherent of philosophical idealism, Zhitlowsky appreciated the
lasting values embodied in the Jewish religion. He did not consider Judaism a means for survival, but a permanent branch of human culture
which gives meaning to, and is a *raison d'être* for, the individual's existence. To base membership in the Jewish people upon religious affirmation is "an offence against truly pure religious faith, as a force per se." [21]
It would degrade true religion to transform it into an instrument for perpetuating Jewish existence.

Zhitlowsky refuted the socio-psychological approach to religion, which minimizes its intrinsic value and intellectual aspect, and sees it mainly as a cohesive, a means of identification with the group. This is, according to Zhitlowsky, a falsification of the true essence of religion. In line with this thinking he proposed a program leading to a "national-poetical renaissance" of the Jewish religion, whose "purified sancta should become the foundation of a free religious life for those Jews who are bound to the destiny, needs, tribulations, and yearnings of their people."[22] He therefore held that an important segment of humanity cannot be satisfied only with the ideals of truth, justice, beauty, and human dignity as they are reflected in everyday struggles; that this segment must "elevate these ideals to their apogee, which can be achieved by longing for eternity, infinity, and holiness," which comprise the essence of all religion, and are also embodied in Judaism. We should, he insisted, transmute Judaism and extract from it those ingredients which are acceptable to modern Jews, thus retaining intact "that content which may become the basis of a Jewish, humane atmosphere in which every educated, modern, thinking, and nationally aware Jew may breathe freely."[23]

In Zhitlowsky's opinion, a secular Jew may celebrate most Jewish holidays, resting on the Sabbath; observance of the holidays should be mandatory for him. He analyzes the history, the symbols, the significance of each Jewish holiday, and reaches the conclusion that all of them contain national, lofty moments which render them worthy of celebration by secular Jews. "Humanity as a whole," he proclaims, "ought to celebrate the Jewish Passover; should Jews forget it?"[24]

The Jew must be left with the choice to reject or to accept Judaism,

> for we have not any religious "do's" or "don'ts"; we are permitted everything, even to be saddened on the 9th day of Ab (when the Temple in Jerusalem was destroyed), to fast on Yom Kippur, to light candles in honor of the Sabbath, and even "worse" things, if we but discern in them a "national-poetic" content, a human thought, whose logic and justice do not disconcert us.[25]

In the year 1909, when Zhitlowsky expressed these sentiments, American Jewish radicals were still dominated by cosmopolitans (i.e., assimilationists) of all sorts, and in that ideological climate Zhitlowsky's "heresy"—urging Jewish agnostics and atheists to identify themselves, in a sense, with religious Jews—came as a breath of fresh air. It took many years before this idea was put into practice.

In the middle of the 1930s, when immigration from Eastern Europe ceased; when Jews had struck deeper roots in American soil; when the impact of America on Jewish life became evident; when the Jewish community in Eastern Europe sensed with foreboding the coming Nazi onslaught—then many American Jewish secularists, disciples of Zhitlowsky, became disillusioned with their mentor's teachings. Numerous questions were heard, questions that stemmed from the experience of three decades with modern Jewish education. Educators realized that the ideologue of Jewish secularism had built an imposing theoretical structure upon a flimsy foundation. Could the Yiddish language be relied on as the best means of assuring survival? And if linguistic secularism ceased to be the invulnerable strategic base of the Jewish group in America, should it not erect new defense lines to assure the cultural survival of the group? At a time when the main reservoir of their people in Europe was threatened with extinction, should they not take a fresh look at the "invincible rock" —the Jewish religion? A new day of *heshbon hanefesh* ("soul-searching") dawned upon many Jewish secularists.

Zhitlowsky, the old, ardent fighter on behalf of Yiddishism and secularism, no longer possessed his early theorizing vigor, and he had, in addition, become alienated from many of his disciples. But even then, in 1941, two years before he died, he asked:

> Who gave the Neo-clericalists the right to say that secularism is the antithesis of religion? Secularism is not the opposite of religious faith and living; it is the antithesis of clericalism, of actual or spiritual compulsion. . . . In secularism we should differentiate between two altogether different contents. First, external secularity as a political principle that must be embodied in every type of Jewish autonomy or public activity. Second, an internal secularity . . . which is present in the intimate sphere of our spiritual life. . . . The crisis which Jewish secularism is now undergoing is a turning point in the intimate sphere that is bound up with the life of the Jewish individual, and with his linkage to the Jewish group.[26]

One may infer that Zhitlowsky realized that the altered environment and the new spiritual climate warranted a reexamination of his theoretical structure. But he died before he accomplished this task. Others worked to rebuild or demolish the secularist ideology which he had devised with brilliance, and with a masterly hand.

Dubnow's Conception of Jewish Secularism

While Zhitlowsky had formulated his theory of progressive Jewish nationalism from the vantage point of socialism, Simon Dubnow's (1860–1941) philosophy of Jewish existence grew directly out of his historical studies, and what he had to say about the problem of Jewish survival was shaped by his evolutionist approach as a historian. His Cultural Nationlism, or Autonomism, was developed in a series of *Letters on the Old and New Judaism,* which was published in Russia—in book-form—in 1907.

There were, Dubnow believed, three stages in the growth of nationality —race, territory (which involved political sovereignty), and culture. The progress of a people could be measured by the degree to which it depended for survival on each of these elements. Thus, a people held together mainly by race was at the lowest stage of national development; a people held together mainly by territory was at the intermediate stage; and a people held together by culture—like the Jews of the Diaspora—was

> the very archetype of a nation, a nation in the purest and loftiest sense. . . . And the Jewish people could reach this apex because of a combination of factors that molded the Jewish nation so that the physical and the materio-cultural elements were compounded with a greater proportion of the spiritual-cultural ingredients than among other nations. The intensiveness of the spiritual factors has here always compensated for the diminution of the political factors, as, for instance, the lack of sight with the blind is compensated for by the proportional intensification of the sense of touch or hearing.[27]

Dubnow maintained that the cohesive factor which is decisive in the people's destiny is not the political power, but rather its spiritual strength, which "is the essence of its culture and the internal cementing of its members."[28]

By spirit Dubnow did not mean religion alone; his conception of the spiritual included attitudes, values, and folkways. Thus he refused to grant that religion was responsible for the survival of the Jews in the Diaspora. What had kept them together, he believed, was a collective will to live— a will nourished by a common historical destiny.

> We are welded together by our glorious past. We are encircled by a mighty chain of similar historical impressions suffered by our ances-

tors, century after century pressing in upon the Jewish soul, and leaving behind a substantial deposit. . . . The Jewish national idea is based chiefly upon the historical consciousness. What is the power that welds us into a compact organism? Religion and race do not account for our survival, because the agnostics are in the front ranks of all our national movements. The"something" that holds us together is the common historical destiny of all the scattered parts of the Jewish nation.[29]

The most important aspect of Dubnow's nationalist theory lies in the dichotomy that he sees between *land* on the one hand and *people,* or nationality, on the other. This distinction is the cornerstone of his philosophy of Jewish national existence, and nationalism, he held, is actually *collective individualism.* In the development of a nation, the elements of race and land play a smaller part than the cultural historical components. As proof of this thesis he cites the Jewish spiritual nation, which has survived without a land of its own for almost two thousand years. In the ancient victory of the Pharisees over the Sadducees, Dubnow saw the triumph of spiritual and cultural nationalism over political and military nationalism— from which he concluded that the Jewish nation was essentially defined by spirit rather than territory even before it was driven into exile and scattered over the face of the earth.

It was a struggle about the very essence of the nation, about whether the Jewish people should be . . . an average, or a unique member of the international family of nations. . . . The nation is the kernel, and the land is but the shell; the shell may be broken but the kernel remains intact, and if the seed is a healthy one the nation will always be able to preserve its autonomy against the heteronomy of the alien surroundings, and will be able to serve as a standard for all the nations as a model of spiritual steadfastness.[30]

The essential characteristic of Jewish nationalism is therefore, according to Dubnow, its spirituality; and bravery on behalf of cultural and social progress is the central motive in Dubnow's conception of Jewish nationalism. He distinguishes between two varieties of nationalism, an imperialist-despotic one and a progressive-humanitarian one, but as a Jew, Dubnow holds, "I utter the word *national* with pride and conviction because I know that my people, due to the special conditions of its life in the Diaspora, cannot strive anywhere to primacy or to dominance. My nationalism can be only purely individualistic and therefore completely ethical."[31] He points out the confusion that the early Marxian Socialists brought about by using synonymously the concepts of internationalism and cosmopolitanism. Now, however, they have realized their error and know that true internationalism is compatible with cultural nationalism. The fighters for social emancipation should join hands with the fighters for national freedom. Dubnow concludes his third *Letter* exclaiming, "It is fitting and proper for the descendants of the Prophets to raise aloft the banner of the pure national ideal which combines the visions of the Prophets of truth and justice and the lofty dream of a united humanity."[32]

As a corollary to these basic tenets, Dubnow develops his attitude to the Jewish religion. As a cultural evolutionist he holds that "Judaism was formed by the social conditions of the people, and not vice versa."[33] Jewishness is for him the whole gamut of Jewish culture, of which religion is but one aspect, although a very important one—Jewish nationalism in its totality is a cultural-historical entity, which includes, beside religion, other ethical, social, and philosophical elements. He therefore feels that Jewish nationalism may embrace in its orbit all Jews, religious as well as secular.

In accordance with this philosophy, Dubnow believed that the tragedy of Spinoza would have been avoided if, in the seventeenth century, Sephardic Jewry had adopted the concept of Jewish secularism. Spinoza would have remained a member of the Jewish community if, during the "fatal unfolding of Jewish history, the national idea had not been fused with the religious idea to such a degree that an exit from the religious community was identical with an exit from the national collectivity. Three centuries since Spinoza's birth had to elapse before the generation of secularist Jews was able to postulate that one may remain a member of the Jewish nationality although he is completely agnostic in religion."[34]

In spite of that, Dubnow insists that a Jew cannot abandon the religion of Judaism and still remain a Jew.

> In our striving toward secularism, toward the separation of the national idea from religion, we aim only to negate the *supremacy* of religion, but we do not wish to eliminate it altogether from the people's cultural treasures. When we wish to preserve Judaism as a cultural historical type of nation, we should remember that Judaism is one of the integral foundations of national culture, and anyone who seeks to destroy it undermines the very basis of national existence.

> Between us and the Orthodox Jew there is only this difference: they
> recognize a Judaism whose forms are permanent, while we believe
> in an evolutionary Judaism that takes on new and discards old forms,
> and that keeps adjusting itself constantly to new cultral conditions.
> . . . To forsake Judaism by acceptance of the Christian religion means
> exit from the Jewish people.[35]

The concept of the Jewish People (*Klal Isroel*) is a central doctrine in
Dubnow's theoretical structure.

> When secularized in the spirit of our time, the Jewish national idea
> signifies that all politically scattered parts of Jewry represent a homo-
> geneous cultural-historical world-people, which should together with
> other national minorities in the multi-national states always protect
> its national rights—autonomy of the community, of the school, and
> of the language. That which we safeguarded throughout the centuries
> in the garb of religion, should now be separated from the external
> form, and should come forward in its true physiognomy.[36]

This implies that the center of Jewish autonomy, which once resided in
the synagogue, should now be replaced by the all-encompassing, secular,
democratic Kehillah comprising social, educational, political, religious, and
other functions. The collective will of the Jewish people to live expressed
itself, in all the lands of the Diaspora, concretely in the creation of an
autonomous community which was separated from the general community
by the spiritual "fences" of religion, ethics, and folkways; in Eastern Europe
Jews were able to achieve self-government through the Kehillah.

The central position which autonomism occupies in Dubnow's thought
is explicitly stated in his introduction to *Pincas Hamedinah:*

> The secret of Jewish survival is dependent on the positive command
> of the ancient prophecy; "The sceptre shall not depart from Judah."
> In each country our people builds a miniature state. Our enemies in
> all generations cry out: "There is a certain people scattered abroad,
> and dispersed among the nations, in all the lands of your kingdom,
> and their laws are diverse from those of every other nation." But
> the Congregation of Israel goes on in its historical path, and says:
> An internal autonomous group within an external political group,
> and the nature of things sanctions it.[37]

In common with all the other great nineteenth-century historians, Dubnow freely applied the central currents of contemporary thought to the writing of history. From Comte and Spencer he learned to think of history as moving progressively along a line of inevitable evolutionary development (though, being a student of *Jewish* history, he was bound to become more cautious in his optimism than his mentors). From Ernest Renan he adopted the idea of nationality as determined by subjective will and national awareness, rather than by the external characteristics of state, territory, and language. And from Hegel he borrowed the dialectic (while taking care to distinguish his "naturalistic" use of the evolutionary triad of thesis-antithesis-synthesis from Hegel's). In Dubnow's scheme of Jewish historical development, the thesis is represented by the Orthodox Jewish masses, the antithesis by the assimilationists, and the synthesis by the new Jewish intelligentsia—presumably men like himself and Ahad Ha'Am— who harmoniously combined ancestral and European culture.

This intelligentsia, he believed, would emerge as the guiding class of Jewry in the twentieth century, and would create a new mode of autonomous Jewish life. Just as Jewish life once revolved around the synagogue, so in the twentieth century it would be centered in an all-embracing secular Kehillah, democratically organized and responsible for educational, religious, and social functions. Every Jew would be a member of this Kehillah.

On the question of language, Dubnow was a pluralist. He encouraged the emerging Yiddish literature and believed that Yiddish, Hebrew, and Russian should be instruments of the autonomous Jewish Kehillah. He considered that Zhitlowsky had overrated the nationalizing value of Yiddish In his polemics against Zhitlowsky he said:

> The Yiddish language is here [in Zhitlowsky's national program] the only national cultural value that our people has created in its history, and which may guarantee its survival in the future. But this is only a legacy of several centuries, and what shall we do with our millennial heritage? About one third of our people does not speak Yiddish today, and several generations later another third may disregard it (especially in America); should we abandon them to complete assimilation? History shows us that had the Jewish people rested only on language no trace of it would have remained by now. For even in ancient Judea, and in the Levant, the people could not resist linguistic assimilation, not only in its daily living, but even in a great part of its literary creativity. The future of a people must be built upon all

pillars of its cultural autonomy, and not solely upon one of them—
one which has endured only for a few centuries, and which may,
within a few hundred years, lose its power of sustenance. Yiddish is
precious to us, and we must utilize it as a means of uniting the greater
half of our people in the coming generations. But to erect our entire
national culture upon "Yiddishism" means to cast off from us immediately millions of Jews who do not speak this language, and to
prepare millions of others for bankruptcy at a later time.[38]

One may sum up Dubnow's conception of Jewish secularism thus: Jews
represent a nationality that has reached the apex in its development; it is
the most *historical people,* which has created cultural values that have put
their stamp upon all of humanity.[39] The religious and ethnic components
in Judaism have been so strongly merged that they seem identical, but
actually "this is the result of the growth of the national organism and of
its adjustment to unusual, exceptional historical conditions." [40] It is apparent
to Dubnow that the two ingredients, the religious and the ethnic, are not
indissoluble, and that one may be considered a rooted Jew without accepting the religious component of the Jewish heritage, for "every type of Jew
may select from our culture whatever element or current is more pertinent
to him."[41]

Thus, while the socialist ideologue of secularism—Zhitlowsky—maintains that the Jewish religion may, in our day, be superseded by the Yiddish language, the historian—Dubnow—knows that language alone is insufficient as a guarantee against cultural disintegration; the *total historical
culture* of the people should be accepted, for Jewishness is more than religion. Religion must not dominate Jewish community life, but neither
should it be excluded from the people's storehouse. All kinds of Jews,
religious and nonreligious, are of equal worth, but as soon as a Jew for-
mally gives up his religion and becomes a Christian or a Moslem, he automatically excludes himself from the Jewish people. To Zhitlowsky, who
stressed *normalization* as the chief goal of his program for Jews, the
"Jewish Problem" did not differ much from the Czech or the Polish problem. Dubnow, on the other hand, is convinced that the intricate Jewish
dilemmas cannot be resolved by general prescriptions. The history of the
Jewish people, and the social conditions under which it lived, he believed,
have produced a unique group, one that is supernormal rather than sub-
normal.

Dubnow's concept of Jewish secularism and Zhitlowsky's variant have been vital forces in shaping the Jewish secular milieu and its institutions. In addition, the novelist and essayist Y. L. Peretz, the poet and thinker Abraham Liessin, and many others have played an important part in molding modern Jewish culture. Each contributed his share and nuance to the manifold of Jewish secular culture in America.

The Ideological Crisis in the Thirties and the Religious Framework

On the eve of the Second World War—when it became apparent that the gains which the Emancipation had brought to European Jewry were about to disappear, when many sensed that the Dark Ages were returning for European Jews, when the darkest recesses of human nature opened up —it seemed that the pillars of Jewish secular culture were about to collapse. In the American Yiddish press, modern, sophisticated Jewish poets gave expression to the temper of the times: for example, a poem by Jacob Glatstein, "Good Night World; Back to the Ghetto," was not meant as a program of action, but it did reflect a mood.

Many Jews became disillusioned with their faith in progress and humanity, and sought comfort in the ancestral creed. The Jewish historian A. Tcherikover outlined in bold strokes the mood of that period:

> The nationalist movement could never cope with the dominant role that religion has played in our history, and even its best and most sophisticated representatives did not succeed in formulating an ideology of group survival based solely upon the principles of rationalistic nationalism, and secularity. Among Jews, nationalistic emotions and religion are inseparably interwoven. . . . Now, at a time of soul-searching, the atavistic religious emotions have surged forth from the depths and seek an outlet, and demand their rights. . . . We realize that the call to return to the past is futile. The old springs of religious faith are quite dried up. . . . But neither can we completely free ourselves . . . from envy of the harmonious religious world of past generations. . . . It is the tragedy of a generation that is wrestling with itself, struggling between modernism and its heritage.[42]

There were also some internal Jewish-American factors that sharpened the crisis in Jewish secularism. The growth of the American-born Jewish population manifested convincingly that the Yiddish language could not be relied upon to remain for long the cohesive force uniting the Jewish community in America. Most of the Jewish children attending Yiddish schools no longer knew the language. Many teachers and school-workers had lost their old faith in the Yiddish language and literature as means for a meaningful Jewish continuity in America. It became evident that the Jewish home of the second generation was devoid of Jewish content: the Sabbath and the Jewish holidays were rarely celebrated or observed. The spiritual "capital" which had been brought over from the old country was gradually being squandered, and little was produced here. For how long, Jewish secularists asked, will we be able to subsist on this imported cultural "capital"?

In addition to these altered factors within the Jewish community, the general climate of opinion in America was radically different from what it had been in the twenties. Modern man—including Jewish secularists— became disillusioned with technical, material progress. It did not satisfy his hunger for genuine loftiness; it did not give him a *raison d'être;* it left a void in place of the old faith that had promised immortality, permanence, and tranquility. Modern man has been deeply affected by what Walter Lippmann called the acids of modernity. He resists faith, but he cannot live without it. His soul is corroded by skepticism and by an ethical relativism which undermines all metaphysical and religious certainties, and yet he cannot give up the search for absolutes.

Many disenchanted Jewish intellectuals yearned for anchorage in the permanent soil in which generations before them had found roots and inner security. But the modern Jew, and the non-Jew, while they yearn for the "lost paradise" of their ancestors, find the religious faith of the past no longer tenable.

This background gave rise to a reevaluation of Jewish secularism, and an attempt to "Americanize" it was undertaken by several prominent Jewish scholars and writers. And just as Zhitlowsky's and Dubnow's thought was colored by the European thinkers of the nineteenth century, so revisions during and after the Second World War aimed to modify Jewish secularism in accordance with the current trends in American social science, to formulate a Jewish rationale consistent with the pragmatic psychological or sociological theories which were prevalent in America at that time.

Accepting the psychological approach to religion—that the individual's psychic experience is the essence of religion—the psychologist Leibush Lehrer, at the end of the thirties, propounded the thesis that religion and Judaism are dissimilar, for the quintessence of general religion lies in the

private experiences of individuals, whereas Judaism is primarily a code
which regulates the lives of Jews as belonging to a collectivity. The term
Jewish religion is to Lehrer a discordant note. "Our creed (*Dath*) is a
constitution of commandments, an all-embracing system in which survival
of the people is the leading motif. It is false to designate Judaism as religion. . . . Judaism is altogether unlike any of the existing world religions.
It comprises different ends and means."⁴³

Presupposing, then, that religion and Judaism are disparate concepts,
Lehrer believes that one cannot qualify Judaism with the terms *religion*
or *secularism,* since essentially it is not a religion, and consequently it is
not necessary to secularize it. In Judaism the core is not theological but
rather legalistic, not metaphysical sanctions but sociological functions, not
whether you have faith in God but whether you are observing the sancta
(*Mitzvoth*). Which is another way of saying that the true substance of
Judaism is expressed in folkways, in observances, in culture and tradition,
in Law (*Halakha*) and conduct, not in "fear of the Lord," not in piety or
in creedal dogmas. "Judaism is primarily a folk idea, a concept of conduct."⁴⁴

According to Lehrer, the dichotomy between religion and secularism is
not applicable to Jewish life, for secularism is a negative concept, a denial
of the old Jewish patterns of living which the so-called Jewish religion has
imposed upon the Jews,⁴⁵ "unless we interpret the term secular [*weltlekh*]
not as a negation of some kind of religion, but rather as the opposite of
traditional inertia or rigid orthodoxy."⁴⁶

Lehrer's doctrine, which was promulgated during the period of the decline of East European Jewry, reflected the reaction to Zhitlowsky's "normalization." It rendered an important service by calling attention to the
fact that not all *general* concepts may automatically be applied to Jewish
phenomena; that Judaism is not identical with other religions, but is rather
a unique intricate fabric wherein many strands intersect. But when one
analyzes the implications of Lehrer's thesis, one realizes the inadequacy
and invalidity of his approach.

First, his basic conception takes for granted that while the essence of
religion lies in the psychic experience of the individual, the substance of
Judaism does not deal with the individual, nor with his psychic experience,
since Judaism, according to Lehrer, is essentially a way of life for the
collectivity. This interpretation represents, however, but one side of the
coin, and is questioned by eminent scholars of religion and Judaism. For

an intellectual approach to religion reveals that every faith is centered in a system of ideas that obliges the adherent to give his consent to some particular beliefs.

The *Oxford Universal Dictionary* defines religion as the "recognition, on the part of man, of some higher unseen power as having control of his destiny, and as being entitled to obedience, reverence and worship." This definition makes it clear that one's adherence to a religion presupposes his *recognition,* or *knowing,* or *consenting,* that there is a power above man. The *Oxford Dictionary* also defines religion as "action or conduct indicating a belief in, reverence for, and desire to please a divine ruling power." Here, too, the element of belief is included. Similarly, in *Webster's New World Dictionary* (college edition, 1955), religion is defined as "a *belief* in a divine or super-human power or powers to be obeyed and worshipped as the creator(s) and ruler(s) of the universe."

Lehrer is not unaware of Maimonides' Creed, of Albo's Dogmas (*ikkarim*), of the Karaites, of the Hasidim, Misnagdim, and Orthodox Jews, who fought each other over dogmas and over theological doctrines and beliefs—all of which deny his basic contention. But he attempts to remove all of these stumbling blocks which refute his conception of *Yiddishkeit* by explaining them away as exceptions to the rule, as anomalies. He is also misled by the vogue among the sociologists of religion that it is of no importance whether one has faith in God as long as one observes His commandments. But would it have been possible to pray, or to be an observant Jew, if behind it all there had not been a deep faith in the One? And is it not true, as is pointed out by some Jewish scholars, that even from the point of view of Jewish survival, faith in God is more important than praying?[47] For would so many Jews have been martyrs for the sake of their religion if the element of creed had constituted so insignificant an ingredient in the whole complex denoted by the term *Judaism?*

The fact that Judaism is not solely a system of observances, but also comprises central dogmas, has been pointed out by many Jewish scholars. Solomon Schechter states that, although he cannot define "the infinite called Judaism," he is certain that the "highest motives which worked throughout the history of Judaism are the strong belief that God, the God of Israel, will be the God of the whole world."[48] He then cites from the Talmud the statement that those who do not believe in Resurrection or in Revelation are heretics (*Apikorsim*), and none of them will enter the Hereafter. This is Halakha, i.e., a basic law.

Similarly Harry A. Wolfson emphasizes that religion has three aspects—

it is a way of knowldge, a way of salvation, and a way of life—and that while Judaism seeks to express itself in some concrete form of life, it is "a religion of faith . . . and a view of life."[49]

Another Jewish scholar and publicist, I. Efroikin, in discussing the current trend to regard the essence of Judaism as a way of life rather than a system of beliefs, writes:

> Without fear of God, without love of God, there are no precepts or commandments, and therefore no way of life. And if a Jewish way of life could be preserved for thousands of years in an alien and hostile world, it was due only to the fact that it was sanctified by faith. You will therefore not find a single Jewish sage who would deprive Yiddishkeit of its creedal foundation. Whether this foundation is built upon thirteen dogmas, or upon six, or upon three or only upon one—upon the prophet Habakkuk's saying "and the righteous shall live by his faith"—without faith there can be no Judaism.[50]

In summary, then, if religion in general consists of a set of creedal doctrines, Judaism is no exception to that rule; it belongs to the same category as other religions, although it consists of additional elements. Second, in Judaism the universal elements are also of paramount importance. True, the people of Israel are the central axis around which the Jewish faith revolves, but "mysticism is not an esoteric plant on the soil of Judaism. . . . There was always in Judaism a certain tendency towards mysticism of one kind or another."[51] The *Zohar*, the *Duties of the Heart*, the Psalms, the Prayers— all of these and many more assuaged the hunger of the soul of the individual in the Jew, who yearned to surpass his finiteness; and the Jew's craving for redemption reflected not only his longing for *national* freedom, but in addition his longing for *universal salvation*, to bring about the Kingdom of God on earth. All of these central and peripheral motives were incorporated in historic Judaism.

Let us now examine Lehrer's doctrine that only Judaism is ethnic, whereas the religions of other nations remain neutral to the critical events in their history. Is this really so? It is correct to assert that among no other people is it as difficult as among Jews to differentiate between religion and nationality. But can one be unmindful of the role and nationalistic individualization of religion among the Irish, Italians, Czechs, or Poles?

More subtle, but no less decisive was the permeation of the new European nationalism with the religious fervor of medieval Christianity, illustrated by frequent borrowing of religious ideas and terms by leaders of oppressed nationalities. The mystic Andrew Towianski and the great poet Adam Mickiewicz saw in the Polish people a personification of the suffering Messiah, and ascribed to it an Israel-like mission of the redemption of humanity. Under Mickiewicz's influence, Mazzini, on his part, proclaimed the Italian nation to be the divinely instituted Messiah destined to overcome the dualism between Heaven and Earth, Spirit and Matter, Thought and Action.[52]

Evidently, among these nations, as among the Jews, one cannot draw a sharp line of demarcation between religion and nationalism as Lehrer does.

Most of these important points do not altogether escape Lehrer, but because of his pragmatic-functional approach, he minimizes them. Had he not overlooked the central position of *creed* in Judaism, and had he not overstressed the ethnic elements, he could not have propounded such a dualism between religion and Judaism. His psychological approach obstructed his view of the universal and the intellectual components in Judaism. Religion, then, in all its aspects, is a major ingredient in the composite of Judaism (Yiddishkeit) and secularism among Jews, reinforces the other strands in the fabric of Jewish culture; it is not a negation of Jewish tradition and continuity, but rather a synthesis which accentuates "the fusion of the religious, the ethnic, the mores, in historical Jewishness."[53]

Jewishness in a Religious Framework

The old maxim "as the Christians do, so do Jews" has been confirmed in the United States much more than in Eastern Europe, for here Jews have become more integrated into the culture, economy, and politics of the land than in any other land of the Diaspora. Every student of the American Jewish scene can perceive the impact of general American cultural and even religious fashions upon Jewish living. Conforming to the American pattern, according to historian Henry Steele Commager, the Christian religion became

> disentangled . . . from history and authority and metaphysics, and made to rest honestly upon one's own feelings, and one's indomitable optimism and trust in life. Religion came to be largely a matter of observing certain formalities and of doing good. . . . It had largely

ceased to be a fact of spiritual experience. . . . Professors of the sternest creeds temporized with sinners, and did what might be done to win them to heaven by helping them to have a good time here.[54]

In this climate of a utilitarian, institutionalized, social religion, two sociologically trained Jewish writers, Samuel Margoshes and Charles B. Sherman, expounded their thesis that American Jewish community life, including its secular-cultural ingredients, should be put into a religious framework.

This theory may be summarized as follows: In order to preserve a creative Jewish community in America, we must adjust it to the prevalent ideas of the general environment; otherwise, the group status of the Jewish community will not be sanctioned by the majority, by the American consensus of opinion. However, to win the approval of America for Jewish group survival, we must declare ourselves to be a *religious* rather than an ethnic community. But will the non-professing Jews be accepted into this "religious community"? To this question, the proponents of a "religious framework" theory reply that we should redefine religion, for "religion in general and especially the Jewish religion is . . . a very flexible concept that leaves room for various changes and interpretations, even regarding the belief in God. . . . The religious framework encompasses not only all aspects of Jewish culture, including the secular, together with Jewish folkways, but also Jewish doctrines and beliefs, which the modern Jew can conceive of and accept fully." [55] It follows from this thesis that the synagogue should become the central institution in the religious American Jewish community, but the synagogue would be much broader in scope.

Sherman argues that

> as a program of Jewish national survival, pure secularism has not struck roots among American Jews, for they are obtaining all the secularism they desire from the non-Jewish environment. . . . Except for the state of Israel, secularism can preserve Jewish identity only in a ghetto, and not in the free land of America. . . . With the exception of the Jewish communities between the two world wars, of Latvia, Estonia and Lithuania, I am not aware of any Jewish settlement that was ever organized within a nonreligious framework.[56]
> Over three thousand years of Jewish history attest to the sustaining power of Jewish faith, but we have yet to see a Jewish community survive on a purely secular foundation for a long period of time.[57]

The remedy, according to Sherman, lies in a community structure that fits the American multireligious (rather than multinational) pattern.

> The Jewish community will have to find its place in the American social pattern which excludes nationality divisions and allows for only two types of group organizations: religious and racial. Since we cannot accept a racial designation or status, we have no alternative but to function as a community within a religious framework. There is nothing in this kind of organization that is violative of the nationalist principles of the secularist Jew, since he can observe Jewish holidays and follow certain traditional practices not as religious institutions but as expressions of Jewish culture and part of Jewish folkways.[58]

It is important to bear in mind that both Margoshes and Sherman, expounding the "religious framework" viewpoint, approach Jewishness via sociology. "Jewish organized life in America is not a theological but rather a sociological problem."[59] More concisely and explicitly, Margoshes states:

> For me religion is as important . . . as the value of its social functions. If the *most sacred interests of the group are transformed into the highest sanctities of religion* [emphasis added] . . . then I am inclined to accept such a religion not only as a guarantee for the survival and continuity of the group, but also as my personal faith as a member of a religious community. . . . What I ask of religion is to give a guarantee of immortality—not of myself—but of the group with which I have linked my destiny.[60]

The italicized clause—"the most sacred interests of the group are transformed into the highest sanctities of religion"—is the cornerstone of Mordecai Kaplan's Reconstructionism. In other words, God, the Law (Torah), and the Jewish Sancta (*Mitzvoth*) are means for the survival of the people, for in accordance with this interpretation,

> a group religion is least of all a philosophy of life. Its function, primarily, is to invest with sanctity not life in general, but specific objects, persons, places, events, days, etc., and specific codes of Law, customs, and morals. Collective religions . . . being to the group what self-consciousness is to the individual, derive their *raison d'être* from their ability to further the existence of the group and to develop its spiritual potentialities.[61]

This approach to religion, originally advanced by the French sociologist Émile Durkheim, is, however, questioned by many scholars as untenable. To the degree that it is valid, it can only be taken as a criterion for *primitive religion,* in its early stages. It is wholly inadequate and implausible when applied to Prophetic or Talmudic Judaism as in terpreted by Maimonides, by the Baal Shem, by the Gaon of Vilna, or by Rabbi Kook of Jerusalem. Moreover, many secular Jews cannot accept the adjective *religious* as denoting the heightened consciousness of the group, as Kaplan and his followers insist. Not only the above-mentioned Jewish rationalists and mystics, but such general philosophers and theologians as Kierkegaard, Reinhold Niebuhr, Morris R. Cohen, and Jacques Maritain, would not accept the Kaplan-Margoshes definition of religion.

As the literary critic and thinker Shmuel Niger pointed out, secular Jews need not profess religion, because

we are Jews even though we are not religious and do not profess any faith. . . . If these Jews who form, perhaps, the majority of the American Jewish population should proclaim themselves as Americans of the Jewish faith, they would deceive themselves and the world. . . . A Jew is a historic ethico-cultural, and socio-politico-economico-psychological phenomenon. A Jew is a Jew, a Jew, a Jew. . . . And if the third generation will truly desire to remember what the second generation wanted to forget, it will remember that its Jewish identification is not a screen for Jewish theology, but the truth of Jewish history.[62]

Religion as a guarantee of Jewish group survival in America is challenged even by religionist Mordecai Kaplan.

If proof were needed that the survival of Judaism fundamentally depends on the survival of the Jewish people, we would have only to point to what has been happening to the Jewries of those countries in which their only distinctive bond of unity has been Jewish religion. In France, England, Germany, Holland, and the Scandinavian countries, the Jews have been gradually disappearing. How ineffective religion alone is in keeping itself alive is shown by the fact that even the moral and financial encouragement of government is unable to sustain it.[63]

But the adherents of Jewishness in a "religious framework" cite, in support of their thesis, the so-called religious upsurge in America during the forties, and particularly among second- and third-generation Jews. They argue that in the suburbs, where American-born Jews live, it is being amply demonstrated that only religious Jewishness is viable in this country. Here, they point out, many new temples, synagogues, and centers are springing up.[64] The theory, then, must be adjusted to practice.

Will Herberg goes even further and states that a religious framework is an all-American phenomenon. He believes that we have a national religion with three creedal variants: Protestant, Catholic, and Jewish; and that one demonstrates his loyalty to the national religion by identifying with one of the creeds: "Being a Protestant, a Catholic or a Jew is understood as the specific way, and increasingly perhaps, the only way, of being an American and locating oneself in American society. . . . Americanness today entails religious identification as Protestant, Catholic or Jew in a way and to a degree quite unprecedented in our history."[65] He even goes so far as to claim that "the same basic values and ideals, the same underlying commitment to the American Way of Life, are promoted by parochial school and public school, by Catholic, Protestant and Jew, despite the diversity of formal religious creed."[66]

Many will take sharp issue with Herberg's views. Some will question the reliability of the sources upon which his sweeping assertions are made. What is more significant is Herberg's admission that American religious life has become so secularized, and that the Christianity or Judaism one finds in church or in synagogue

> is an other-directed gospel of adjustment, sociability and comfort, designed to give one a sense of "belonging," of being at home in the society and the universe. It is thus not too much of a paradox to assert that many of the inner-directed "unbelievers" of the nineteenth century in a sense stood closer to, or at least less distant from, authentic biblical faith than do so many of the religious people of our time, whose religion comes to them as an aspect of other-directed conformism and sociability.[67]

If that is so, is it not, then, a very arbitrary assumption to designate this institutionalized "religion"—without faith, dogma, theology, or content—as religion? Is a thing of social utility to be designated as religion?

And assuming that Herberg was describing the true state of affairs in the 1950s—that there was a revival of "religion" in America—are we, then, justified in supplying a theory to validate and to interpret this reality? One may question "whether replies to questionnaires, or even the facts of life should be considered the highest authority in determining such fundamental problems as religion, culture, and similar things."[68]

Let us, however, assume for the moment, as our sociological religionists believe, that this is the right *theory* for the future; what, then, is the *practice* within the Jewish religious framework? According to the Reconstructionist Kaplan, this is the true state of affairs:

> We should not confuse increase in membership or institutional strength with a return to religion, nor the growth of parochial schools, nor the multiplication of synagogues and synagogue centers—all a manifestation of what has been termed the Jewish Edifice complex.
> . . . Despite the noise about the increase of religious schools, only a limited number of parents give their children some kind of Jewish schooling and only in rare instances does that schooling give a positive Jewish bent to their way of life. The Jewish religious schools are like subway trains always full, with people constantly getting on and getting off at every station. The number of men and women who are qualified to teach Jewish subject matter is shockingly small. And what about our gifted Jews, how many of them are affiliated with a synagogue? How many attend? Can names like Brandeis, Einstein, Hillman, Lilienthal, Oppenheimer, etc., be associated with any type of normative Judaism? . . . Do the great synagogue buildings express greatness of soul, or fatness of purse? How many Jews live in their Judaism? Ask any Orthodox or Conservative rabbi how many of their people observe, really observe, Kashrus and the Sabbath, which they profess to believe in. Ask any reform rabbi the extent to which his congregants' lives are directed by Judaism.[69]

A basic fallacy is also noticeable when we analyze the comprehensive character of Jewishness in a religious framework. This framework would encompass the total Jewish heritage: the Yiddish and Hebrew languages, and literature, culture, and other nonreligious matters. Our religion, then, does differ from Protestantism and Catholicism. An Italian Catholic is bound to Catholics of other countries only by religion, not by language or culture. Jews living in various countries, though they may vary in their attitudes to religion, are nevertheless conscious of belonging to the same people. In other words, the Jewish collectivity differs from the Protestant and Catholic churches. Why should we proclaim ourselves a purely religious group similar to Protestants or Catholics, and then reveal that our religion is inextricably bound up with ethnic historical ancestry, with secular culture, with politics, and that the whole aggregate is indissoluble? "Shouldn't we rather declare from the outset that we are a distinctive historic community and that our uniqueness comprises, in addition to our creed, other things, as well, this being the truth? . . . Our distinctiveness differs, therefore, from the other religious groups."[70]

However, the proponents of a religion framework question whether America would sanction ethnic and cultural separateness. The answer, it seems to me, must be sought in the *real* America—the spiritual and social climate of the 1960s and 1970s—and in the *ideal* America—what the term *America* signifies to representative American leaders and thinkers.

The Social and Spiritual Climate of the Sixties

All who have observed the turbulence of American life in the 1960s know that the movement for cultural pluralism has been on the upsurge, and that the "new ethnicism" among Blacks and Puerto Ricans has spurred a Jewish ethnic awareness among American Jews. Many have been asking: Would a synagogue and philanthropic Jewishness satisfy and give meaning to today's socially conscious Jew? And could an anemic Jewishness guarantee a creative Jewish continuity in America? Would a contemporary Jew concerned with universal and "eternal" problems be content merely with parochial and fund-raising activities?

The third generation of young Jews born in America has been reaching for leadership in American Jewish life. The sixties was a time of decline for all ideologies and utopias; nihilism or absurdism became the prevalent fashion in literature and in the theater. Many felt that technological civilization had brought about a depersonalization of the individual. "Meaningfulness! Relevance!" became the general cry. What spiritual sustenance do *I* get out of allegedly sacred values that are *not* observed?

Adjustment to society—the educational goal of John Dewey—could no longer inspire, for society was sick. It must be transformed, not adjusted to. After Auschwitz, many lost faith in the values advocated by the Establisment. If such crimes are possible, should one obey the law? Should not one rather obey his own conscience? "Conscience is above the law!" rebelling youth cried. To kill systematically an entire people (Auschwitz), do not these horrible events signify that ethical beings must first of all be responsible to their own conscience?

In our own Jewish world, the Six-Day War in Israel in 1967, the expulsion of whites—which often meant Jews—from the ranks of the "Black Revolution," and the disillusionment over Communist anti-Semitism in Russia and East European countries, all have helped awaken an ethnic consciousness among American Jews. Many young Jews "discovered" Peretz, Ahad Ha'Am, Borochov,[71] Medem[72]—Jewish secularists whose philosophies blended Jewish ethnic awareness with social consciousness.

Many radical Jewish students in America have been learning that self-affirmation and avowal of one's ethnic identity are not in contradiction with universalism. In the intellectual ferment on the campus, one can hear the voice of the Jewish student expressing a positive attitude to Jewish continuity in American society. The common denominator of many journals and newspapers published by Jewish students throughout the land has been the bold assertion that universal ideas are in consonance with ethnic identity, with a concern for the future of the Jewish world community and of Israel. These publications have been filled with quotations from the works of Jewish secularist culture heroes. The present young generation is actually seeking anew what Yiddish-speaking secularists have found in an earlier epoch—a fusion of Jewish thought and humanism, progressivism and Jewishness. They are in search of a Jewish lifestyle, a *Jewish* humanism, in the cultural setting of the last quarter of the twentieth century. They cannot accept the authoritarian doctrines of religious creeds, or ready-made ritual forms. In the open society of America they are seeking a Jewishness that is rooted in Jewish spiritual soil and facing, at the same time, the whole world.[73]

If one wants to look at the statistics—although one should never take them as criteria of "right" and "wrong"—as an indication of a "trend" or a mood, one could cite the Gallup poll of December 1966 about attitudes to religion. The question asked was: How important is religion to you? Ninety percent of Protestants, and only 30 percent of Jews answered that they consider religion important. This, then, is the "real" American Jewry.

Horace Kallen, the American Idea, and the Right to Be Different

The "ideal" America, the America that is epitomized in the Declaration of Independence, in the thought and writings of Jefferson, Theodore

Parker, Louis Brandeis, and Horace Kallen, the America that represents the *American idea,* the idea of the equality of the different, has not forgotten that liberty includes also the right to be different. And here we come to the eminent Jewish American philosopher Horace M. Kallen (1882–1974), expounder of cultural pluralism as the American idea, and a secularist who stressed the need to harmonize the Jewish heritage with the world-view of modern, humanist Jews.

The concept of cultural pluralism that Kallen developed at the beginning of this century postulates that whoever believes in true democracy, in the "American Idea," must also recognize the right to be different, and must accept multiplicity in faith, ability, occupation, and taste. For this difference between people is natural, creative, and therefore desirable.

> The democratic faith affirms the right to be different; it aspires to assure equal liberty and equal justice to all individuals, and associations of individuals as different. Whatever be the ground on which human beings come together with one another—religion, work, play, sport, art, science, ethnic origin, or political purpose—the societies so formed continue without fear or favor, equal in right to the protection of the laws.[74]

To be and *to be different* are identical, because no human life, Kallen emphasizes, needs any sanction from another existence, be it human or divine, natural or supernatural. This right to be different applies to both individuals and groups. For the Declaration of Independence, articulating that all men are created *equal,* could not have meant that all of them are alike or have one character. Its authors meant *equal* though *different.* They recognized that equality does not abolish diversity in nature, in culture, in language, in mentality, but rather preserves all of these differences in order that human beings become liberated to live and to grow in consonance with their abilities.[75]

> For difference and freedom are two words for one process, and the first is the manifestation of the second. Hence, as Mr. Justice Hughes once pointed out: "Where we lose the right to be different, we lose the right to be free." Free enterprise, free speech, free assembly, free belief, free thought—all the freedom you can list, become modes of the right of the different to equality as different.[76]

The profound student of human nature and society knows that uprootedness and assimilation are not conducive to the development of wholesome and creative human beings. He is aware of the value of anchorage in and identification with the ancestral group through which the individual realizes his potentialities. The ethnic group is "the efficacious natural milieu or habitat of his temperament . . . the center at which he stands, the point of his most intimate social reactions, therefore of his intensest emotional life."[77]

Kallen is convinced that Jewish assimilation is not only anti-American but also crippling to the individual personality, mentally and spiritually.

> The consensus of scientific students of the human person . . . appraises personality as a continuing growth whose any present moment is its living past participating somehow in the formation of its unformed future. Not remembering any phase of this past is not the same as extirpating or annihilating it; rather is forgetting a sort of ghettoizing, a segregation and suppression of a dynamic component of the forgetter's individuality that keeps pushing toward the light of consciousness, and seeking its own free support and growth. The energy of suppression is a diversifying psychosomatic tension. . . . Persons in such a state are not whole, not truly in good health. . . . With the best will they make neither good parents nor good neighbors. . . . On the record persons who, however involuntarily, have begun life in a Jewish milieu, get set on a gradient of human relations that moves most certainly toward that organic union of inner peace and outer freedom which signify happiness, in a Jewish community.[78]

In addition, assimilation is for Kallen anti-democratic, for democracy implies pluralism, variety, diversification.

> This diversification and manifoldness of association, whereby any individual may freely figure as a member of even more different groups with different roles than he can possibly function in, is one quality which distinguishes the American Jewish community from any other. Indeed, it is a central aspect of its Americanization, for it signalizes a major difference between the United States and other lands. It is the principle of a pluralistic society which rests its unity not on "dual allegiance" merely, but on multiple allegiances. As de Tocqueville

noted more than a century and a quarter ago: "In no country in the
world has the principle of association been more successfully used or
applied to a greater multitude of objects than in America." And, of
course, the success is shared by the Jewish communities of the United
States.[79]

Citing the most important documents in American history, and the pro-
nouncements of its illustrious leaders from Jefferson to Franklin D. Roose-
velt, Justices Hughes, and Warren, Kallen concludes that "the tension between an ancient authoritarian monism of culture and the free cultural
pluralism intrinsic to the American Idea has been the vital spring of the
nation's history. Throughout this history the American people's fighting
faith in the Idea has kept it the preponderant force in their altering cultural
economy." [80] For Kallen the American Idea implies the preservation of ethnic cultures: "the pursuit of happiness"—postulated in the Declaration—

> is the creation of cultures, and the sporting union of their diversities
> as peers, and equals; it is the endeavor after culture as each com-
> munion, and each community, according to its own singularity of
> form and function, envisions its own cultural individuality, and strug-
> gles to preserve, enrich and perfect it by means of a free commerce
> in thoughts and things with all mankind. Cultural pluralism signa-
> lizes the harmonies of this commerce at home and abroad. It de-
> signates that orchestration of the cultures of mankind which alone
> can be worked and fought for with least injustice, and with least sup-
> pression or frustration of any culture, local, occupational, national
> or international, by any other.[81]

It goes without saying that Kallen's concept of cultural pluralism had to
put up with a fierce antagonism. Some of his opponents maintained that
if his ideas were implemented they would bring about a polarization of
America. Others, who were sympathetic to cultural diversity, argued that
cultural pluralism had "missed the bus"; that the American-born generations have not demonstrated the will and the interest to preserve their
ethnic identity here; that without languages there will not be a cohesive
force that could hold together the separate groups. The resurgence of an
ethnic consciousness among American minorities during the last decade
refutes all of these categorical assertions. Cultural pluralism has demonstrated its viability in contemporary America, notwithstanding the fact

that we are living in a radically different world than the one which existed when Kallen promulgated his theory a half century ago.

Only several years ago the United States Congress enatced the Ethnic Heritage Studies Program Act, authorizing the federal commissioner of education to subsidize programs, develop curriculum materials, and disseminate information regarding the history, culture, and traditions of the various ethnic minorities in America. This Act is the result of the new spiritual climate in America, the belief that the "melting pot" theory of assimilation is bankrupt and that ethnicism is a positive, constructive force in contemporary American society. This change in outlook is undoubtedly due in part to the fact that many people have lost the important values of community, identity, traditions, and family solidarity.

The Act also implies that the fear of polarization which was used by the opponents of cultural pluralism is groundless. For if American youth will learn about the specific problems, the various life-styles, the livelihood, the contributions to America on the part of all our minorities, all of this would not fragmentize our country.

But should one remain skeptical as to the will of the non-Jewish ethnic groups to maintain their cultural identity, one must nevertheless admit that the American Jewish community has manifested its determination and capacity to preserve Jewish cultural identity and uniqueness. In the course of millennia, and in some eras and countries—in Spain and Germany during medieval and modern times—without a specific Jewish language, Jews have learned to maintain their identity. With or without a separate, spoken Jewish language, there is a more persistent will among American Jews than among some other minorities to maintain a specific cultural Jewish continuity.

Neither should it be forgotten that ethnic identity not only is an expression of the craving of the group to survive, but also answers an inner need of modern man to protect himself against alienation, uprootedness, and impersonality.

The sense of ethnicity has proven to be hardy. As though with a wily cunning of its own, as though there were some essential element in man's nature that demanded it—something that compelled him to merge his lonely individual identity in some ancestral group of fellows smaller by far than the whole human race, smaller often than the nation—the sense of ethnic belonging has survived. It has survived in various forms and with various names, but it has not perished.[82]

Whatever the cause of the survival of ethnicity, it is an undeniable fact that the American Jewish community is making strenuous efforts to continue as a unique collectivity.

At the present time America consists of numerous ethnic, racial, and religious minorities in addition to Jews. There are today in the United States many secular Jews, nonconformists of the second and third generations, seeking to identify themselves with the Jewish people through secular institutions such as the American Jewish Congress, the Zionist Labor Alliance, the Workmen's Circle, the American Jewish Committee, the Zionist Organization, and many more. Many of these Jews are non-religious and nonobservant; they are Jewish secularists or secular Jews who are reinterpreting Jewishness in harmony with the *Zeitgeist,* and modifying Jewish humanism, retaining, however, the core of Jewish secularism: that membership in the Jewish community does not presuppose any religious faith or observances.

Jewish secularism in the Diaspora, for modern Jews who cannot affirm theistic religion—and Judaism is God-centered—aims at underlining that Jewishness is so complex, profound, unique, and comprehensive that every Jewish individual may find in that symphony the melody that captivates him and those motifs which find the deepest echo in his personality. And if secular Jews, on occasion, long for the values which gave meaning and sustenance to the existence of their ancestors, if they are sensitive to the beauty and the insights of the religious creativity of their people, they are not thereby denying their secularist professions, but rather manifesting that both terms in the expression *secular Jews* are of equal importance. They confirm thereby that Jewish secularism bears the imprint of the collective Jewish experience, and that it looks upon the world, in the words of Peretz through Jewish eyes.

Jewish humanists or secularists realize that their most precious ideals and values, if they are to answer their needs for solace and sustenance in times of crisis, must spring from their people's unique experience, must be rooted in the spiritual soil of their ancestry. For secularism, like Judaism, if it is to give the Jew a sense of belonging to his group, must draw its inspiration from the people's sages, martyrs, traditions, hopes, and aspirations. A secularism that is meaningful to the modern Jewish individual must be the result of an organic development and the fruit of a particular cultural climate. Only secularism, with deep roots in the culture and history of his ethnic group, can give the modern Jew the moorings he seeks. Otherwise we will add a new ism, competing with other isms for its survival, instead of helping in the survival and enrichment of its adherents, for whom it was devised.

To the secular Jew, the chief characteristic of religion in general, and of Judaism in particular, lies in a personal faith, a divine power, that rules the universe, and he cannot impose that faith upon himself by virtue of being born of Jewish parents. However, this does not imply that he is a complete stranger to the loftiness, the poetry, the universal insights which his ancestors have woven into historic Judaism. And if he ever experiences moments of exaltation and yearns to transcend the limitations on the spirit of its material nature, in the words of Henri Bergson, then the God of the Prophets, of the Kabalists and the Hasidim, may come closer to him. But Judaism cannot be normative for him as it is for a religious Jew. Jewish secularism suggests a philosophy which perceives all that is good and valuable in non-Jewish cultures, but as seen through the prism of Jewish history, which shaped both the Jewish collectivity and the individual Jew. It recognizes that the modern Jewish secularist is *linked* with the Jewish tradition, but not *shackled* by it. For as long as traditional observances and customs are not obligatory for him but are of a voluntary nature—for the sake of an anchorage for his children or because of a sentimental reverence for ancestral values—then they are not inconsistent with his secularist philosophy.

Let us also note that although Jewish secularism was in the modern period associated ideologically with the Jewish labor and socialist movements, this match is not indispensable for the survival of either. In America, particularly, Jewish secularism was also linked with Yiddish, but this too is not an indissoluble marriage, for Yiddishism and secularism are two currents that may for a time become confluent and at other times run separately. The Hebraists Ahad Ha'Am and Jacob Klatzkin, the Populist (non-socialist) Dubnow, the Pragmatist Kallen were all secularists. Jewish secularism is not dependent on language, or on any "ism." Secularism is a universal phenomenon, an ideological current in the modern history of all civilized nations, and this current is not about to disappear. On the contrary, it is getting broader among all advanced nations.

But while this is irrefutable, one must also bear in mind that *now,* when Jews have become integrated into American society, Jewish secularism should include a substantial *Jewish extract;* it cannot only acquiesce in negativism to superannuated values and institutions; we must accentuate the positive. Our Jewish secularism selects from the rich Jewish spiritual heritage *everything* that is valuable, meaningful, and relevant; and there is much that is perennially relevant for modern Jews in all the currents of Jewish history: in the Bible, in the Talmud, in the Kabala, in Hasidism, surely in the Haskalah, and in our modern Yiddish and Hebrew literatures—the crowning achievements of secular Jews.

Religious Secularism as a Philosophy for Jewish Humanists

Were we to give an American twist to the concept of Jewish secularity, we could designate it "religious secularism." This apparent contradiction is easily resolved when one remembers John Dewey's definition of *religious*. In *A Common Faith* Dewey differentiated between the noun *religion* and the adjective *religious*. *Religion,* he says, signifies dogmas, institutions, rituals, precepts, and practices, whereas *religious* denotes an attitude, a disposition, a commitment. "Any activity pursued in behalf of an ideal, and against obstacles, and in spite of threats of personal loss because of conviction of its general and enduring values is religious in quality."[83]

In view of this definition, it follows that when a Jew bets his life on the survival of his people, when he makes an effort to inculcate Jewish values in his children, or when he is deeply involved in Jewish cultural activities, all of these experiences are religious in character. Jewish secularism in America at the present time is, then, in the Deweyan sense, *religious secularism,* for this Jewish rationale obligates one to foster Jewish concepts and ideals—ideals that are reflected in Jewish literature, in Jewish history, and in all emanations of the Jewish ethos.

The Jewish secular conception is an attempt by all who are seeking to identify themselves with the Jewish people through modern means to harmonize the prevalent ideas of Western culture with the historic Jewish heritage. It is confluent with the mainstream of Jewish thought explored and deepened by Philo, Maimonides, Moses Mendelssohn, Ahad Ha'Am, Peretz, Zhitlowsky, Dubnow, and many more Jewish thinkers who laid the cornerstone in the edifice of Jewish secularism, which, if renovated in each generation, may serve as a satisfactory rationale for modern Jews in the Diaspora and in Israel.[84] In the words of Horace Kallen, "Jewishness or Hebraism is a focus of modernity. It is the Jewish way of life become necessarily secular, humanist, scientific . . . without having ceased to be livingly Jewish."[85]

We may sum up the evolution of secular Jewishness thus: While the first generations of Maskilim strove to combine secularity with Judaism, the present generation, stemming from these enlightened ones, has evolved the formula of *religious secularism*—although both terms in this expression differ in their implications from what they signified for the pioneers of the Haskalah. For, as we have tried to demonstrate in this essay, Jewish secularism was born in a different era, and on another continent from ours; and because of the dissimilarities in both time and place, the complex of ideas known as secularism has been evolving and altering.

The evolution of Jewish secularism adapting itself to time and place parallels, in some respects, the development of Judaism. For just as the Jewish religion has throughout the centuries absorbed alien influences and changed forms, institutions, and ideas, so has Jewish secularism been modified by modern concepts and by the American way of life. Living in pragmatic, pluralistic America, the Jewish community cannot impose a preconceived faith on its members, but must grant them the right to choose freely those parts of the heritage which are pertinent to their struggles and ideals.[86]

As each truly religious person must find God for himself, so each individual may seek his own way toward identification with his group, and each generation is justified in reexamining hallowed values in the light of its own experience. That is why all Jewish philosophies aiming at the preservation of the group and at the anchorage and enrichment of the individual with the intrinsic values of his ancestral culture have their *raison d'être*.

NOTES

1. L. Finkelstein, *The Pharisees* (Philadelphia: Jewish Publication Society, 1938), 1:93–94.

2. W. Latsky-Bertoldy, *Erdgeist* [Earth-spirit] (Riga, 1932), pp. 38–39.

3. Hans Kohn, in *Universal Jewish Encyclopedia* (New York, 1942), 6:126–28.

4. Leo Kenig, *Folk un Literatur* (London: Arbeiter Ring, 1947), pp. 39–40.

5. Ben-Adir, "Modern Currents in Jewish Social and National Life," in *The Jewish People: Past and Present* (New York: CYCO, 1948), 2:285–92.

6. Sh. Niger, *In Kamf far a Nayer Dertsiung* [The struggle for a new education] (New York: W. C. Education Committee, 1930), p. 3.

7. Ibid., p. 4.

8. Baal-Dimyon [N. Shtif], *Hoomanizm in der Elterer Yiddisher Literatur* [Humanism in the older Yiddish literature] (Berlin: Klal-Farlag, 1922), pp. 27–28.

9. Ibid., pp. 61–62.

10. Niger, *Nayer Dertsiung*, p. 6.

11. A. Tcherikover, ed., "Revolutsyonere un Natsyonale Ideologyes fun der Russish Yidisher Intelegents" [Revolutionary and national ideologies of the Russian Jewish intelligentsia], in *History of the Jewish Labor Movement in the United States* (New York: YIVO, 1945), vol. 2.

12. A. Menes, ibid., pp. 205–6.

13. Ibid., p. 501.

14. L. Shpizman, ed., *A Geshikhte fun der Tsionistisher Arbeter Bavegung in Tsofn Amerika* [A history of the Zionist labor movement in North America], 1:81–84.

15. *Niger, Nayer Dertsiung*, pp. 8–13.

16. The conference of Jewish writers and scholars held in Czernowitz in 1908, which proclaimed Yiddish as a national language of the Jewish people.

17. Chaim Zhitlowsky, *Gezamlte Verk* [Collected works] (Warsaw: Farlag Bjoza 1929), 4:181.

18. Ibid., p. 183.

19. Chaim Zhitlowsky, *Der Yid un di Velt* [The Jew and the world] (New York IKUF, 1945), p. 60.

20. Chaim Zhitlowsky, in *Oifn Shaydveg* [At the crossroads] (Paris, 1939).

21. Zhitlowsky, *Der Yid un di Velt*, pp. 190–95. See also Jacob B. Agus,

Guideposts in Modern Judaism (New York: Bloch Publishing Co., 1954), pp. 332–35; also M. Boraisha in *Der Tog,* May 2, 1948. Ben Halpern writes: "What then is our quarrel with the American religious ideologists? Paradoxically enough . . . it is that they offer us God too cheaply. We do not want Him as a solution for the problem of the Jewish Diaspora in America. . . . To make such a use of God seems to us respectful neither to Him, nor to our problem" (*Midstream,* Spring 1956).

22. Zhitlowsky, *Gezamlte Verk,* 4:245.

23. Ibid., p. 246.

24. Ibid., p. 250.

25. Ibid., pp. 268–69.

26. Zhitlowsky, *Der Yid un di Velt,* pp. 290–99.

27. Simon Dubnow, *Letters on Old and New Judaism* [Hebrew] (Tel Aviv: Dvir, 1937), pp. 12–13.

28. Ibid., p. 7.

29. Simon Dubnow, *Jewish History: An Essay in the Philosophy of History* (Philadelphia: Jewish Publication Society, 1903), pp. 30–31.

30. Simon Dubnow, *Velt-Geshikhte fun Yidishen Folk* [World history of the Jewish people] (New York: Elias Laub Publishing Co., 1948), vol. I:15–17.

31. Dubnow, *Letters,* p. 48.

32. Ibid., pp. 50–51

33. Dubnow, *Velt-Geshikhte,* 1:15.

34. Ibid., 6:213–14; and *Letters,* p. 19 n.

35. Dubnow, *Letters,* pp. 18–19.

36. Dubnow, *Velt-Geshikhte,* 3:338.

37. As quoted by K. Pinson in *Jewish Social Studies,* October 1948, pp. 347–48. See also S. Rawidowicz, in *Simon Dubnow: In Memoriam* [Hebrew] (London and Jerusalem: Ararat Publishing Society, 1954), pp. 20–21.

38. Chaim Zhitlowsky, *Zamlbukh* (Warsaw: Farlag Bjoza, 1929), p. 194.

39. *Simon Dubnow: In Memoriam,* pp. 137–40.

40. Dubnow, *History* 1:19–20.

41. Dubnow, *Letters,* pp. 18–19.

42. A. Tcherikover, in *Oifen Shaydveg* (Paris, 1938).

43. Leibush Lehrer, *Yidishkayeit un Andere Problemen* [Jewishness and other problems] (New York: Farlag Matones, 1940). pp. 29.

44. Ibid., p. 57.

45. Ibid., p. 51.

46. Ibid., p. 91.

47. Yudel, Mark, *Shul-Pinkes* (Chicago: Sholem Aleichem Institute, 1946), pp. 45–46.

48. Solomon Schechter, *Studies in Judaism* (Macmillan Co., 1896), vol. 1; also, A. J. Heschel, *God in Search of Man;* Jewish Publication Society; 1956, pp. 151–52, 322–25.

49. H. A. Wolfson, *Escaping Judaism* (Menorah Press, 1923), pp. 47–48.

50. J. Efroikin, *A Kheshbon-Hanefesh* [Soul-searching] (Paris, 1948), pp. 161–62. See also C. J. Ducasse, *A Philosophical Scrutiny of Religion.* After having examined all the aspects of religion, Ducasse reaches the following conclusion: "The beliefs are then for man what gives meaning to all the other aspects of his religion. Without the beliefs, he might go through the motions of it, but only as an automaton" (pp. 131–32).

51. Schechter, *Studies in Judaism,* 3:18.

52. Salo W. Baron, *Modern Nationalism and Religion* (New York: Harper & Bros., 1947), pp. 18–19.

53. Mark, *Shul-Pinkes,* p. 41.

54. H. S. Commager, *The American Mind* (New Haven: Yale University Press, 1954), pp. 167–68.

55. S. Margoshes, in *Der Tog,* April 7, 1951.

56. B. Sherman, in, *Der Yiddisher Kemfer,* July 13, 1951.

57. Ibid.

58. B. Sherman, in *Judaism,* January 1952.

59. Ibid.

60. S. Margoshes, in *Der Tog,* May 5, 1951.

61. M. M. Kaplan, *Judaism as a Civilization* (New York: Macmillan Co., 1934), pp. 318–20.

62. Sh. Niger, in *Der Tog,* Novemeber 5, 1955.

63. M. M. Kaplan, *A New Zionism* (New York: Theodore Herzl Foundation, 1955), p. 107.

64. W. Herberg, *Protestant-Catholic-Jew* (Garden City, N.Y.: Doubleday & Co., 1956), pp. 204–5 and 220.

65. Ibid., p. 274.

66. Ibid., p. 258.

67. Ibid., pp. 277–78.

68. Sh. Niger, in *Der Tog,* November 26, 1955.

69. Kaplan, *New Zionism,* pp. 39–40.

70. Sh. Niger, in *Der Tog,* November 26, 1955.

71. B. Borochov (1881–1917), founder and leader of the Poale Zion party in Russia and the United States.

72. Vladimir Medem (1879–1923), leader of the Jewish Socialist Bund in Russia and Poland.

73. Sarah Feinstein, in *Dimensions in American Judaism* 4 (Winter 1970); 2; also, J. A. Sleeper and A. L. Mintz, eds., *The New Jews* (New York: Vintage Books, 1971), pp. 4–14.

74. H. M. Kallen, *Democracy's True Religion* (Boston: Beacon Press, 1951), and *Secularism Is the Will of God* (New York: Twayne Publishers, 1954), pp. 29–32.

75. H. M. Kallen, *What I Believe, and Why—Maybe* (New York: Horizon Press, 1971), pp. 171–73.

76. H. M. Kallen, "American Jews: What Now?" *Jewish Social Service Quarterly, Fall* 1955, p. 22.

77. H. M. Kallen, *Culture and Democracy in the United States* (New York: Boni & Liveright, 1924), p. 200.

78. Kallen, "American Jews: What Now?" p. 21.

79. Ibid., pp. 17–18.

80. H. M. Kallen, *Cultural Pluralism and the American Idea* (Philadelphia: University of Pennsylvania Press, 1956), p. 99.

81. Ibid., p. 100.

82. M. M. Gordon, *Assimilation in American Life* (New York: Oxford Press, 1964), pp. 24–25.

83. John Dewey, *A Common Faith* (New Haven: Yale University Press, 1934), pp. 9–10 and 27.

84. See *Encyclopedia of the Social Sciences* (1942), s.v. "Secularism," where it is underlined that secularism in Protestant countries differed in form from secularism in Catholic countries.

85. H. M. Kallen, *Judaism at Bay* (New York: Bloch Publishing Co., 1932), pp. 4–5.

86. H. M. Kallen, *Of Them Which Say They Are Jews* (New York: Bloch Publishing Co., 1954), pp. 104–6.

II
Varieties of Affirmation Among Jewish Secularists

CHAIM ZHITLOWSKY

Chaim Zhitlowsky was a philosopher, essayist, and orator—in Yiddish, Russian, and German—who played a major role in the Yiddish cultural movement in America. He was one of the foremost exponents of Jewish secularism and Yiddishism, and a founder of the Jewish Seymist party.

Zhitlowsky was born in a small town near Vitebsk in White Russia in 1865. His traditional Jewish education ended when he was thirteen. He entered a Russian Gymnasium (high school), where he absorbed the the ideas of the Russian Folk Revolutionaries, and at twenty-one he went to Petersburg, where he published his first book in Russian, *Thoughts on the Historical Destiny of the Jews.* In 1888 Zhitlowsky left Russia and settled in Switzerland, where he lived for about fifteen years. During that period he graduated from the University of Bern in 1892 with a Ph.D. in philosophy, and became a central figure among the Russian Folk Socialists, participating in debates and symposiums, and contributing to socialist periodicals.

In 1904 Zhitlowsky came to America, and four years later he settled in New York, where he established and edited the Yiddish magazine *Dos Neie Lebn,* which became the most important vehicle for his ideas, and for those of the Yiddishist intelligentsia. Zhitlowsky traveled the length and breadth of the United States and Canada, lecturing to ever larger audiences, who were spellbound by his oratory. He attracted many admirers, who looked up to him like Hasidim who revere a Rebbe. He died in 1943.

In his essays and lectures he expounded an ideology that routed the socialist assimilationists of his day; he was the architect of a secularist philosophy for agnostic Jews which is, in essence, still tenable.

WHAT IS JEWISH SECULAR CULTURE?

We shall consider Jewish secular culture here in its modern image, in its linguistic form of *Yiddish*. This is not the first fashioning of secular Jewish culture. In very ancient times, Israelite cultural life, including literary creativity, was almost entirely secular. Only with the rise of the so-called sacred books, which are filled to the brim with purely secular episodes and considerations, did there arise a differentiation between sacred and "external" (apocryphal) books,[1] "secular," as they may now be called.

Also a great deal later, in the Hebrew drinking and love songs, in the elegies and humorous songs of the Spanish-Arabic period, in the poetry of Immanuel Romi,[2] and still later in the neo-Hebraic literature of the Haskalah period until the present time, Jewish literary and cultural creativity bears to this day a purely secular character which has nothing to do with one or another official religious belief.

All the more so with the non-intellectual branches and products of human culture among the Jewish people, in their economic and social life as well as in their political life, when this was still possible for us. Here the religious element occasionally played an important role, but not such as to impose its character on the entire substance of Jewish cultural life and Jewish cultural creativity.

Jewish secular culture is, accordingly, no novelty in our history. "From Egypt until the present" it did not desert the Jewish people. What is novel for us is modern secular culture in *Yiddish*. Here, too, it will do no harm to bring out a little more clearly wherein the novelty consists.

The language itself—Yiddish—is not regarded by the Jewish people as *sacred,* nor as a language for purely religious purposes and rituals, but as *secular,* a "mundane" language for all the needs of a human life that occur in a definite linguistic sphere. After all, the language itself was an acquisition from the outside world.

This does not mean that Yiddish was not used for religious purposes. Not only by women with their blessing of the candles, with their "God of Abraham,"[3] with their special prayers for women, and their *Tsenerene,*[4]

49

not only the simple masses, who swallowed the edifying sermons of the *Magidim*[5] in Yiddish but also the Jewish devout scholarly world could not use the holy language, the *loshn koydesh*,[6] for the entire "oral culture" of the Jewish people in the German and Eastern European lands.[7] Both in education, in the *hedorim* and yeshivahs,[8] in the scholarly sermons, casuistries (*pilpulim*), religious speculations, Hasidic sayings of the *Tsadikim*,[9] rabbis and *khoyzrim*,[10] and in the higher ethical interpretations—the language of instruction and religious clarification was *Yiddish* and to a larger degree is so to this day.

And nevertheless, regardless of the tremendously great area that religious life occupied among the devout generations and still occupies to this day, the language and the linguistic sphere in Yiddish did not lose their secular character. The devoutly religious "written" culture is written to this day chiefly in the "holy" language, in *loshn koydesh*. Every piously religious piece of writing in "the holy language" is a holy book. The same devoutly religious piece of writing in Yiddish is a *secular* one and is regarded as holy only by devout women.

In this very fact inheres the *novelty* that is connected with the language itself and which began to prevail as early as the fifteenth century. If you compare our entire written culture in the Hebrew linguistic sphere and in the Yiddish one, throughout the whole course of our historical life, you notice that in Hebrew cultural creation the trunk, with all the most important branches, is religious, and the secular creation is only one branch on that tree. In the Yiddish linguistic and cultural sphere the case is exactly the opposite: From the fifteenth century to the present day, the trunk with the "oral" culture and the most important branches are *secular,* bearing no relation to the official religious faith, whereas religious creativity in Yiddish is only a branch on the tree, and even this branch, as far as its language is concerned, cannot lay claim to any religious sanctity.

What is new here concerns the *secularization* of Jewish national and cultural life. This denotes a complete *revolution* in it. Previously, to live a full life as a Jew denoted only living a full life in one or another religious Jewish sphere; it also denoted, already in the secular-national period, living a full life in the sphere of the Yiddish language. The more traditional religion began to lose its dominating power over Jewish minds and hearts, the more it becomes virtually a private matter for every Jew, the more cultural needs are satisfied in Yiddish that have nothing to do with Jewish religious faith—the more there becomes rooted, flourishes, spreads, and branches out the purely *secular* trunk of our present cultural life in Yiddish.

This is what constitutes the *revolutionary* newness in our cultural and national life. This makes up the characteristic feature of the new historical epoch into which our people has entered. Previously, both in the devout-national and the progressive-assimilationist epochs of our historical life, belonging to the Jewish people was linked with belonging to the Jewish faith, to Judaism in one form or another. Secession from the Jewish faith meant secession from the Jewish people. Now without any doubt every Jew belongs to the Jewish people who lives with his own people in its linguistic sphere—regardless of whether he believes in the *Jewish* religion, whether he believes in God or is an atheist.

When a Jew satisfies his spiritual-cultural needs in Yiddish, when he reads a Yiddish newspaper or a Yiddish book, goes to a Yiddish lecture, when he attends a Yiddish play or a Yiddish movie, or sends his child to a modern Yiddish secular school, when he listens to a Yiddish radio hour or carries on a conversation in Yiddish about Jewish or non-Jewish matters or problems—he is without doubt a Jew, a member of the Jewish people. People of non-Jewish ancestry who become accustomed to the Yiddish linguistic sphere and become part and parcel of it, almost *assimilate* with it—such people also occur, but they are such rare exceptions that we can disregard them entirely.

And such Jewish integration into a purely secular intellectual linguistic and cultural sphere grows and expands in all countries of the world where larger or smaller communities of Eastern European Jews are to be found.

It would certainly be of great interest if we could obtain a clear survey of the *scope* of Yiddish in the Jewish world. It is very possible that *Yiddish* as a colloquial language among Jews, the *spoken* Yiddish language, has lost a certain part of its domain in the last thirty years since the [first] World War, or has remained stable, notwithstanding the increase of the Jewish population. We can, however, assume that a certain decline of that area has really taken place, thanks to the objective assimilationist tendencies in Jewish life, and even more thanks to the assimilationist and Zionist-Hebraist ideology. In accordance with the fate of the ethnic linguistic spheres among the other minority peoples, we must also assume that among us this very ideological factor plays everywhere, and also in America, a strong historical role both as a destructive force as well as a perpetuating and developing one.

If we have this circumstance in mind, we can state with a certainty that the assimilationist ideology is at the point of disappearing and not increasing among our people. The innermost logic of our objective situation among nations since the World War brings about a strong process of nationalization, in many ways linked with a revival of religious Jewishness. This process, however, impels attachment to the Jewish people, and in the innermost logic of this nationalization process lies the rapprochement to the *Jewish folk masses,* to their life and their linguistic sphere in Yiddish. We can assert such a rapprochement in a considerable number of what were formerly purely assimilationist circles. The shrinking of the area of the Yiddish linguistic sphere can turn out with us, as with a great many other minority peoples, to be a temporary phenomenon which can be transformed, in the course of the nationalizing and democratizing historical process, into its exact antithesis.

There exists also another "however" in the matter of area shrinkage. *If* we have lost something in *breadth,* we have gained from this in depth and in height and in the nationalizing force of our "secular" language. In the Yiddish language a *Yiddish cultural sphere* has been created in its various ramifications which we have noted before. And here everyone must admit that these *conscious* creations in Yiddish, both in written culture, in literature with its books, newspapers, and periodicals, and its oral culture with its theater, lectures, movies, radio hours, these conscious cultural creations in the linguistic sphere are continually growing, both in the quantity of the Yiddish word used as in the significance of this absolutely new cultural sphere for our national and cultural renaissance.

This, however, also means that thanks to the rise of Yiddish secular culture, we begin to assume equality in our national cultural character with all other cultural nations in the world. A people is a culture-creating quasi-organism that sits at its own loom and weaves human culture according to its style and form. Language has the psychic threads that extend from individual to individual and connect all parts of the people in cultural creation.

From these psychic connective threads of the popular language, which at the same time is the national language, the people weave on their own loom their own written and oral culture. As is the case with all other nations in the world, so it becomes now also with our Jewish people. In this lies the chief significance of that national cultural revolution that the Jewish secular culture brings into our life.

I just said that we begin only now to assume equality with the cultural nations of the world. We are standing only at the very beginning. And because the new, the progressive national epoch of our historic life has not shed the old skin of previous epochs, and because the Jewish secular culture still has so many opponents, and because the plight of the Jewish people is such an awkwardly twisted one—the conscious creators of secular culture in Yiddish are confronted by problems which are foreign to the nations of the world, because with *them* the answers to the problems are elementary truths, and with *us* they are still baffling ones, which open the way to quite subtle argumentation. European nations, for example, elevated their popular languages to the level of *the* national languages several hundred years ago. With us it is still a debatable issue.

It is impossible for me to touch on all the problems of Jewish secular culture. A few of them must, however, be brought up and elucidated because they have a direct bearing on the activity of our cultural leaders. One problem is about the *content and the form* of Jewish secular culture.

The French have a secular culture in France which is one of the most progressive in the world. Have you ever heard that one should split hairs about what the *French* content of French secular culture should be? With us, however, we still have swordplay with regard to the question as to what the *Jewish* content of our Jewish secular world should be. In practice it is indeed a very important question, but in theory it is a survival of the epoch when Jewish existence was bound by the condition that one should believe in a definite religious content. A heretical, illegitimate [*tref*] national *random* existence in the world, living and creating freely without a fixed purpose like all other nations was simply incomprehensible. The same attitude was even aggravated among those assimilationist intellectuals who became nationalist and Yiddishist penitents: *for what reason* should one refuse the rich cultural fleshpots in the different Egypts and go away into the sandy desert of the Yiddish linguistic sphere? In order to find pleasure in the Yiddish nursery rhymes? If *we*, the high and mighty aristocrats, go to the people and proceed to create for it, it is surely on account of a serious *content* that should be sacred and dear to us, not on account of the empty linguistic form.

Among many of our cultural creators and activists, *secularism* has become a synonym of the term *anti-religious*. Belief in God and a longing for a religious life is regarded by the majority of our activists as a mortal sin against *secularism,* a mortal sin that must be exterminated root and branch. Among other nations, where the *secular* governments, even if they are atheistic, support religious institutions at their expense, there probably predominates quite a different idea of secularism than among Jews. With us trappings of the concept that prevailed during the assimilationist pseudo-radical era of "Yom Kippur balls" still adhere to it.

In reality the concept "secularity" is never and nowhere connected with anti-religiosity, not in France, nor in America, nor in England, where the cultures are also purely secular. Secularism has two meanings: one for the general life of the state, the other for the educational system and the conscious cultural activity in general that bears a general national character. In the general life of the state this denotes: *Religion is a private affair, and anti-religion is also a private affair.* It is forbidden for anyone to be discriminated against for this or that belief, or for this or that struggle against any kind of religious belief.

In the educational system, and in the free cultural activity in general, secularism denotes the exclusion of everything that comes in the name of any revealed superhuman, supernatural *authority,* a "divinity," and demands one thing or another from man in order to carry out the will of this supernaturally revealed, superhuman authority, or in order to find favor in its eyes, or to receive a definite reward from it, or to avoid a definite punishment from it.

This and nothing else is secularism. Atheistic materialism, which is often considered the essence of secularism, is only a definite variant of it, regardless whether it is correct or false. When someone comes to a person and says: "Thus God spoke to me and this he bade me demand from you!"—his entire activity, borne by this spirit, becomes a religious, sectarian one, and it has to be excluded from secular education and secular cultural activity. However, if someone comes to us and says, as some of us do: "According to my human understanding and feeling, it seems that a divine power exists in the world and that to believe in it is good for man, and that in order to live in the sphere of this power, one has to strive for something that should be sacred and dear to *man,* as a *human being,* regardless of whether he believes in God or not"—this is not excluded from the concept of "secularism." This is a metaphysical, idealistic, *secular* doctrine, that runs counter to the other secular doctrine, the atheistic-materialistic one.

According to my opinion both philosophies must not be imposed upon the minds of children in the elementary educational institutions. They must, however, both be free and undisturbed in the higher educational institutions and in secular cultural activity in general. And the same is applicable with regard to the observance of religious holidays, or even certain religious ceremonies.

If the Jewish Passover, for instance, is celebrated because a people was liberated from slavery and goes to seek a land in which to carry on a free life of its own—although the whole story of the "Exodus of the Jews from Egypt" is perhaps no more than a legend—the holiday is a *human* one, and has very great human significance.

(1939)

NOTES

1. Given in Hebrew as *sforim khitsoynim,* i.e., "outside" the Bible.

2. Immanuel ben Solomon of Rome, Italian-Jewish poet and scholar (1270–1330).

3. A prayer said mainly by women at the close of the Sabbath.

4. A Yiddish translation of the Pentateuch, enriched by illustrative stories, traditionally read chiefly by women.

5. Preachers.

6. Holy Tongue, i.e., Hebrew.

7. *Shebal Peh* = here it implies folk-culture.

8. Elementary Schools and Institutions of higher Talmudic learning.

9. Hasidic rabbis.

10. A person appointed by a Hasidic rabbi to repeat and explain the sermon given by him.

MORRIS R. COHEN

Morris Raphael Cohen, the Russian Jewish immigrant boy who became one of the foremost American philosophers and one of the greatest teachers of our time—"a modern Socrates"—was born in 1880 in the city of Neswish, near Minsk, White Russia. He was brought to the United States in 1892, graduated from the College of the City of New York eight years later, and received his Ph.D. at Harvard in 1906.

Cohen taught philosophy at City College from 1912 to 1938, becoming famous for his use of Socratic irony, and at the University of Chicago until 1942. His influence, through his students and his works, has been far-reaching, and he is considered one of the most original American philosophers since William James.

Cohen's mother tongue was Yiddish, for which he always maintained a special love. He said he owed a great deal of his education to the Yiddish press. In the early 1920s Cohen became active in ORT (an abbreviation of the Russian name of the Society for the Promotion of Crafts and Agriculture Among the Jews), and in 1933 he organized the Conference on Jewish Relations, to which he dedicated himself during the last years of his life. He had a role in establishing the important quarterly *Jewish Social Studies,* and became one of the founders, and the first chairman, of the Research Institute on Peace and Postwar Problems of the American Jewish Committee. He died in 1947.

Piety as defined by Santayana—"reverence for the sources of one's being"—was for Cohen, as he says in the first paragraph of the following selection, a necessary corollary of the Socratic maxim "know thyself." If a Jew is to know himself, he must know the history of the Jewish people. Cohen rejected monotheism and all other forms of theism, for he was not able to reconcile the reality of evil with the idea of a benevolent and omnipotent God.

In his moving autobiography, *A Dreamer's Journey,* Cohen describes how in his later years he came to appreciate the role of ritual in human life.

> For each of us the symbolism of our childhood offers paths to peace and understanding that can never be wholly replaced by other symbolisms . . . and though I have never gone back to theologic supernaturalism, I have come to appreciate more than I once did the symbolism in which is celebrated the human need of trusting to the larger vision, according to which calamities come and go but the continuity of life and faith in its better possibilities survive. [p. 218]

THE PIETY OF AN AGNOSTIC

Santayana defines piety as "reverence for the sources of one's being." In this sense, if not in any more orthodox sense, piety has always seemed to me a necessary corollary of the Socratic maxim "know thyself."

None of us are self-made men, and those who think they are, are generally no credit to their makers. The language in which our thinking moves, the ideals to which our hearts are attuned in the formative years of our childhood, our habits, occupations, and pastimes, even our gestures, facial expressions and intonations, are so largely the social product of generations of teaching, that no man can understand himself and his own limitations unless he understands his heritage; and it is very difficult to understand one's heritage, or anything else, unless one approaches it with a certain amount of sympathy.

No ordinary human being deliberately chooses the country or household into which he shall be born. Hence none of us justly deserve any credit for the deeds of our remote ancestors any more than we can be blamed for their misdeeds. Nevertheless we are born not only as individual men and women but also as members of historic groups; and we are brought up to take pride in the achievements of anyone who in any way belongs to our race, nation, or family. Such pride sustains our self-respect, by supplementing the poor record of our individual lives with the glories of the larger unities with which we identify our being; and in some cases this spurs heroic achievements on our own part. The members of any hereditary group which, like the Jewish, is regarded as in some way inferior by dominant opinion are apt, by way of reaction, to intensify this pride. But in some cases they naturally wish to escape their handicap and become absorbed in the dominant group, if not for their own at least for their children's sake. I have never joined the outcry against such individuals as "traitors," or "deserters." I see no justification for condemning intermarriage or the conversion of Jews to Christianity. (It is of course contemptible to crawl into any church for your belly's sake, but this applies also to many of those who remain in the church of their fathers.) Still a realistic view shows that for the most part we must accept our heredity and do the best we can with it. In any case we cannot achieve self-respect if we are afraid of self-knowledge, of knowing the history of our ancestors and how we came to be what we are.

One of the most serious consequences of the declining influence of the synagogue is that the great mass of Jews has lost contact with the traditional substance of Jewish education. Not only those who wish to forget their Jewish origins but others remain ignorant of the historic background which has molded their own being. This has produced, most regrettably, the type of Jew interested in everything except his own history. Because none of us can escape the influences of our ancestry and the traditions in which we are brought up, it is important for a Jew living in a predominantly non-Jewish world to understand the actual history of his own people, the conditions which have brought about his present position, and the main factors that are effective in maintaining or changing these conditions. In other words, to lead a dignified self-respecting life, a Jew must know the history of his people, not merely in the Biblical period, which is generally just as well or even better known by his non-Jewish neighbor, but also in Talmudic and more recent historic eras. He must know enough to understand the real sources of the difficulties which he will encounter and to meet those difficulties with understanding rather than with blind resentment or cowardly complacency. And for an American Jew it is important to understand the large role which the Hebraic tradition has played in the development of American thought and American democracy from Puritan times to the present day.

The history of the Jews has always had, for me, a peculiar fascination. Even in the years when I was most consciously rejecting the supernaturalism of Orthodoxy I was devoting a large part of my thinking to Biblical history, Biblical criticism, and comparative religion. Beginning in 1899 and for many years thereafter as a volunteer teacher of the Thomas Davidson School, I gave courses in the Book of Job, the Hebrew Prophets, and other religious subjects. When I entered the Graduate School at Harvard, courses with Woods and G. F. Moore in the Hebrew religion and the history of religions formed a major part of my studies. In later years a considerable part of my reading and lecturing was directed to Jewish problems. The literature of the Old Testament which I studied as a child has never ceased to grip me, and in days of depression when I have had little energy for writing or study I have found the books of the Bible and Old Testament criticism most absorbing reading.

Interest in Jewish affairs, however, has never been for me a purely intellectual matter. At all periods of my life I have seen fellow human beings, sometimes dear friends, close relatives and cherished students, suffering and facing all sorts of perplexities because they were of the Children of Israel. This was not always a matter of creed. Anti-semitism, in its modern as in its more ancient forms, does not generally draw distinctions between Orthodox, conservative, Reformed, agnostic, atheistic, or even converted Jews, between conservative Jewish bankers and fanatical Jewish revolutionists. The blows of oppression, contempt and discrimination generally fall on all Jews alike, even into the third and fourth generation. Out of this reality comes a call to rise to the defense and help of one's fellows.

To the sensitive humanitarian this call may sound across all the gulfs that separate peoples and civilizations. I have always had the greatest admiration for Gentiles like John Haynes Holmes who have come to the defense of Jews as of any other oppressed people. And I have always felt the same admiration for Jews like Julius Rosenwald, Louis Marshall, Walter Pollak, Osmond Fraenkel and Nathan Margold, who have enlisted gallantly in the struggle for the rights of other oppressed racial and religious minorities. But such sympathy is a rare flower of civilization. The eighteenth-century philosopher who said, "The world is my country, to do good my religion," expressed an ideal which few humans have ever achieved. For most men the cumulative force of social tradition and the enormous difficulty of overcoming the momentum of social institutions limit the horizon of effectiveness, even of effective sympathy. He who would call upon the better nature of his fellow men must recognize these human limitations.

Humanitarianism can become a potent force in the real world only as it builds outward from group relations in which sympathy is normal. He must be narrow-hearted indeed who cannot feel for those with whom he grew up, whose heritage is his heritage, whose misfortunes are his misfortunes. Humanitarianism ceases to be thin and other worldly when it is bound up with men and women whose roots are intertwined with one's own. When, in the days of the Russian famine of the twenties, a distinguished American Zionist warned that "man does not live by bread alone," that "Palestine was the only salvation," and that it was "useless to give bread" to the Jews of Russia, I could not forget my own cousin, who starved to death before help from this country could reach him. Massacres in Czarist Russia or Nazi Germany are very close when one knows that, but for the good luck or unconquerable fortitude of parents or grandparents, he and those who are dearest to him might be among the victims. When, in the months before our marriage, Mary Ryshpan headed a drive to aid the victims of the Russian pogroms of 1905, who of us did not recall the words of the Puritan who said, when he saw a man led to the gallows, "There, but for the grace of God, go I."

So it was again in the years of the First World War, when on the Eastern Front every Russian defeat and every German defeat was blamed and visited upon the Jews, and when every Russian or German victory was celebrated with an offering of Jewish blood or a bonfire of Jewish homes. So it was again in the days of Hitler. In the face of these realities I have never been ashamed to identify myself with fellow Jews who suffered, and I have tried not to let differences of religious belief or politics or other ideologies stand in the way of practical co-operation in the struggle against injustice or in the endeavor to relieve suffering. After all, what is distinctive about a civilized man is that he can work with others who have different ideals, so long as there exists an underlying human sympathy.

Still, it is sometimes hard to live up to the civilized ideal when one's fellows resort to the attacks on character and integrity with which we Jews so often embellish our differences of opinion. Perhaps this habit is evidence of a peculiar capacity for hatred; perhaps it is but a modernization of the art of cursing, which was already highly developed in Old Testament times but certainly reached a pinnacle of perfection on the East Side of my youth. It has sometimes seemed to me that we need a special Anti-Defamation League to protect Jews against the libels and slanders of their fellow Jews. In fact some fruitless efforts in this direction were made in the days of my youth by my godfather, Reb Meier—a *rov,* who never accepted any fees for answering ritual questions, or other service, and who always when solicited for advice urged women to refrain from cursing. Cursing was not only a form of attaining relief from their many troubles but it developed into a fine art, and I do not know of any language that is as rich as Yiddish in that respect.

A single story that I heard from one of my teachers may illustrate the possibilities of cursing as a fine art. There was a contest among three men as to who could invent the most terrific curse. The first man started off with the following: May you have as many sores as there have been perforations in all the *Matzoths* which the Jews have eaten since they left Egypt. (To prevent fermentation in the dough, every *Matzo* has many rows of thin perforations in it.) The second contestant then produced the following: May you be as rich as Korah (the Jewish equivalent of Croesus) and may all that money be spent on salt to rub into these sores. Whereat the third countered with the decisive one: May you have all that fools have wished on themselves.

Many of these curses contained strange words that had no definite meaning, but were all the more terrifying for it. I remember the rage I felt when my sister in angry quarrel with me called me "Brahman"—a word of whose meaning I had no idea whatsoever. But perhaps these childhood experiences helped to inure me to the epithets that would be hurled at me in later years by men and women who deemed themselves endowed by God or Lenin with authority to solve all human problems and to smite unbelievers with the wrath of His indignation.

I do not believe that there is a "Jewish Question" or a "Jewish Problem" any more than there is a "Christian Question." Indeed when I was scheduled once to speak on "The Jewish Problem" at a meeting of the Menorah Society, I rose and said, "Gentlemen, there is no Jewish problem." Then I sat down. After having shocked the audience into thinking, I did rise and explain why I thought that there is no "Jewish Problem." There are, of course, many human problems, of which Jews, as human beings, have perhaps more than their share. But these problems, traced to their ultimate roots in reality, are also the problems of other minority groups, and what group of human beings is not a minority in one situation or another?

For most of these problems I know no answer. But I believe that one of the essential elements of civilization is the division of labor. I have faith that some problems which are beyond my powers and beyond the powers of any one of us may be solved by the co-operation of many. In the words of Rabbi Tarphon, "The day is short and the task is great. It is not incumbent upon thee to complete the whole work, but neither art thou free to neglect it." And so, for each of us who is able to recognize his own limitations, comes the question, "How can I best contribute to that which is beyond my power to complete?"

To me the choice of ways in which to express my respect for the sources of my being has always been very simple. Never having been afflicted with wealth, I have never had to trouble myself seriously about what causes or institutions I ought to endow or support. I have never had the talents for raising money in good causes which my dear friend Jacob Billikopf has put to such good use. I have never had the strength to address and fire large crowds. All that I have ever been able to offer to my people is that which a teacher and scholar can give.

In my younger days, such offerings as I could hope to make on the altars of social understanding were fired by the dream of Thomas David-

son of a school or movement which would combine the underlying insights of religion with the knowledge of science and the wisdom of philosophy. In the first articles of mine that ever found their way into print,
articles published in 1901 and 1902 in the old *Alliance Review,* I struggled with these problems—the problem of religion and science, the loyalty
that we owe to the past and the loyalty that we owe to the future, the
problems of a lost or liberated generation on the East Side, which are,
seen in true perspective, the problems of every generation in a changing
world. And for some seventeen years after Davidson's death I did my best
to keep alive the rare combination of intellectual study and spiritual com-
munion that had taken shape in the Thomas Davidson School at the Educational Alliance.

When in 1902 I began to teach at City College, and for thirty-six years
thereafter, I naturally shared in the struggles of my students against the discrimination that faced so many of them as they sought to establish their
careers. And as a citizen I could not be silent in the face of the great
campaign to repudiate the declaration that all men are created equal which
culminated in the racist immigration laws of 1922 and 1924. Along with
Jane Addams, Isaac Hourwich, Felix Frankfurter, Father John Ryan, and
other unregenerate liberals, I joined in the battle to expose the false science
on which this anti-semitic and anti-Catholic legislation was based. Our
efforts in 1921 to raise money and to enlist scientific bodies to support
studies and publications in this field came to naught in the face of the
postwar hysteria with its nightmare of an immigrant threat to 100 per cent
Americanism.

In later years there were other ventures in the field of Jewish scholarship
and education to which I could not refuse what small contribution I might
offer. As Chairman of the Talmudic Library in 1928–29, alongside Dr.
Chaim Tchernowitz, I did my best to bring into being an encyclopedia that
would make the Talmud intelligible to all readers. But the prevailing cult
of unreason had made of "Talmudic disputation" a popular term of contempt—even among Jews. It was hard to find among Jewish intellectuals
the sort of enthusiastic support for this project that we obtained from
non-Jews—among them Dean Roscoe Pound, Dean Shailer Mathews, Professor Dewey, Professor Torrey, and my old teacher of religious history,
George Foote Moore of Harvard. At all events, I was unable to persuade
more than a handful of my fellow citizens that the Talmud is a unique
achievement in the history of civilization and one that throws a white light
upon the historic value and general significance of Jewish contributions to

world civilization. The Talmud had been my first teacher. Now the Talmud was in low estate, and it would have been gratifying had I been able to repay it in the only coin a teacher values.

Not quite so hopeless were the efforts in the field of vocational education that my wife, the devoted companion of so many of my labors, and I put into the development of the work of the ORT. To both of us, as old teachers, ORT presented a continuing challenge: What could vocational training, administered with sympathy and understanding, do to help oppressed people to surmount the degradations of poverty and hatred?

With the help of my son Felix my philosophical outlook had been formulated in *Reason and Nature* in 1931, and the bearing of this philosophy on law and society had been fairly outlined in a volume published in 1933 under the title *Law and the Social Order*. With the help of my colleague and former pupil, Ernest Nagel, the implications of my philosophical approach for the teaching of logic had been reduced to what was later to prove a "best seller," as logic books go, *An Introduction to Logic and Scientific Method*. Our work on this was drawing to a close in the spring of 1933. I could now look forward to retirement from college teaching with a feeling that what I had to contribute to the world of philosophy would not entirely perish with me. With this sense of relief, I could look about me to see what, if anything, the meager offerings of a logician could contribute to the future of my people here and abroad and to the cause of human freedom, with which the fate of the Jew has been so intricately bound for so many centuries.

(1949)

HORACE M. KALLEN

Horace Meyer Kallen, the exponent of cultural pluralism, was an eminent American philosopher who formulated a secularist rationale for Jewish humanists. In the course of seventy years he manifested creativity in both Jewish and American cultures.

Kallen was born in Germany in 1882. His father, an Orthodox rabbi, brought him, at the age of five, to Boston, where he received his general and Jewish education. He graduated with a Ph.D. in philosophy from Harvard University, where he had become the favorite student of the philosopher William James. He also studied at Oxford University and at the Sorbonne, and taught at Princeton, Wisconsin, and the New School for Social Research. Kallen died in 1974.

Among Kallen's numerous books are *The Book of Job as a Greek Tragedy, Judaism at Bay, Culture and Democracy in the United States, Secularism Is the Will of God, Art and Freedom,* and others on a wide range of intellectual interests and learning.

As a pragmatist Kallen evaluated Jewishness not in terms of definitions or historical correctness, but rather in its consequences for a stronger and richer Jewish life. He was of the opinion that Judaism comprises not *a* view of life, but *views* of life—views in the plural. Each grouping in Jewish life—Orthodox, Conservative, Reform, Zionist, Bundist, Yiddishist, or Hebraist—may, according to Kallen, emphasize in the texture of Jewishness whatever is pertinent for its struggles and ideals. All intellectual currents in American Jewry, all religious and secular philosophies, have their *raison d'être* in maintaining a meaningful Jewish continuity.

In his appearances at Jewish education conferences, Kallen never tired of stressing that Jewish education, if it is to be relevant for the young, not only has to be a record of the past, but must include Hebrew *and* Yiddish, Israel *and* the Diaspora, Zionism *and* all other movements and achievements of Jews.

IS THERE A JEWISH VIEW OF LIFE?

Albert Einstein says that there isn't, "in the philosophic sense." He may be right. But also, he may be wrong. The question does not admit of a single, unambiguous answer.

For the Jews are an ancient people, and their history is long and varied. Their religion, Judaism, is not so old nor so varied as the history of its creators and adherents, yet its own life-history is marked with at least as many crises and alterations as the life-story of the Jewish people. And it could not be otherwise. For Judaism, like Hebraism, is an indefinite manifold. Its existence consists of the coming together and the moving apart of great numbers of diverse and contradictory items of thought, feeling and conduct. Each and every one of these items has a claim upon the consideration of any person endeavoring to establish what Judaism is or what Judaism is not.

But this claim is hardly even honored. The definition which any citizen gives Judaism depends on his loves and hates, on his wishes and frustrations. Those cause him to react selectively to the entire shifting aggregate of which living Judaism is composed. They will lead him to affirm qualities which others deny, and deny qualities which others affirm.

To this rule, Einstein is no exception. In science, a specialist in astronomical mathematics; in human relations, a democrat, an internationalist and a pacifist, the loyalties and rebellions these terms imply determine in advance what items from the manifold of Judaism he will choose in order to make up an exclusive definition of "the Jewish view of life."

With Dr. Einstein's selection I have no quarrel. On the contrary, it is quite in harmony with the type of selection I myself make, as those well know who have read my works on this subject, especially my *Judaism at Bay,* where I have endeavored to show why some such view of Judaism may be held as peculiarly representative of the high place in the rise and fall of the Jewish tradition.

But demonstrating and establishing this definition call for the simultaneous recognition that there exist other opinions, other views of Jewish life, other and quite contrary definitions, each one of them an alternative demanding to be refuted and cast aside. Refuting them and casting them

69

aside meant acknowledging that they had a place in the aggregate which is Judaism. Some of them include Maimonides and shut out Spinoza. Others include the Bible and exclude the *Siddur*. Some include the *Shulhan Arukh,* but exclude Maimonides, Spinoza, the *Siddur* and the Bible. Others combine them all with the *Shulhan Arukh*. Still others exclude the *Shulhan Arukh,* mutilate the *Siddur* and include a "mission of Israel" an "ethical monotheism" and at the same time glorify Maimonides and patronize Spinoza.

Who is right? Who is wrong? The answer does not depend on the intrinsic character of the definition nor on its historical correctness nor its religious sanctions. The answer depends entirely on its *consequences* to the strength, the enrichment of Jewish life.

Now in life, quite otherwise than in mathematics, consequences belong to an unpredictable future. They can not be established in advance. They are not foregone conclusions.

History, which can be written only by survivors in the struggle for life, is the judgment which the survivors pass upon both their struggle and their opponents'. Thus, Jewish history as written by Jews embodies the judgment of the victorious Elohist upon the defeated Yahwist, the victorious priest upon the defeated prophet, the victorious Pharisee upon the lost Sadducee, the persisting rabbi upon the transient dissenter, the effortful nationalist upon the sentimental religionist, and so on. Contemporary parties in Israel employ or reverse these judgments in order to rationalize their own ends and to justify their own struggles. For example, the very reverend Dr. Cyrus Adler, President of the Jewish Theological Seminary, President of Dropsie College, President of the American Jewish Committee, etc., etc., will put together and invoke one set of historic judgments to justify his mortuary policy and attitude in Jewish life. The less reverend Drs. Albert Einstein or Stephen Wise will invoke another set to justify their vital ones. Their compositions, their invocations, their demonstrations, their arguments are not revelations of the facts. Their compositions, their invocations, their demonstrations, and their arguments are only invidious uses, special applications of the facts. The facts themselves remain everlastingly neutral to all the causes that employ them, stubbornly elusive to all the meanings which are imposed on them.

We may get some inkling of the character and implications of the facts when the observer who studies them has no passionate concern about their use.

Thus, we may take it as being pretty close to the truth when George

Foote Moore tells us, in his magnificent *Judaism,* that the Judaistic tradition owns no theology in the Christian or Greek sense of the term; that its dynamic essence was the rule of life or the system of observances which were finally codified in the *Shulhan Arukh* and were the same wherever in the wide world Jews could be found; but that "basic human relations are without measure or norm and left to the conscience and right feeling of the individual"; that they are *masur lalev,* committed to heart.

But Moore was writing of what has sometimes been called "normative Judaism." He had also made a selection. He paid attention to nothing outside of this traditional historic complex which the generations kept on reliving until the middle of the last century. He ignored the variant, the new, the heretical, which had arisen and struggled to establish itself within the complex. But he knew he did so, and he did not endeavor to have anyone take the part for the whole. A complete science of Jewry cannot ignore those things. A complete science must include everything that any Jew has ever identified as Jewish in life and quality. But Jews laboring in their struggle for a life and a living, are prevented from dealing with this all-inclusive total. The time and place and circumstances of their struggle, its passions and its ideals dispose them to seek one item and reject another, so that their passions may be gratified and their ideals realized.

Thus, it is Dr. Einstein's necessity and his right to select from the Jewish inheritance that which seems to him pertinent to his struggle and his ideals. His opponents have the same necessity and right to make their own selections. But both he and they would be wrong if they treated their selections as accounts of the entire Jewish reality, as descriptions of the historic content of Judaism and Hebraism. In the nature of the case, such selections can be nothing of the sort. First and last, they are personal and class valuations, special pleas made by means of data lifted thus out of their original contexts, and employed to express the feelings and to realize the ideals of those who have so lifted them. Judaism or Hebraism is not any one of them by itself. It is all of them together—and then some.

Is there, then, a Jewish view of life? No. There is not *a* Jewish view of life. There are Jewish *views* of life. The views are many. Life, with all its conflicts and antagonisms and hates, indeed through them, makes itself somehow one.

(1938)

LIEBMAN HERSCH

Liebman Hersch was a phenomenon in the Jewish world—an East European Jew who became a noted scholar in Geneva, Switzerland; a Bundist (Diaspora-Socialist) who wrote important studies in French and contributed to Yiddish periodicals and encyclopedias. Born in Lithuania in 1882, he was the son of a Hebrew writer and Maskil (enlightened person). In 1904 Hersch migrated to Geneva, where he received his Ph.D. in the social sciences. In 1927 he became a full professor at Geneva University, and he published numerous studies of Jewish migrations and population trends in many lands.

During the Second World War he was active in helping Jewish refugees from Nazi-occupied European lands, and was also an active worker in the Jewish Socialist Bund, and its representative in the Socialist International. In 1947 Hersch toured Palestine and returned with a profound affection for its Jewish community. The following year he came to New York as a delegate to the Congress for Jewish Culture, impressing everyone as a broad-minded thinker, an intellectual aristocrat, and a warm human being. Professor Hersch died in Geneva in 1955.

MY JEWISHNESS

I am a positivist. For me only the empirical world is suited to be an object of knowledge. We do not possess the necessary senses to comprehend what lies beyond the world of experience, nor do we possess the words that would be necessary to formulate such knowledge for ourselves or transmit it to others.

Regardless of the fact that the barrier separating the conceptual (what is comprehensible by reason) and the non-conceptual is sufficiently vague, and that the very concept of experience is, therefore, a relative one (as are our concepts in general), experience nevertheless has quite a substantial meaning for me. My positivism is restrictive and exhaustive at the same time—or, if one wishes, both modest and bold. It is restrictive because it places the entire "other world" beyond the conceptual; it is exhaustive because it excludes every interference of "other-worldly" powers into the events of this world. This, however, does not mean that our spirit stops absolutely at the limits of the positive empirical world. The only thing is that, being unable actually to transcend these limits, we create for ourselves in regard to the extra-empirical world very inaccurate and exceptionally subjective pictorial conceptions that assume different forms according to the inclinations of our character and intelligence, according to our ethical concepts, according to our artistic tastes, according to our age, education, social position, and the like. Therefore man creates his God in his image and after his likeness, according to his own image. Goethe already forged the sentence, which people would have attributed to Voltaire if it had been written in French:

Man his God views as his kin,
Hence He's oft derided been.

This positivism is literally a form of my intellect; it would have been impossible for me to liberate myself from it, even if I had wished to. It is not the result of study of facts, but a manner of behaving in regard to facts. And it is as a positivist that I also regard religion in general and the Jewish faith in particular.

This attitude comprises agnosticism, which declares "that which is

75

above" to be inaccessible to human reason. It dictates an absolute tolerance in regard to religious feelings and ideas, even when they are very far from our own, because it sees in them expressions of the human personality, just as in art, for instance, the person who loves music can and should respect the taste of another for sculpture, or as the lover of symphonies should be able to comprehend that someone else can like operas. For the positivist, on the other hand, religious beliefs, feelings, and institutions, are facts which change with the social conditions of the historical milieu, which develop together with it, and which are subject particularly to the influence of the progress of positive science. Religions, beliefs, and religious institutions are thus a product, and at the same time an element and a factor, of social life. Very strong is the effect of scientific achievements on the element of superstition and magic that is found, in smaller or larger measure, in almost all religions, which are nothing else but a mixture of the two domains of "this world" and the "other world," in the realm of beliefs and all sorts of religious ceremonies, and which shrink with the progress of science.

As far as ethics and morality are concerned, which occupy such a large place in all religions, one should disregard smaller differences and recognize that all great religions of civilized mankind possess one common ground. This is the morality whose basis is love of man and truth and which is expressed essentially in the last six commandments of the Ten Commandments. Moreover, even modern secular morality is based on the same foundations. It differs only in two important points from the so-called religious morality: (1) Religious morality regards the earthly world as a "vale of tears," or at best as anteroom to the life of the hereafter, which is the true eternal life, whereas for secular morality life in this world, on the earth, is the entire life and the goal of everything. (2) Religious morality regards humility as one of the greatest human virtues, whereas secular morality cultivates, on the contrary, the feeling of individual dignity. These two factors of religious morality are, in my opinion, responsible for the fact that socialism opposes religion in general, that it is regarded by it as a sort of "opium of the people"; because, instead of propelling the oppressed and underprivileged of contemporary society to fight for their liberation, this morality tries, on the contrary, to lull them to sleep with the hope of an alleged happiness which awaits them after death, and all this in order that they acquiesce in their bitter fate in this world. Concerning this the positivist can only agree with socialism.

The positivist cannot have any other attitude vis-à-vis Jewish religion than the one he has vis-à-vis religion in general. I, therefore, regard the Jewish religion as a product of Jewish social life, which at the same time is also an important factor of this life. Like every social phenomenon, Judaism also constantly developed in the course of time. How could it, then, have been otherwise?

From "Moses to Moses,"—i.e., from Moyshe Rabeynu to the Rambam—twenty-five centuries elapsed, a duration of time similar to the one which separates the Europe of today from the Europe of the sixth century B.C.E. It would really have been the greatest wonder if a social phenomenon had remained unchanged in the course of such a long time. And, in truth, the Jewish religious ideal actually changed; from this the numerous contradictions in the Scriptures arise; and this is the case not merely between the Jewish Bible and the later religious books, but even between different parts of the Bible itself.

Beside this the Torah is not merely an expression of social life and its evolution, it also represents the historiography of Jews in the most distant past, which is rich in legends, as are the ancient histories of all nations. Legends, however, always remain legends, even if they are based on historical facts. Nevertheless they were included in the Scriptures. Thus, for example, they describe the Exodus from Egypt, life in the desert, the conquest of Palestine, etc. We therefore find in the Bible a considerable number of fantastic stories, naive superstitions, and magic—elements that are characteristic of the primitive mentality.

For this reason, when I was still a boy I not only ceased to observe commandments and religious customs, but also, in the depths of my consciousness, felt myself entirely outside the religious community; and when people used to demand from me a declaration of my religion (during censuses, the prepartion of personal documents, etc.), I always used to answer: without religion.

And yet, for a few years now, my answer to the same question has been: Jewish religion.

Deep inside me for several years now I have had more and more serious doubts concerning my "non-religiousness." A whole series of questions came more and more distinctly to my consciousness, torturing my thoughts, demanding clear replies from me:

1. Does *everything* in the Jewish Scriptures consist merely of legends and superstitions? To pose the question actually meant to answer it. One cannot accept such a premise from the outset, for if this were true, how was one to interpret the unique case in the history of mankind that

these very books served as a foundation for the three great religions of the white race and of a considerable part of other races?

2. Is it really absolutely correct that there are merely insignificant, basically unessential differences? If it were really so, how can one explain why, in the course of long centuries, generations of Jews preferred to be slaughtered or burned alive rather than to accept the Christian religion?

3. Is every religion absolutely a result of the confusion of the two domains, of the "natural" empirical world and the "supernatural" extraempirical world? We know, nevertheless, that one of the greatest religions of mankind, Buddhism, is basically a religion without a god.

4. Finally, is my "non-religiousness" really just as remote from Judaism as from other religions? Am I not a religious Jew in the same measure as I am not, for instance, a Catholic? Once again, to have posed the question, means to have answered it. For after all, it was clear to me that my deviation from religious Jewishness cannot be compared to my enormously greater distance from Catholicism, for instance.

This has brought me, and brings me now, to the point that I should analyze the essential differences that exist, in my opinion, between Judaism and Christianity, particularly in its Catholic form.

According to an opinion—a commonplace one—which is widespread not only in the Christian world but also in some "liberal" Jewish circles, Christianity is supposed to represent a higher ethical stage than Judaism, and in this, indeed, the fundamental difference between the two religions is supposed to consist. In connection with this one often hears it said that Judaism in relation to Christianity is like justice relative to love, vengeance relatve to forgiveness, the dry "word" relative to the "spirit," and so forth. One is sometimes amazed to see what wild ignorance helped this opinion take root, and what false ideas it created. More than once I have had occasion to hear from Jewish intellectuals, and even those who are endowed with a considerable cultural-secular ballast, that "thou shalt love thy neighbor as thyself" is not to be found in the Torah but only in the Gospels; at the same time the people say it with such assurance, as though it indeed were a question of a very generally well known matter.

Not committing such serious errors, one often commits the perhaps less explicit but nevertheless major error of conceiving Judaism as some petrified thing, ignoring its evolution, disregarding the level that Judaism attained at the beginning of the Christian era, and comparing the Gospels with fragments of the archaic texts of the Torah, which were written ten or fifteen centuries earlier. Certainly, these texts were, and have remained to this day, sacred for Jews (incidentally also for Christians). However, with the development of Jewish religious thought, these texts were "interpreted" according to the ideas of the given epoch; and in the epoch of Christ the ethical ideals of the sages of Israel were those which serve as a foundation for Christian morality. Very often even the words are the same. And this is quite natural, because the creators of the New Testament and the creators of the Talmud both drew from one and the same source: from the Jewish Bible, from Jewish tradition, from the maxims of those times.

The fundamental differences between Judaism and Christianity belong to completely different categories:

First of all, *the differences of opinion in regard to matters of principle.* There are three, in my opinion:

1. As a world-view, Judaism differs by its *absolute* refusal to apply in relation to God any concept whatever of the empirical world. Hence the *absolute incorporeality* of God (I emphasize incorporeality, not to be confused with immateriality): *He* is not corporeal: that no bodily accidents apply to Him; and that there exists nothing that resembles Him (in the third of the thirteen credos [principles of faith formulated by Rambam] which every devout Jew repeats every day with the morning service. Hence also the *absolute uniqueness* of God: "Hear, O Israel, the Lord is our God, the Lord is One," says the Torah.[1] For thousands of years, in the morning and in the evening, the Jew recites this verse in the *Krishma*),[2] and with "Hear O Israel" on their lips our fathers, the martyrs, used to breathe their last on the funeral pyres of the "Holy Inquisition." *He* is unique, and no uniqueness exists like unto *Him,* under any form whatever, the second credo also says. It is the absolute One, the "unity of the Creator," in which, first of all the firsts, that Judaism differs from Christianity, and especially with Catholicism, with its doctrines of divine incarnation, of God-the-Father and God-the-Son, of immaculate conception of the trinity; in short, doctrines in which I can by no means see anything else than a mixture of conceptions that belong to two domains, as a confusion of ideas from the empirical world with those beyond any experience.

I will add that in this, as in many other details, the Reformation was a significant return to the Jewish Bible. I will also add that the entire modern metaphysical thought, by its approach to the absolute, to *infinity,* seems to me to be inspired by the Jewish Bible.

2. In the sense of a norm for practical execution, Judaism is both a

moral doctrine and a law in the strictly juridical sense of the word, whereas *Christianity is exclusively a moral teaching*. The religion of Moses is based on the ethics of the Torah, on ethics whose principle is the sanctity of God, and therefore also the sanctity of the human being, who in accordance with His spirit has been created in the image of God, as the verse says, "God's light in the soul of man." The first three of the Ten Commandments establish the essential principle of divine holiness, the last five are derived from the sacred character of the human being; the fourth commandment (rest on the Sabbath) and the fifth (honoring your father and mother) combine in one the idea of divine sanctity with the sacred character of man. The entire Torah is, in essence, merely the expansion, interpretation, and application of these Ten Commandments.

As is known, there is an immense difference between ethical imperatives and legal duties. Ethics is entirely an internal matter. To observe it or not to observe it is a matter of the indiviual conscience; for the believer it is a matter between man and God. The violation, however, of legal statutes provokes the intervention of one's fellow men. Ethics stands on the basis of the pure ideal to which the individual should strive. Law, however, does not abandon the material basis of human reality, and formulates obligations that man must not violate on any account, if he does not wish to be exposed to the danger of being led back to the path of righteousness by public power. Translated into political language, morality is the maximum program and law the minimum program for our conduct.

Some think they can prove the superiority of Christian over Jewish ethics by juxtaposing certain passages of the Gospels with certain texts of the Torah. Thus, for instance, one quotes, in connection with this, Jesus' famous Sermon on the Mount and compares it to the Ten Commandments or to some laws and judgments of the Law of Moses. What a confusion! Instead of comparing the Christian ethical rules to the identical Jewish ethical rules (which, by the way, are for the most part almost the same), one compares an ethical ideal to a paragraph of a legal code, which is an exceptionally strict one in general, and often provides for very draconic punishments.

Actually, Christianity, although it set up very far-reaching moral requirements, divested them of every legal power. Through its lack of interest in the legal order of society, through its declaration that its kingdom is not of this world, Christianity gave its consent to the divorce of ethics and justice, morality and law. Justice and the law were, therefore, relinquished entirely to the authority of the stronger ones.

3. I see still a third essential difference between Judaism and Christianity: the Jewish religion is in a large measure a *national* religion, whereas the Christian religion is a universal one ("Catholic" in the actual sense of the word). A large part of the Jewish Bible is devoted to the history of the Children of Israel. The Jewish people is designated there as the Chosen People. The Law of Moses, particularly the religious laws that pertain to the holidays, is considerably interwoven with national historical events of remembrance. Incidentally, it is part of the nature of a code of laws to be limited in space and in time; the only thing is that its principles may have a universal character.

In this regard Judaism appears to be narrower and more limited than Christianity. However, this is only correct with two essential reservations. In the first place the "Chosenness" concept among Jews has quite a definite meaning. It is by no means a question of any practical material superiority; about a superiority comprising in itself any special privileges or rights over other nations. In truth, it is a question here of special commitments the Jewish people (and those who join it) have taken upon themselves; it is a question of the sacred burden of the Torah, of the burden of the Torah and the commandments which has been imposed on it as "a Kingdom of Priests and a Holy People," appointed to carry to the world the doctrine of One and eternal God. And secondly, if it is true that from the beginning and in the very first texts, the impression arises of a Jewishness that is confined within the narrow circle of the people of Israel, it also cannot be denied that Jewish religious thought developed in the course of time and ripened to the conception of humanity, to universalism. This universalism, however, did not consist of the will to impose its own Torah on other nations, but, in the great hope with which it sustained itself, that the *spirit* of this Torah, its ethics, its fundamental principles, its "ways," would become the general property of humanity.

I draw your attention particularly to the last sentence of Micah: "For all nations shall go each in the name of its god, and we shall go in the name of the Lord our God forever and ever." Although it preserves its national character, Jewry really identifies itself here with universalism by the fact that its very principle comprises respect for freedom and the individuality of all nations in their general striving for justice and peace.

Until now we were speaking chiefly about the Jewish Bible. And the Talmud? The Talmud is in very bad repute not merely in the Christian

world but even among a great many Jews with European culture. If
Christianity also included in the totality of the Scriptures the Jewish Bible,
which was completed before the Christian era, it renounced altogether
the Talmud, which originated partly during the Christian era, partly even
later than the Gospels. Most of the secularist Jewish intellectuals do not
have a more positive attitude to it; they judge it so severely for the very
reason that they themselves had much to endure from the fanaticism of
rabbinical Orthodoxy, from its leaders and adherents, whom one meets
constantly in the camp of social reaction, both Jewish and non-Jewish.
For these intellectuals the Talmud and the later rabbinical literature means
only one great retrogression in comparison to the Bible.

And indeed reasons for retrogression were not lacking in Jewish history
since the Jewish Bible was completed. Jewish national life was utterly
destroyed. From all sides persecutions began to heap upon the Jews,
which perforce degraded their Jewish and spiritual level, narrowed their
horizons, developed feelings of suspicion and hostility in relation to the
non-Jewish world.

Nevertheless, in my opinion, the great progressive work that the Talmud accomplished, regardless of its formalistic casuistry [*pilpul*] and even,
indeed, with the help of this dialectic, consisted in *humanizing,* making
the laws of the Torah in consonance with the essence of the Torah itself.
The law of the Torah is often very strict, literally draconic. "An eye for
an eye, a tooth for a tooth." The pitilessness of those desert times begins
finally to insult the ethical feeling of the Jewish people, which was brought
up in the spirit of a merciful God and love of one's fellow man. Inas-
much as one was forbidden to change the Torah itself, the source of the
code of morality and the foundation of the existence of the nation—the
Talmud began to 'interpret" the Torah. From the necessity of carrying
further the evolution which was sown in the Torah itself, to change it
according to the ethical conceptions and requirements of the time, while
at the same time not altering a single letter of the Torah; from this necessity the specific Talmudic interpretation was born. And the authors of
the Talmud were real artists in this.

There are a considerable number of sins for which the death penalty
is prescribed according to the Torah. The Talmud, however, prohibits
the issuance of such a verdict with countless preconditions, so that in
practice it should become only rare. It goes so far that, according to
the Talmud, "a Sanhedrin[3] that condemns to the death penalty once in
seven years deserves the name of a murderous court."

It is time I should summarize and come to conclusions.

For me, the Jewish religion, like every other religion, is a social product. Not God created man according to His image, but man creates his God according to his own image. It is not God who chose the people of Israel, but Israel selected its God, fashioned its conception about the world and life and its rules of practical conduct.

Everything, however, that comes to us from the past bears, of necessity, a historical imprint. Everything that was created and experienced in the course of different generations, bears the traces of different periods. According to my hypothesis, the Jewish conception of the world and the Jewish religion did not remain unchanged, but, on the contrary, evolved with the times. However, this evolution resembles the development of a fruit tree: the kernel from which it has grown to the fruit that it bears on its branches. The double fundamental nature of Jewish religion, its metaphysical nature—the transcendental character of God—and its ethical nature—the sacred character of the human being—was the internal factor that determined its evolution. This historical fate of the Jewish people, on the other hand, determined the level of development achieved, the purity of the concepts, as well as the concrete rules for its practical behavior. The manner in which our people interpreted for itself the origin of its world-view and its rules of conduct, the supernatural elements with which it infused it, were dependent upon the historical conditions and especially its cultural level, and were certainly not the same in different social strata. The essential nature, the internal spirit, however, did not change. It was and remained an integral component of our being which cannot be uprooted any more.

(1940)

NOTES

1. Deut. 6:4.
2. The prayer said by Jews upon going to bed, and as part of the morning and evening prayers.
3. Highest Jewish tribunal at the time of the Second Temple.

SHMUEL NIGER

Shmuel Niger—critic, literary historian, and journalist—epitomized the modern Yiddish renaissance in Eastern Europe and the struggle to transplant it to America.

Shmuel Charney, who took the pseudonym of Niger, was born in Russia in 1883, in a family of learned Hasidim. He received the traditional East European yeshiva education but also studied secular subjects. He was almost ordained as a rabbi, but his interests in Russian literature, the revolutionary movement, and Jewish group survival prevailed. Niger made his debut as a writer in 1904, becoming for a while the exponent and leader of the Jewish Socialist Territorialists. As the Czarist counter-revolutionary "Black Hundreds" regained the upper hand, they let loose a wave of pogroms and repressions. Niger was imprisoned and was released only after enduring horrible physical torture at the hands of the Russian White Guards.

Niger became the most representative figure of the Yiddish renaissance, which in 1908 was ushered in by the magazine *Literarishe Monatshriftn*— a publication that signalized the coming of age of Yiddish literature and the idea that literature is an end in itself. During the years 1910–13 Niger devoted himself to the study of the humanities at the Universities of Berlin and Bern. In 1913, upon receiving an invitation to become editor of the literary review *Die Yiddishe Velt,* he returned to Vilna, where he transformed this periodical into a first-rate magazine for literature and culture, publishing numerous essays on Yiddish writers and many reviews.

At the end of 1919 Niger left Eastern Europe and came to New York. He resided there until his death in 1955, contributing weekly literary articles to the Yiddish daily *Der Tog.*

Generally considered a Yiddishist, Niger, as his book *Bilingualism in Jewish Literature* manifests, did not minimize the value of Hebrew as a vehicle of Jewish culture. For him "Hebrew and Yiddish constitute a similar couple . . . similarly fated for each other."

Niger was a seminal thinker who did not stand above the battle—he fought Yiddish yellow journalism, chauvinists, and bigots. He took nothing for granted, examining all values, traditions, and intellectual currents with a critical, perceptive intelligence. He discerned no dualism in the categories of Jewishness and universalism, for he knew that each nurtures the other.

WHAT I BELIEVE IN AS A JEW

Ani maamin, I believe first of all in . . . *believing.*
This statement needs at least a short commentary.

One can struggle to be a Jew without the capacity to believe in the Holy One. But it is difficult and perhaps impossible to be a Jew if one does not have the gift of believing in *holiness.* It is as impossible to imagine Jewish history without *tsaddikim* as it is to be a Jew without faith.

It is true that there are Jews who live by virtue of the faith that other Jews profess, but I am speaking of genuine, not spiritually parasitical, Jewishness. True Jewishness, even when it is not religious Jewishness—*Yiddishkeit*—would not have been able to survive had it not been based on faith. In other words, one cannot be even a nonreligious Jew without believing, at the very least, in the spiritual values that are latent in Jewish history. How can one believe in Jewish values if one has no feeling for higher spiritual matters? How can one accept suffering for the sake of Jewishness if one's imagination is too poor to perceive that which it is impossible to comprehend with our senses? One must be as confident of the inner light of the world as one is of the starry sky over our heads, if one wishes to see the hidden light of Jewishness. One is not fit to be a Jew if one is not blessed with the will and the ability to *believe.* And when I say *believe* I do not mean it in the theological sense, but rather in the teleological—in the sense Y. L. Peretz implied when he said that "the world is not chaos"; "the world has a heart." Yes, a Jew must be certain that even if there is no *Judge,* it is unthinkable that there is no judgment

I believe that there is a judgment, that there is a reckoning, or, if one prefers, an awareness of man's responsibility—his responsibility to himself, his responsibility to his own heart and to the heart of the world.

In this sense, as a human being and as a Jew, which is one and the same thing, I cannot imagine any Jewish credo without this first and fundamental belief—to believe in belief. Upon this somewhat shaky yet nonetheless firm foundation, I have built all my other credos! Let me cite the most essential of them.

87

I believe—because I want to and must believe in the survival and in the insupplantable worth of our people. I believe, I want to, and I must believe, in our historic ethnic survival as a people not because there is a biological law of collective perpetuation but because our history has and will continue to have meaning, worth, and significance. Survival for the sake of survival is for the Jews as a people simply unthinkable, not to mention the fact that existence as vegetation is perhaps not important. An individual may live even a bitter and unhappy life only because he does not want to die or because he is afraid of dying. But a collectivity, a people, especially such a people as we Jews are— a people that does not give assurance to its sons and daughters of personal security, a people that by surviving as a people does not alleviate the lot of its members but rather exposes them to danger—such a people must be worthy of their suffering, their sacrifices. And we can be worthy of these sacrifices only if our historical experience provides us with something that no other people possesses and when our present life is a creative continuity of our lofty past. Only the awareness that the great life-experiences, the moral powers, and all the other spiritual treasures that we have accumulated and continue to accumulate for ourselves and for the world could not have been accumulated by other nations, whose existence was more secure and stable, only this belief in our creative spiritual distinctiveness, only the feeling for the specific profound melody that we are contributing to cosmic music has made possible the ecstasy achieved by our great individuals, and for the masses—the burden of self-sacrifice, the self-sacrifice that is often the tragic glory of our history. It seems to me, therefore, that Jews will either live as a people in spiritual creativity, and therefore be culturally different from other nations, or they will not live at all. And when I say this I mean all the Jews, not only those who live in the Diaspora. Even if many of us should have an opportunity to settle in *Eretz Yisroel,* and even if we attain our own economic and political life there, we will not survive as a people whose existence has worth and significance if we become *like all other nations,* and do not continue the unique evolution of our historic experience, which began with our ancestor Abraham and continues down to his youngest great-grandchildren.

Not only "in alien lands," as a minority, but also in its own land, under its own flag, may such a people as our Jewish people assimilate morally. The danger of spiritual slavery, or slavery in freedom, as Ahad Ha'Am labeled it, exists not only in the lands of emancipation, but also in the land of auto-emancipation. The great advantage of having our own coun-try does not lie in the fact, as many think, that there we will be able to shed the burden of Jewish history and become a people like all other peoples; on the contrary, it resides in the fact that in our own country we will have a greater and fuller opportunity to realize our right and our duty to continue developing the main characteristics of our historic in-dividuality.

I believe that the Jewish people as it is today is more a product of the last two thousand years of its history than of the first thousand years. This is so because the Diaspora epoch is more, rather than less, Jewish history and Jewish heritage than the history of the Jewish tribes in *Eretz Yisroel*. For only in the periods of exile did the kernels finally sprout that were sown in our own land, only then did they bring forth ripe fruit. In *Eretz Yisroel* stood our cradle; as a people we matured in the world, in the Diaspora. Only there did Israel, the Torah and God become one. Only there did *Israel* become what it is, and the Torah, Jewish cul-ture, what it is. The Prophets were the forecasters, the promisers, and the preparers of this spiritual maturation, and it is true that they revealed themselves in *Eretz Yisroel*. But it is also true that prophecy was the mightiest protest against the Jewish reality of the time. Prophecy man-ifested the *potential* spiritual moral possibilities of the Jewish people. But these divine potentialities became manifest only in the epoch of the Tannaim and Amoraim,[1] among whom there were as many Diaspora Jews as Palestinian Jews.

If during the epoch and in the milieu of the Prophets were revealed the hidden foundations of the Jewish people's spiritual edifice, it was in later epochs that they built it and lived in it. It was in the Diaspora that the dream of the Prophets was translated into the language of reality. Never-theless, when we seek in our past the sources that should and do water our life and our creativity, we should not be concerned with whether they originated in Palestine or in the Diaspora. We should rather consider their intrinsic worth—whether they have dried up and are empty or whether they are still full and ebullient. From each epoch, each stream, each current in our historic life we should select those religious and ethical values or those intellectual and artistic achievements that can help bind us to our historical tradition without our being bound by it.

I believe that all the currents of our past creativity can and should nur-ture and fructify our creativity now and always. I believe that all their apparent contradictions are a passing phase. They are a transient expression of the kind of extremism that defines every faction when it is new, when on the one hand it meets bitter opposition or on the other, indifference. The new faction must by nature be militant, fanatical, and extremist. Later, however, the situation changes, the edges of the rigid young ideas are gradually rubbed off; the contradictions between the old and the new philosophies are more or less reconciled, and yesterday's enemies themselves hardly notice that they have become partners.

We have a clear example of this in the social cultural history of the European Jews in the nineteenth century. During the first half of that century a war flared up between Orthodoxy and Reform in the West, between Hasidism and Haskalah enlightenment in Eastern Europe; in the second half a new controversy arose between the social and the national ideas. All these disputes and controversies were eventually settled. Hasidism stirred up religious feelings that were in danger of congealing, and, by opening new sources of faith, Hasidism enriched the Jewish folk-imagination as well as the creative imagination of individuals. Haskalah for its part liberated our thought and pointed the way to modern culture. The liberated thought of one part of Jewry and the awakened religious mood of another part erupted into a war between the Maskilim and Hasidim. It seemed that it would be a war of life and death; at least that is how it looked in the first half of the nineteenth century. But then, during the second half, two other intellectual currents appeared in Jewish life. On the one hand, moden national consciousness began to stir. On the other hand, the social idea penetrated the Jewish milieu. Here were two new forces, each fighting to be sole ruler. And again it looked as if one or the other, nationalism or socialism, would have to yield. But soon it became evident that this, too, was not so. Moses Hess' teachings began to shine through, and faced with their bright light, socialism *recognized* Jewish national Messianism and they fraternized with one another. It became obvious there was no contradiction between the struggle for social justice and that for the Jewish national renaissance. On the contrary, a partnership developed; social and national motifs merged and became one. What is more, not only were these two streams joined together, but the once antagonistic ideas of Hasidism and Haskalah flowed into the newer life-currents and were absorbed by them. In the Jewish national movement, Hasidism's deepened yearning for redemption was fused with the youthful, cultural ideas of the Haskalah. Similarly, in the Socialist-Revolutionary Jewish movement the self-sacrificing spirit, the ecstasy, the redemptive dreams of Hasidism were combined with the secularity and universalism of the Haskalah. The psychic types of a Jewish Socialist, a Folkist, a Halutz were a product of the melting pot that the fires of Jewish history had ignited with social and national self-consciousness.

This historical example proves that it is not only necessary but *possible* to be nourished by all the currents that have watered and fructified our folk-soil. And it does not matter that in the past these currents flowed in opposite directions.

Another example is the story "If Not Higher." It is a genuine product of the Hasidic folk-fantasy recreated by Peretz, a modern writer, a product of the Haskalah. In other words, the story represents a true synthesis of Hasidism and Haskalah. The moral of Peretz's story is social-ethical—the Rebbe's helping a poor woman is a superior achievement to flying to heaven. Its significance is national-cultural. Thus we have a harmonious blending not only of Hasidic and Haskalah motifs but also of social and national ideas.

Modern Jewish culture has been and is the sum of all those forces that once quarreled among themselves and later were reconciled. I believe it is especially important to emphasize this now, at a time when, because of the great tribulations that we are experiencing, there is a tendency among us to become extremist, one-sided, and to destroy the synthesis, to pulverize the totality that we have achieved at such a great cost.

It is fashionable nowadays to speak contemptuously of the Haskalah epoch, the great epoch of our modern social history. People speak disparagingly and resentfully not only about its transitory faults, but about its great achievements. Because of the husk that has shriveled, they want to discard the essence, the healthy kernel, that has remained. *Therefore,* let us go back, they say, to good old Orthodoxy! Now is the time to remember that just as we could not and would not return to the extremism of the "Epoch of the Antithesis," as Simon Dubnow called the Epoch of Emancipation and Assimilation, so we cannot and must not revive the one-sided *thesis* of the isolated and half-congealed, although deeply Jewish, ghetto-life before the period of Emancipation.

I believe that the compromise we have achieved after such difficult wrestling, the compromise between the past and present, between tradition and reform, between Jewish national self-awareness and civil rights—this reconciliation between Jew and human being, people and humanity—this compromise can and must remain.

Our auto-emancipation is, as the name indicates, a continuation of Emancipation, and only as such will it retain continuity. Even today's

Orthodox Jew, especially the Neo-Orthodox Jew, cannot get along without the means that the Haskalah and the modernization of Jewish life have given him, although he may indulge in belittling their goals.

As to the other manifestations of contemporary religious and national Jewishness, it is not necessary to point out how much they owe to the ideas and movements that have brought us in contact with science, literature, art, and the milieu of enlightened non-Jewish society. Without this creative encounter we would have had neither the Science of Judaism, nor our new literature in both languages (in Hebrew and Yiddish), nor our theatre, nor all those manifestations that reveal our universal spirit, our vital rhythm, and our hunger for the plastic arts.

It seems to me that we are giving too much attention to the question We and They, and too little attention to ourselves. Our social and even our spiritual activities are directed too much to the *outside* and not enough to our inner selves. We should turn our face to our inner life. Surely we must protect ourselves, but woe to a society that is so busy with self-protection that it has not enough time and energy left for self-criticism and self-improvement. When I speak of our inner life, I mean by that our whole life, not only this or that part of our life, and our life *everywhere*—both in the lands of the Diaspora and in *Eretz Yisroel*.

(1946)

NOTES

1. *Tannaim* were the Jewish scholars who lived during the first two centuries of the common era. The *Amoraim* were the Jewish scholars in Palestine and especially in Babylonia in the third to sixth centuries.

YUDEL MARK

Yudel Mark was a man of many talents: a noted Jewish philologist, a folklorist, a historian of Yiddish literature, an educator, and the editor of the *Great Yiddish Dictionary*. Born in Lithuania in 1897, Yudel Mark received his education in Vilna and at Petersburg University. He was a leader of the Jewish Folkists and later became secretary-general of the Jewish National Council of Lithuania. He was also a founder of the Yiddish Scientific Institute in Vilna.

In 1936 he came to America, and in New York he became the consultant on the Yiddish schools for the Jewish Education Committee. Thereafter he became a central pillar of the Yiddish secular segment of the American Jewish community—acting not only as a writer and scholar but as the ideologue of the Yiddish cultural movement. He was a Yiddishist—i.e., he believed that the perpetuation of Yiddish is essential for Jewish creativity, and that Yiddish, though no longer the mother tongue of the American Jewish child, should be preserved as a special tongue for that area of our life which is permeated with "insular" Jewishness, such as celebrations of Jewish holidays, and other special Jewish activities and occasions.

This does not mean that Mark was a language fanatic who considered Yiddish the cure-all for ethnic survival. No, indeed! Yet he believed that in order to be culturally creative, there must be some separation from the majority culture, and this is only possible by means of another language—Yiddish. To teach Yiddish is not only to teach a language but to open the gate and point the way to Jewish folk-culture.

Mark was not only a theoretician of the Yiddish secular school but also a practical educator. He published a series of grammars, texts and workbooks for Yiddish schools on the elementary, secondary, and college levels, as well as pedagogic materials for teachers. He has made a significant contribution to Jewish education in Eastern Europe and America.

In 1970 Yudel Mark settled in Jerusalem, where he edited the *Great Yiddish Dictionary* and occupied a central position among the Yiddish writers and scholars of Israel. On a visit to the United States in August 1975, he died.

JEWISHNESS AND SECULARISM

All forms of Jewish differentness are forms of Jewishness. All Jewish mores and customs, all beliefs and commandments, all specific social attitudes, all unique Jewish ideas—all of this is included in the great concept of *Yiddishkeit*.

It is of no importance where these life-styles stem from; it is only important that they differ from the life-styles of the non-Jewish neighbors. In the seventeenth century, the *kapote* [long coat] did not embody even a shred of *Yiddishkeit* but later the *kapote* embodied Jewish differentness and was associated with the Jewish pious life-style in Eastern Europe.

This differentness preserved us as a people. Without it we would have been crushed long ago, and no trace would have been left of the living, suffering Jew. They would have relished the books that were left by us, and extolled our ideas and accomplishments for world culture. We should apparently have had a grand tombstone instead of a bleak fate among the nations of the world. But we would have been buried in the cemetery of nations and languages together with the Babylonians, the Persians, and so forth. But we never ceased creating forms of *Yiddishkeit* under all sorts of conditions, circumstances, under the various transformations of our history. Jews created Jewishness, lived with it, and due to it have survived.

Is Jewishness (*Yiddishkeit*) a religious creation? Yes and no; yes, if you look at it from the vantage point of the Jewish religion that embraces everything, or if you look at Jewishness through the eyes of a pious Jew. But *Yiddishkeit* is not a religious creation, but a much broader sort of product if you measure it by the criterion of other religions.

Is Jewishness an ethnic creation? Yes and no; yes, because the Jewish nationalist, the survivalist, the one who wants to preserve Jewish differentness under all conditions, in all the Diasporas, everywhere, discerns and *could* interpret all customs, all ideas, all life-styles of the Jew as deliberate or nondeliberate means to dissociate them as a separate nationality, an independent nation among the nations of the world. Jewishess is the way

97

of living among the nations of the world. Jewishness is the way of living among the Gentiles not as Gentiles. Surely this was implied by the one who expressed the opinion that with the coming of the Messiah all the Practical Commandments will be annulled. Therefore, Jewishness is the Jewish ethnic creation. But it cannot be measured by the general nationality criterion of Europe, nor can it be measured by the American nation concept, for Jewishness is an immensely rich and variegated creation. Jewishness is a concept that includes everything that belongs to the sphere of ethnicism, but in addition, also, everything that belongs to the realm of religiosity, and that is included in additional spheres.

Perhaps it would be more correct to say that Jewishness is religiousness of a high grade plus ethnicity on a very high level. But even then the formula is not a complete one, because we must add to it other ingredients—for instance, the fact of being a minority, i.e., the social and psychological elements of being a minority group. The Latin terms *religion* and *nation* did an unintentional wrong to the researcher who wanted to find out the character of Jews. The concepts *oomah* [Hebrew for "people"] and *emunah* [Hebrew for "faith"] would have been more flexible. The one who forged the idea: Israel and the Torah are identical, expressed profoundly the essence of the Jew; in our free translation it would imply: Jews and Jewishness create one whole.

When we bear in mind the complexity of Jewishness and the impossibility of transferring non-Jewish categories to Jewish life, then we comprehend our kind of *Yiddishkeit*. We cannot say that we are discarding everything religious because then we would discard almost everything; neither can we say: we are accepting everything of an ethnic nature, for then we would have to accept almost everything. Apparently we cannot apply one criterion.

Our Jewishness is decidedly not Orthodox. Even though we may have the finest expressions of infatuation for the old-time, perfected traditional Jewish differentness. Even when we yearn for the genuine, all-embracing God-fearing way of life. Even though we should think that only a hundred percent tradition would preserve us—we apparently will not be able to make such a sacrifice. We are too individualistic, too free, we have learned too much history, sociology, and psychology to think that every religious "don't" could be sacred, and each of the Practical Commandments of significance. We cannot stop being analytical, we cannot follow blindly a sacred book, paragraph by paragraph. As long as we remain true to ourselves, we cannot jump out of the influences and results of the last two hundred years of Jewish history. Of our own free will we shall not lock ourselves up behind ghetto walls, and we will not accept the burden of all the 613 [*Taryag*] Commandments. Perhaps we are too sophisticated, but that is what we are. Adjustment to the environment is not at issue, for we are, up to a certain degree, the products of a process of adjustment that has taken place, and we cannot get out of our skin. We will not grow beards and earlocks, and put on skullcaps.

Our moderate Jewishness is a Reform Jewishness. Since we do not accept everything within the tradition, but we analyze, we select and adjust to our ambience, we are, of necessity, reforming Jewishness. Our reform is surely not of the kind that the German Jews introduced and that was later exported to America and other lands. Their Reform movement was the movement of rich Jews and those who take alien and cold Protestantism as a model. Our Reform movement is, first of all, a different social milieu of poorer Jews, of Jews who love their people and wish forever to be attached to it. We do not wish to compare the Jewish religion to Christian religions, and we do not wish to imitate alien models. The survival of the Jewish people is our chief goal, and we wish to preserve, as much as possible, Jewish differentness. But we are also faced with the problem of the *impossibility* of persisting in the old ways in their inviolability and entirety.

Our kind of Jewishness should be characterized as an attempt to reach a new synthesis between radical Reformism and Orthodoxy; as a blend of intellectual values, and a way of life—a blend that does not forget that deeply rooted Jewishness is a fusion of religious, ethnic, and folkways. And this synthesis is created by a group that speaks in behalf of the people's interests, that remembers both the social advancement of the common man and his spiritual development and his role in preserving and in the forging ahead of Jewish history. This is the synthesis that our Yiddish literature has already, to a large extent, found (primarily in the works of Y. L. Peretz), but our social thought has not as yet attained. This is the synthesis of everything that is constructive, that may serve in preserving our people, that may render meaningful and beautiful its existence. This should be the synthesis of separating ourselves in differentness, and at the same time facing the whole world—even if it is hostile to us—in order that we may take from it whatever is worth taking, and in order to improve it eventually, so that it would be worthwhile to live in this world.

Secularism then is anti-dogmatism, it is the need and the possibility of thinking more or less freely. *It is the theory that there can be a Jewishness that is viable without the walls of a spiritual ghetto.* Secular culture is that Jewish culture that develops, grows, and thrives under a spiritually free heaven, under all kinds of influences: it is authentically Jewish, rooted, but also from indirect sources, and non-Jewish ones.

Secularism implies accepting the whole world, facing it. Secularism means taking over everything valuable, essential, that has been created spiritually by non-Jews, and first of all taking over scientific technical achievement, but also the profoundest and finest of the cultural peaks of all the nations. But secularism would be uncritical and superficial if it pursued everything that is alien, or that is in vogue spiritually. Secularism can and should be critical, without losing heart, without servility, without enthusiasm for things non-Jewish; it can and should be exceedingly fastidious, and should weigh and measure upon the scale of our perennial ethics, and reach only for the best flour from alien mills.

We always had single followers of secularism among us. There were even whole eras when secularity was outstanding and almost dominant. But Ashkenazic Jewry was less secular than Sephardic Jewry, perhaps because of the fact that the neighboring peoples were more malicious and backward than those with whom the Sephardim came in contact. Since *Gzeyres Takh V'Tat* [the Chmelnitzky pogroms of 1648–49], since the Sabbatai Zevi movement, the dominant current in *Yiddishkeit* became harsher and more dogmatic, whereas the secular ingredient became weaker and persecuted. The Maskilim [Enlightened Ones] were those who started among us, ardently and uninterruptedly, the current of secularism.

Our modern culture in Yiddish is the most vivid expression of secularism throughout the Jewish world. But not the only one. Modern Hebrew literature is also secular, and in various languages we have in the last two hundred years genuinely Jewish secular creations. Language or partisan ideologies do not determine the secular character of creativity. Herzl and Ahad Ha'am were surely secular, as were Moses Hess[1] and Pinsker.[2] Dubnow and Shipper[3] were as secular as Zunz[4] and Graetz.[5] Neither were Hillel Zeitlin[6] or Franz Rosenzweig[7] free from secularity. And the Jerusalem University is no less secular than YIVO (Yiddish Scientific Institute).

Secularism does not imply the negation of what is Jewishly traditional, but rather complements it. Secularism has not come to repudiate all that is old, but rather to create new additions. Secularism does not turn aside from old sources, and does not wish to sever itself from roots, but rather aims at getting more sunrays for the leaves of our tree, and wants our roots to get nourishment with juices from all kinds of soil. And secularism believes that we will be able to digest all juices and bask in all these rays, so that our four-thousand-year-old tree should be able to bear new fruit, Jewish fruit with a Jewish taste. One need not be ashamed of the term *secularism* any more than of the expression *Yiddishkeit*. They are both precious words. They can both be sacred words.

(1948)

NOTES

1. *Moses Hess* (1812–1875), Jewish social philosopher and Zionist precursor in Germany who wrote the Zionist classic *Rome and Jerusalem*.
2. *Leon Pinsker* (1821–91), pioneer Zionist who wrote *Auto-Emancipation*.
3. *Ignacy Shipper* (1884–1942), Jewish historian in Poland, and one of the founders of the Poale Zion (Labor Zionists), murdered by the Germans in Treblinka.
4. *Leopold Zunz* (1794–1886), founder of the "Science of Judaism" in Germany.
5. *Heinrich Graetz* (1817–1891), Jewish historian and Bible scholar in Germany.
6. *Hillel Zeitlin* (1872–1943), Jewish philosopher and publicist in Poland, killed by Germans in the Warsaw Ghetto.
7. *Franz Rosenzweig* (1886–1929), Jewish philosopher in Germany.

TSIVYON (DR. BEN-ZION HOFFMAN)

Dr. Ben-Zion Hoffman, a very popular journalist writing under the pen-name Tsivyon, was an erudite contributor to the *Jewish Daily Forward*. He was born in Latvia in 1874 and died in New York in 1954. At eighteen he was ordained as a rabbi; coming under the influence of the Haskalah, he went abroad, and in 1906 he received his Ph.D. in Berlin. Two years later he came to America, where he devoted himself to journalism.

At first he became the editor of the Hebrew daily in America, *Hayom* (1909), and later, one of the prominent contributors to the *Jewish Daily Forward,* for which he wrote on political, literary, and scientific topics.

Tsivyon, a student of the socialist and labor movements; well versed in old and new Hebrew literature, was distinguished by a lucid, simple, and somewhat humorous style. A man of skeptical temperament—a rare phenomenon in his milieu—he was more of a thinker than a fighter, more an observer than an activist. With humor, clarity, and logic he championed modern, secular Jewish culture, Yiddish, and the Yiddish cultural movement. Being more of a pragmatist than a dogmatist, he won many followers for his ideas.

JEWISHNESS AND FAITH

Not long ago we heard an appeal: "Jews, return to the ghetto!" However, the Jews did not obey and did not go there. Presumably they waited for the summoners to go first and show them the way. The summoners, however, never intended to go. For them it was merely a rhetorical phrase. The appeal was issued not by religious Jews but by nonreligious Jewish intellectuals who had once had ideals and lost them.

Therefore, the wiser among them soon realized that it had been a foolish, impractical summons, and they became silent. And the fools? They always have a paradise of their own in which they live. The main point, however, is that the Jews in America remained where they were.

Everything, then, seems all right. But it is not. We are indeed not asked to return to the Jewish ghetto—incidentally, who knows where the Jewish ghetto in America is located?—for this, however, they make a great fuss about "Jewish content." "Jewish content" is a much older contention than the appeal: "Return to the ghetto!"

And again the same point: it is not believing, devout Jews that are seeking a content from you, but unbelieving Jewish intellectuals, who once had ideals and then lost them, have undertaken to look for a Jewish content, and some of them have reached such a state that they have begun to cry: "Jews, return to the synagogue!"

I have nothing whatever against their appealing to Jews to return to the synagogue. They do not drag one by the coattails, and everyone is free to disobey them. I just have one complaint: why do they not go themselves when they bid others to go?

I understand when a devout Orthodox Jew comes and says that we should go to the synagogue because the essence of Judaism is God and His Torah. This is a point of view against which it is difficult to argue, because the strong arguments will be on the side of the devout Jew. He will be able to prove by various examples from Jewish history that only the Jewish God and His Torah have preserved the Jewish people. And I understand such a Jew very well when he says that Jewishness can be maintained only when Jews will believe in God and His Torah. And

105

one must not merely believe in the Torah but also observe it. And there
is a great deal to observe. There exist not merely 613 commandments
which one must observe, but more sins against which one must be on
one's guard. What, however, can those unbelieving Jews tell you about
a "Jewish content" when they attempt to nourish you with their philosophy of the Jewish God and His Torah?

The philosophy about the Jewish God and the Torah, about the ethics
and morality of the Jewish religion, may perhaps sustain a few individuals
in their Jewishness, but cannot sustain a people.

I will not attempt to enumerate all the factors that have had an effect
in preserving the Jewish people until today. It will suffice if I admit that
the Jewish religion was a very important factor. However, Jewish religion
does not mean the philosophy about the Jewish God and the ethics and
morality of the Jewish Torah. Jewish religion means to pray, to observe
Kashruth, to keep the Sabbath, to fast on Yom Kippur, and to obey everything that is written in the *Shulhan Arukh.*[1]

When the enlightened Jew begins truly to believe in God and attains
the conviction that his Jewish content depends on the Jewish Torah, he
must do what Dr. Nathan Birnbaum[2] did: he put on a skullcap, began
to pray three times a day, to observe all 613 commandments, and became a member of the devout *Agudath Yisroel.*[3] This is consistent.

Dr. Birnbaum knew previously the entire philosophy about the Jewish
God, about the ethics and morality of the Jewish Torah, and about the
entire mysticism that was created around the Jewish Messiah. He could
have written whole books about it; but he understood that Jewishness
cannot sustain itself on the philosophy of enlightened Jews concerning
God and His Torah. If Jewish religion helped to preserve the Jewish
people, it was not the philosophy of Jewish religion, but the "practical
everyday precepts," *mitsves maysies* as they are called, the fulfillment
of all commandments and the guarding against all transgressions.[4] He
therefore put on a skullcap and subordinated himself to the burden of
the Torah.

The God of the everyday Jewish person is far from a philosophic One.
He is anything but the God of the Rambam,[5] which is expressed by
everything *that He is not:* He does not have the shape of a body and
is not a body, He has no beginning and no end, no one can see Him
because He is concealed from all human eyes, and the like. It is difficult
to portray such a God to an unsophisticated person. The God of the
ordinary Jew is expressed through everything that he can imagine *that*

He is: He sees everything, He hears everything, and He punishes and rewards, He makes a person sick and healthy, He gives long years and shortens the years, He makes a person poor and makes him rich—in short a God that simple human reason can imagine. He is a humanized God. And it is clear that one must fear such a God, one must pray and weep in His presence, because He can do good and can also do evil. He is the God of the *u nesane toykef*.[6]

And it was for this God that Jews endured all afflictions, anguish, and sufferings. Ordinary Jews would not have suffered so much for a philosophic God whom an average person finds it difficult to conceive.

The philosophic God was created by nonbelievers who are seeking a faith. And it is the same, as well, with the ethics and morality of the Jewish religion. They lack the faith and will to harness themselves in the yoke of the Torah and to observe every day all the commands and commandments that they impose on the Jew. They therefore make the matter easy for themselves. It is merely a question of ethics and morality. In this way one is a Jew with Jewish content. However, they have no need to pray, fast, observe the Sabbath with all its prohibitions, and bear on their shoulders the heavy *Shulhan Arukh* with its innumerable laws.

If the existence of Judaism has to depend on this unbelieving Jewish faith, I do not believe that Judaism can long endure, even if these unbelieving Jews should put on an act and observe the seder or shake a lulab.

The truly devout Jew does not even ask why we have to suffer all these afflictions on behalf of Jewishness. Such a question cannot occur to him at all. Can he cease to be a Jew? After all, God created him to be a Jew.

The question whether it pays, and for what purpose one should bear the afflictions, can only occur to an unbeliever. And if he attempts to seek the answer in the Jewish God and His Torah, he is in a bad way: because he really does not believe in God. For such a person the best and strongest answer is that one is a Jew not because he wishes to be a Jew but because he cannot give up being a Jew.

If it were a question of calculating whether it pays or not, we would be very badly off. Many would surely reach the conclusion that it does not pay. But it is not a question of making a calculation. The existence of a people does not depend on calculating whether it pays to exist and suffer or not.

An individual Jew may reach a conclusion that it does not pay for him to be a Jew. And in former years a Jew had a way out—he became converted to Christianity. True, he remained a Jew after that as well; however, there was at least a method to deceive oneself. But today that method does not exist either. Conversion is of no avail. One can neither deceive oneself nor can one deceive others. But however things may be, an entire people cannot do what an individual can. An entire people cannot reach a conclusion that it must become converted.

And let us attempt to imagine the impossible, that the entire Jewish people has reached a conclusion that it does not pay to be Jews and suffer. What will it do then? It cannot help itself in any way, it must continue to exist. Sixteen or seventeen million Jews cannot cease to exist.

But what about the so-called Jewish content? Or should the question be posed in a simpler way: what exactly comprises the Jewishness of those who do not observe God's Torah?

It is difficult to give an answer on behalf of such Jews. However, one can formulate the answer in this way: their Jewishness consists in their awareness that they were born Jews and have to remain so. This applies to all. After that come the differentiations. There are those whose national consciousness is more developed, and they feel an attachment for the Jewish people. They cannot even state a definite motive why this is so. In the case of others their national consciousness is clearer. They will tell you that it is influenced by Jewish culture, by Jewish literature or Jewish history. Then they follow up with a theory that various nations should exist and as a matter of course the Jewish nation should also exist. And those who wish to become even more absorbed in theory can indicate to them that there are special reasons why the Jewish people should exist. But the truth is that a people does not exist because of theory, just as it does not exist because of logic. There would not have remained a trace of the Jewish people long ago if it would have had to exist because of logic. There is absolutely no logical reason why Jews had to suffer so many afflictions for the sake of their national existence. And it cannot be explained logically how they have continued to exist.

(1940)

NOTES

1. The collection of laws and prescriptions governing the life of an Orthodox Jew.

2. Nathan Birnbaum (1864–1936), a Jewish author and thinker, former Zionist leader and Yiddishist, who was the president of the Czernowitz Conference in 1908, which proclaimed Yiddish as a national language of the Jewish people. Originally a freethinker, he later became a spokesman for Orthodox Judaism.

3. Lit. "Union of Israel," the name of an international organization of Orthodox Jews, founded in 1912.

4. Both the commands one has to perform and those forbidden add up to 613.

5. First initials of Moyshe ben Maymon (1135–1204), the great Jewish philosopher and scholar, known in the general history of philosophy as Maimonides.

6. Lit. "Let us give affirmation" (to the holiness of the day), the first words in a prayer that is said on Rosh Hashanah and Yom Kippur wherein God's omnipotence is described.

ALBERT EINSTEIN

Albert Einstein, the great physicist, mathematician, and humanitarian, was not only an intellectual giant, but a conscious Jew and an active supporter of Zionism.

Einstein was born in Ulm, Germany in 1879, and was educated in Switzerland. After receiving his degree he was appointed an instructor at Bern University. Later he was a professor at Zurich and Prague. In 1914 Einstein became professor of physics at Berlin University, where he remained until the rise of Nazism in 1933. He then settled in Princeton, New Jersey, where he died in 1955.

After the death of Chaim Weizmann (1952), the first President of Israel, Einstein refused an invitation to stand for election as President of Israel. He was deeply interested in Israeli scientific institutions, especially the Hebrew University, of which he was a trustee, and to which he donated the manuscripts of his theory of relativity.

When he returned to Germany in 1914 he became conscious of his Jewishness. His interest may have been aroused by his warm sympathy with East European Jews who, during the war and the postwar period, fled to Germany, craving the assistance of their fellow Jews. He became a Zionist, being repelled by the assimilated German Jews. Einstein the humanitarian believed that concern for man himself and his fate should always form the chief interest of all technical endeavor.

Although Einstein's greatness was achieved in science and mathematics, his writings on humanistic and Jewish topics contain many noble expressions of human feeling, and penetrating insights. Here are some:

Never do anything against conscience, even if the state demands it. My religion consists of a humble admiration of the illimitable superior spirit who reveals himself in the slight details we are able to perceive with our frail and feeble minds. That deeply emotional conviction of the presence of a superior reasoning power, which is revealed in the incomprehensible universe, forms my idea of God. I believe in Spinoza's God, who reveals himself in the orderly harmony of what exists, not in a God who concerns himself with fates and actions of human beings.

111

JUST WHAT IS A JEW?

The formation of groups has a strengthening and refreshing effect in all spheres of human endeavor, made possible mostly by the struggle between the convictions and goals that the different groups represent. The Jews also form such a group, possessing a character of its own, and anti-Semitism is nothing else than the antagonistic, hostile attitude that the Jewish group evokes among non-Jews. This is a normal social reaction. If not for the political exploitation for evil of this phenomenon, it would never be designated by any special name.

What are the characteristic features of the Jewish group? What, first of all, is a Jew? There are no quick short answers to this question. The simplest manifest answer would be the following: a Jew is a man who believes in the Jewish religion. The superficial character of this answer will soon become apparent through a simple parallel. Let us ask ourselves: what is a snail? To this one can give a similar answer: a snail is a small animal that sits in a snail-shell. This answer is not entirely incorrect, but at the same time it is not an exhaustive one. For the snail-shell is one of the material products of the snail. In exactly the same way the Jewish religion is one of the characteristic products of the Jewish community. Moreover, it is known that a small snail can cast off its shell and not cease in doing so to be a snail. The Jew who gives up his faith (in the formal sense of the word) is in a similar position. He remains a Jew. Difficulties of this sort are encountered if one wishes to explain the essential character of a group.

The bond which unites the Jews in the course of thousands of years, and unites them also today, is, first of all, the democratic ideal of social justice, with the addition of the ideal of mutual help and tolerance among all human beings. Even the oldest Jewish religious writings are permeated with social ideals which had a tremendous effect on Christianity and Islam, and exerted a favorable influence on the social structure of a large part of humanity. The institution of a day of rest in the week must be remembered here as a great blessing for the whole of mankind. Moses, Spinoza, Karl Marx—however much they differed from each other—all lived and sacrificed themselves for the ideal of social justice: after

113

all, it was the tradition of their ancestors that led them across this thorny path. The extraordinary achievements of the Jews in the field of charity are derived from the same source.

The second characteristic feature of the Jewish tradition is its high esteem for every form of intellectual striving and spiritual effort. I am convinced that this respect for intellectual work is completely responsible for the contributions that Jews have made to the progress of every type of knowledge in the broadest sense of the word. In view of the fact that the number of Jews is relatively small, and that considerable difficulties and obstacles are put in their path, the broad scope of their contributions deserves the admiration of all sincere people. I am convinced that this is derived not from their having been specially endowed with a treasury of abilities, but the fact that Jews hold in high esteem every kind of intellectual achievement creates the necessary atmosphere for the development of every kind of talent in which they succeed. At the same time they possess a strong instinct which precludes the blind glorification of any moral authority.

I have confined myself here to these two characteristic hereditary traits which, it seems to me, are the most fundamental ones. These standards and ideals find expression both in small and large matters. They are transmitted from parents to children; they give color to the conversations and opinions between friends; they fill the contents of the religious writings, and they give the characteristic stamp to the communal life of this group. I see the essence of Jewish nature in these sharply marked ideals. The fact that these ideals are carried out in actual daily life merely in an imperfect fashion is only natural. Nevertheless, if someone wishes to express briefly the essential character of a group, the approach must be such as takes the ideal into account first.

More than on its own tradition, the Jewish group matured on the basis of the oppression and hatred it constantly encountered in the world. In this lies, without doubt, one of the fundamental causes for Jewish existence in the course of so many thousands of years.

The Jewish group we briefly characterized above consists of about sixteen million souls, less than one percent of mankind. Their significance as a political factor is very small. They are widely scattered over almost the entire world, and in general they are not organized as a single totality, which means that they are incapable of carrying out any collective act.

If anyone wished to create an image about Jews merely on the basis of what their enemies say, he would have to come to the conclusion that they, the Jews, represent a world power. At first glance this indeed looks like an absurdity; and yet, in my opinion, there is a certain meaning behind it. The Jews as a group may really be impotent; however, the quantity of achievements on the part of individual Jews is everywhere a significant and important one, regardless of the fact that these achievements were made in the face of heavy obstacles. The powers that slumber in the individual are mobilized, and the individual himself is stimulated to deeds and a readiness to sacrifice because he is inspired by the spirit that lives in the group.

From this stems the hatred of Jews, which is borne by those who shun the enlightenment of the people. These people fear intellectual independence more than any other thing in the world. In this I see the chief reason for the bestial hatred of Jews that rages in contemporary Germany. To the Nazis the Jews are not merely a means of diverting the irritation of the masses from themselves, their real oppressors; they see in the Jews an unassimilable element, who cannot be driven like a herd to adopt dogmes uncritically; and if such a condition exists, their authority is constantly threatened, because the Jewish character strives absolutely to enlightenment for the masses.

Proof of the fact that this analysis hits the nail on the head can be seen in the "solemn" ceremony of burning books, which the Nazis carried out soon after they seized power. This act—senseless from a political standpoint—can only be understood as a spontaneous emotional outbreak. This act uncovers and reveals more than any other move of a greater goal and more practical importance.

In political life, as I see it: two contrary tendencies are at work which are constantly combatting each other. The first is an optimistic current which is derived from a belief that the free development of the productive forces of individuals and groups leads throughout to a satisfactory state of society. It recognizes the necessity of a central power that ought to stand above groups and individuals, but surrenders to this power merely organizational and regulating functions. The second, a pessimistic current, assumes that the free play and enterprise of individuals and groups leads to the destruction of society. It therefore strives to base society exclusively on authority, blind obedience, and coercion. Actually this current is pessimistic only to a certain extent, because it is optimistic in regard to those who are, or wish to be, bearers of power and authority. The adherents of this second current are the enemies of the free groups and of the development of independent thinking and thought. They are, moreover, the bearers of political anti-Semitism.

(1949)

SAUL L. GOODMAN

Saul L. Goodman, writer, essayist, and educator, was born in Bodzanow, near Plotsk, Poland, into a Hasidic-Maskil family. He received both a traditional and a secular education, simultaneously studying Talmud and the curriculum of a high school (Gymnasium). In 1921 he migrated to America, where he graduated from the Jewish Teachers Seminary, Boston University (B.S. in social science), and the Graduate Faculty of the New School for Social Research (M.A. in philosophy). He subsequently completed all the courses for a doctorate in philosophy under Professor Horace M. Kallen, and also studied intellectual history at Harvard and philosophy at Columbia University.

Since his student days in 1924, Goodman has been active in the Yiddish cultural movement as a lecturer and writer. For twenty-four years he was the executive director of the Sholem Aleichem Folk Institute, the mother organization of the network of Sholem Aleichem Folk-Shulen. In this capacity Goodman prepared pedagogic materials, established and supervised afternoon and Sunday schools, and edited *Derekh,* a bi-monthly magazine in English and Yiddish for teachers and lay-people.

During the last twenty-six years Goodman has been Professor of Jewish Thought and Yiddish Literature on the Graduate Faculty of Herzliah-Jewish Teachers Seminary. He is the author of a book of essays, *Traditsye un Banayung* (Tradition and Innovation), for which he received the Zvi Kessel Literary Prize in 1968. He also edited *Our First Fifty Years,* a historical survey of the Sholem Aleichem Shulen, and several yearbooks of the Sholem Aleichem Folk Institute.

Goodman has lectured to both American-born and immigrant audiences throughout the United States, Canada, and Mexico, expounding his philosophy of Jewishness based on national cultural values that are viable and relevant for our age. "He is primarily interested in convincing the younger generation that, although we are living and should live with Western culture, we possess our own spiritual riches which we dare not reject, if we do not wish to impoverish our lives" (Jacob Glatstein). "Goodman is an intellectual who has absorbed a great deal of both Jewish and American culture. There is no dichotomy between these two cultures with him" (Elias Schulman).

117

THE CREDO OF A JEWISH EDUCATOR

Like many of my contemporaries I belong in two worlds—the Jewish and the non-Jewish. In my case there was no gap between Jewishness and Western culture. I studied traditional sources and Western civilization simultaneously, and both captivated me. In both I found wisdom, brilliance, and beauty. I was, as a youth, enchanted by the poetry of the Bible, the *Siddur,* by the medieval Hebrew poets whose *piyutim* were included in the *Machzor.* Growing up in Poland, in the house of a learned father, a *lamdan,* who had lived for several years in London and New York, the great world was not unfamiliar to me.

As a youth I believed wholeheartedly in the idea of progress—that in the future we would have better human beings. I saw light and promise in Western civilization. Even as a young man, when I probed Marxist dialectics, I was intrigued at the same time by the esoterics of the Kabalah and Hasidism. I sensed even then that I need not accept the philosophies of the various schools in Judaism or in Western thought in order to appreciate and value their insights and visions.

At an early age I realized that *my* people, *my* culture, is the channel that leads me to humanity; that first of all I should be concerned about the fate of my family, of my people. Until the rise of Nazism I was sustained by the ideal of democratic socialism. The Second World War, the monstrous barbarisms of the "secular religions" of our age—Communism and Fascism, the slaughter of six million Jews—all of these cataclysmic events have shattered my faith in all isms, utopias, ideologies.

Sensitive, intelligent Jews cannot, in view of such a cataclysm, go on living "as usual." Confronted with such an "eclipse of conscience," we must reevaluate *all* values. We cannot stop asking: How was it possible? How was it possible, after having gassed human beings—men, women, and children—that the murderers—German officers, officials, doctors—should later go on listening to the music of Bach, Beethoven, Mozart? And how could the "civilized Christian world" look away while an old, creative people was being annihilated? And why are so many intellectuals uttering in the same sentence Auschwitz and Hiroshima? Are these two

119

monstrosities analogous? At Hiroshima two armed camps were pitted against each other, whereas at Auschwitz the German war-machine threw defenseless civilians into the gas ovens. And all of these atrocities were committed with the participation of the German army, professors, industrialists, and clergymen!

But if I became skeptical of all isms and lost my faith in our ability to create an ideal world, it does not follow that we cannot ameliorate the lot of man. Partial solutions, palliatives, are possible; a little can be accomplished. We must not give up laboring on behalf of a world where there will be fewer wars, less poverty, less suffering, more freedom for each individual, more opportunity for everyone to fulfill the best potentialities in his personality.

As a Jew who feels an affinity with all previous Jewish generations, I am filled with reverence when I am confronted with our tragic history. I profoundly believe that Jewish culture is so sublime that it merits eternal life. It is so unique, so lofty, that only a vandal would allow it to die. This holds true also for the modern secular Jewish culture that has been created in Yiddish and Hebrew—in Europe, in America, and at present in Israel. The Yiddish and Hebrew literatures are so insightful, so valuable, so beautiful, that they are worth making sacrifices for, so that they live and grow. And the perpetuation of modern Jewish culture, in both languages, does demand sacrifices on the part of American Jews.

Jewish parents who are concerned about their children's Jewish education will have to put a heavier burden upon the shoulders of their offspring. They will have to provide them with a secondary and higher Jewish education—not merely with an elementary one. Otherwise we in America will become a sterile tribe, and the survival of a stagnating community is not worth struggling for.

As a Jew I live in constant tension between skepticism and faith. We Jews have suffered too much at the hands of the stepmother—the world— not to be skeptical of her promises, of her noble declarations on solemn occasions. But at the same time I also remember that we cannot divorce ourselves from the world. If we want to be true to ourselves, to our ethos, to our path in world history, then we must do more than our share in ameliorating the lot of man. This is also in our own interests. As a member of a people that has produced the prophetic vision of "The End of Days," I should like to believe that the best of all the nations are endowed with a sensitive conscience; that the "Thirty-Six Righteous" for whose sake the world can exist belong to all nations.

Since the days of our ancestor Abraham, our people has been blessed with iconoclasts, nonconformists. Our religion, our ethics, our very existence, is a challenge to the world and to ourselves. We must continue to cultivate our Jewish *chutzpah*—to say NO to many things. Affirmation of Jewishness does not imply accepting all Jewish beliefs or institutions. Innovations are imperative. Every tradition that we cherish was at the beginning new, revolutionary. We should select from Jewish culture everything that is meaningful for us. To affirm my identity as a Jew means to be an authentic human being. To be a Jew denotes having an appreciation of history and rootedness; it signifies an affinity with all Jewish generations—from the one that stood at Mount Sinai to our own.

Central to my Jewish world-view is a modern version of *Tikkun*—self-realization. Each person is "deficient" until he realizes himself, until he "finds" his true self; and he will only find it if he labors to live in accordance with his dream and vision. In Kabalistic terms, he is remote from the divine source until he is reintegrated into the original whole; then only has he found salvation, or *Tikkun*, or fulfillment. *Ahavas Isroel*, love of Israel, means for me loving the ideal values of my people—its ethos, its history—and contributing my share to the *Tikkun* of my people and the world.

There are those who say that our Jewish heritage is not relevant for the younger generation; that the Psalms, the Book of Job, the glorious poetry of Isaiah and Jeremiah, of Judah Halevi, Bialik, and Leivick—have none of them produced essential spiritual vitamins for the contemporary Jew. But whoever is not deluded by the mirage of newness must recognize that Jewish creativity in Hebrew, Aramaic, and Yiddish is a spiritual reservoir from which the younger generations may draw insights, ideas, experiences, and subtleties that are timeless.

It seems to me that the best way to win over the young as "consumers" for our cultural products is not by preaching "loyalty" or "survival," but rather by living with and deriving happiness from our cultural treasures. One who undergoes a Jewish esthetic experience, one who enjoys a Jewish scholarly work, poem, or novel, becomes thereby a minor artist. He cannot rest until he communicates to others what has been "communicated" to him. Such experiences will, as a matter of course, be conducive to a creative Jewish continuity. As the British novelist and essayist E. M. Forster tells us, "works of art do have this peculiar pushful quality; the excitement that attended their creation hangs about them, and makes minor artists out of those who have felt their power."

In a world of a constant race for success and power, the truly creative people are the quiet, the independent, the sensitive—those who produce literature, art, science—or the simple, modest individuals whose creativity expresses itself in their exemplary private lives. And these people have the best opportunity to live satisfactorily in a democracy. But like the historians Tocqueville and Burckhardt, I well know the price of democracy—from time to time the masses succumb to demagogues. Democracy is a gentle plant that must be protected by idealistic minorities, and we Jews should be in the first ranks of this dedicated minority. There is no automatic progress; each generation must be educated anew for democracy, for tolerance, for justice—none of these ideals can be inherited. Eternal vigilance is the price of freedom and humaneness.

Many of our creative, committed sons and daughters cannot affirm religion. These nonobservant Jews have been—in modern times—in the forefront of our national and social movements aiming at our creative survival. We should therefore formulate rationales that make it possible for these secular Jews to remain first-class citizens in the Jewish collectivity. Otherwise we would exclude from Jewish life many sophisticated Jewish intellectuals. And this must not happen! It would be absurd to shut out from our midst those who in modern times have been the founders and expounders of Jewish survivalist philosophies—the Dubnows, the Ahad Ha'Ams, the Borochovs, the Zhitlowskys, the Shlome Mendelsons, the Horace Kallens—all those who forged new weapons in the battle for Jewish continuity and in the struggle against abject assimilation. All of those thinkers, and many more, belonged to the secular segment of the Jewish people.

When pondering the future of Jewish culture in America, I am, however, not unmindful of the fact that most of the exponents of secular Jewishness grew up in Eastern Europe, where the physical survival of Jews was in constant jeopardy. There, Jewish thinkers, because of persecutions and pogroms, were compelled to devote their efforts to averting the threat of extinction. That is why modern secular Jewish thought has focused primarily on our collective survival rather than on the content and meaning of the life of the Jewish individual. Here in American society the situation is, however, altogether different; the Jewish community is not facing any immediate physical threat to its survival. Here in democratic, free America, our urgent concern should be the *meaning* of Jewish survival; the spiritual content and quality of Jewish life. Existence for the sake of existence is not sufficient to assure our future, and, in addition, does not warrant our sacrifices. And Jewish creative continuity in America demands ceaseless sacrifices! Jewish essence, Jewish content is the price of Jewish survival in America. Secular Jews should therefore devote their efforts to evolving a way of life, a philosophy and ritual for the nonobservant Jew.

Religious Jews provide for the believer ready-made answers, philosophies concerning all of life's dilemmas: on the meaning of human existence, on life and death, on this world and the hereafter. And even if, in "normal times," the average Jew does not concern himself with "eternal questions," and does not stop to think whether he believes in or is skeptical of old theologies, he does react differently in times of personal or collective stress and crisis. In such critical times an atavistic impulse reappears even among nonreligious Jews—a longing for the faith of their ancestors that might give them a feeling of rootedness, of security. The Jewish religion has, during its millennial history, fashioned a way of life, a ritual, that links the individual with previous generations. Such a feat Jewish secularism could not match in less than a century. The secular segment of the Jewish people, which has its roots in contemporary Jewish nationalism and socialism, has not as yet evolved a meaningful modern-traditional ritual which would link the secular Jew with the *Klal-Isroel.*

What is worse, Jewish secularists are split organizationally over old ideological nuances and issues that are no longer valid or relevant. American Jews live in a country that is dominated by pragmatism—a philosophy whose primary criterion is the practical consequence that a philosophy has for our life. For the pragmatist, what matters most is what will be the practical difference in his conduct or action if a certain philosophy is true or false. Even in Europe, the birthplace of modern ideologies, it is now widely held that there has come an "end of ideologies," utopias, messianisms. In such a spiritual climate it is no longer tenable for secular Jews of various shadings to maintain separate institutions.

Second, all shadings among Jewish humanists are faced with the same cardinal problems: what extract of Jewish culture will not be dissolved in the American "sea"; what secular Jewish substance will separate us from the non-Jewish milieu and at the same time be relevant and give sustenance to the younger generation of Jews? For even a Jewish secularist recognizes that the Jewish people is a unique phenomenon in many respects, and that general solutions are not always applicable to our dilemmas. The Russians, the Germans, the French do not wrestle with the problem of who is a Russian, a German, a Frenchman. For Jews, however, it is difficult to find one answer that would satisfy all of us.

Even secular Jews cannot completely reject the views and attitudes of the Halakha Jews regarding this problem, for the simple reason that secularists have not as yet found a reliable substitute for the Halakha that would give us such guarantees for survival as Judaism and the Halakha gave us for two millennia. (This does not imply that Orthodox Jews have a monopoly on the interpretation of the Halakha.) It is much more difficult to be a secular Jew than a religious Jew—especially in the Diaspora. But it is also hard to live as an ethical human being. For an authentic Jew, however, it is easier to be a *mentsch,* a humane being.

III

Universalism and the Jewish Heritage

Y. L. PERETZ

Yitzkhok Leibush Peretz, the father of modern Yiddish literature and perhaps its greatest personality, was a sophisticated, Westernized intellectual. He was born in Zamosc, Poland in 1852, and died in Warsaw in 1915.

Reared in the East European religious tradition, he early came in contact with modern learning, and later passed the examinations as an advocate. He began to write poetry in Hebrew, but later turned to Yiddish. In 1889 he settled in Warsaw, becoming an employee of the Jewish Communal Bureau—the Geminah—and continuing to work there to the end of his life. His home in Warsaw became the most important literary center of the East European Jewish intelligentsia.

Peretz, the innovator, the modernist, gave expression in his writings to the ferment that swept Jewish life at the end of the nineteenth century. He was a brilliant, versatile, and original artist and thinker, writing stories, poems, plays, and essays. In addition he was a leader of the Jewish cultural movement then at its height in Poland. "Peretz was"— in the words of the poet Jacob Glatstein—"the Reb Levi Yitschok[1] of the agnostics. He was their advocate. Through his marvelous Hasidic tales, he sought to give the agnostic merit, and to preserve Jewish life for him. . . . Esthetically and ethically we were lonely until Peretz linked us with the world, and demanded that the world listen to the Jewish voice that has something to tell the century of great anticipation."

Peretz, the subtle artist and profound thinker, was a deeply rooted Jew who distrusted the modern world, loved the Jewish tradition, and wished to conserve the moral values of Judaism. He has put his ineradicable imprint on Jewish literature and thought.

---

[1] Levi Yitschok (1740–1809), noted for his profound "Love of Israel," and particularly for the common people.

WHAT IS THIS JEWISH HERITAGE?

In Search of Clarity

Jewishness has been weakened.
But what is Jewishness?
"We are Jews!"
But what does this mean?
We often say: "We want our children and children's children to remain Jewish."
But what do we have which we can hand down to them?
What is this so-called Jewish heritage?
When somebody leaves us, against our will, we say to him: "You have become a renegade!"
But if the question is put: "A renegade from what? What did he forswear? Whom did he abandon? What is this Jewishness of which he became an apostate?"—there is no answer. Instead of clarity, we are treated to several varieties of stammering and different degrees of vagueness. Each stammerer refutes the other and each vague reply excludes the other.

Such a condition is possible because Jewishness is interpreted differently by each age, each social class, and even each individual. Every interpretation lays claim to be the only true form of Jewishness.

Some take institutions in which the Jewish spirit is embodied at a certain historic moment in a certain land and substitute these institutions for Jewishness as a whole.

Others take linguistic symbols that vary with time and space, the *language* of the Jewish religion, philosophy, morality, etc., and substitute these symbols for the living creative content.

Still others substitute for the vital, growing *organism* its shroud, which varies with clime and era.

The *eternal* is jammed and compressed into a fleeting *moment*.

Thus it comes about that people of the same ethnic kinship, who happen to live in different places and at different times, fashion their Jewishness out of their narrow perspective, out of their brief transitory existence.

Moreover, they often succumb to a mirage; they accept *foreign* forms

129

as their own; they deem their imitation of foreign ways to be normal Jewish ways originating in Sinai.

Was not the Polish clerical gown declared most holy by some?

Do not others look upon the sacrificing of a rooster during the week before Atonement Day as of the essence of Judaism?

Do not still others regard as worse than apostasy the disbelief in spirits and in angels, even though the former is Persian and the latter Babylonian in origin?

It is about time to renounce, once and for all, what is merely symbolic, transitory, accidental, and to seek what is eternal, essential, fundamental.

Jewishness is the Jewish way of looking at things.

More precisely, Jewishness is the universal spirit as it is embodied in the Jewish soul.

Jewishness is that which makes the Jews, in eras of national independence, feel free and enables them to fashion institutions as embodiment of their national creative will. Jewishness is, in such times, joy, ecstasy, zestful living.

Jewishness is that which creates, in troubled eras, institutions for defense, for prevention of danger, for protecting itself and its members. Jewishness is, in such times, a call to battle and a challenge to heroism.

Jewishness is that which must, in times of dependence and weakness, retreat into its shell, conserve its resources, endure in silence, and wait for better days. Then Jewishness is hope and pain, messianic dreams and other-worldliness. Then it demands real sacrifice.

This Jewishness, for which we demand sacrifices, must be clearly and precisely defined.

Formerly people thought that a person was born as a *tabula rasa,* a blank slate on which life with its stylus made imprints. Today we know that the individual participates actively in the learning process, that man enters upon the struggle with his environment equipped with a certain heritage, with a certain psychic configuration, with a certain will-power, with traits that determine his success or failure in the struggle for existence.

What is true of the individual also holds for the nation.

With what did we enter upon the world arena? What do we want? What cultural thread do we weave into the web of the world? What is our tone in the universal harmony? What will be lacking, if we were lacking?

What is Jewish and what is non-Jewish? In what way do we differ from others?

What must we protect? For what must we sacrifice ourselves? For what must we battle?

What does our life stand for and what would our death signify?

The Jewish Way

Nomadic blood. A wandering clan in the desert.

Implanted in its blood—honesty and justice. Of these qualities does it fashion its God, a God who accompanies it on all its wanderings and is therefore not formed of wood or stone, a God who moves and lives.

A sublime concept of the deity, a free and breath-taking concept of a boundless, limitless universe.

When the desert is left behind and inhabited lands are traversed, this clan of wanderers cannot mingle with the peoples settled in those lands. There is mutual repulsion. The nomadic clan, therefore, lives apart. Finally, it seeks to escape from tensions and pressures by obtaining a territory of its own.

It conquers a land. The God of the clan becomes the God of the chosen people in the chosen land. The clan ceases its wanderings. It establishes in its land a temple for its God.

It has not the heart to exterminate the native inhabitants. Honesty, implanted in its blood, does not permit it to erect a fence against outsiders or to make their life difficult. Justice, implanted in its blood, does not permit it to attack and to subjugate other peoples. Hence, it remains a little people in a separate state—a state of priests, a holy people.

In the course of time it succumbed.

This people was, however, the creator of its state and not a mere product of a state. It was the builder of the temple for its God and not a group gathered together haphazardly for common worship at a shrine. It was the architect of the social, cultural, and economic forms in the land and not the product of a land's melting-pot. Hence, this people survives the loss of its independence, its state, its language, its temple, and all its cultural and economic forms. It again sets out on its wanderings over the face of the globe and its God continues to wander with it.

Its former instinctive apprehending of God and the world now becomes a conscious concept of greater clarity. Israel becomes a universal people. The God, who does not abandon it and who suffers exile along with it, becomes a God of the universe. The lands of the diaspora, the entire world, becomes the arena of conflict between the one God and the many gods. The one God will triumph!

The world is not yet free of war and bloodshed, of servitude, exploitation, pain, and oppression, since God is still above the world and has not yet entered into its essence.

The time will come, however, the time must come, God will judge all peoples and cleanse the world, Messiah will appear. We will bring him. We, the weakest of peoples! We, God's martyred people! Imprisoned in diverse economic systems, encased in all kinds of social and political structures, suffering under the domination of manifold provincial codes of law, differing local patriotisms, foreign arrogance, and superior force, enduring all the disabilities of minority-status and all the torture imposed upon the weak in a world where might is dominant—our people still persists and still remains true to itself.

It retains the remembrance of its ancient state as a golden memory of its youth and it still has as its guiding-star its vision of the messianic world-state of the future. Out of past memories and future hopes it spins its legends and weaves its symbols. Irradiated by unswerving confidence and by holy faith, it never succumbs to despair. When surging billows loom ahead, it bows its head to let them pass and then it raises its head again up to heaven, to its God. If trouble comes, it endures and then forgets easily and quickly. It wants to carry on, to survive its tortures. It wants to experience Messiah or at least the travails foreboding his approach.

Thus does this people live, hope, and keep faith. . . .

Jewish life must burst into blossom again. With the Bible as germinating seed and with folk symbols and folk legends as dew and rain, the field will sprout again, the people will revive, the Jews will rise once more to suffer anew for their truth and will reaffirm their faith in ultimate victory.

The flag of a Jewish renascence must be raised again, the banner of Messiah, world-judgment, and world-liberation, the symbol of a future free humanity.

This is the mission of the eternal people, the world-people, a mission to be carried through in all phases of Jewish life, by the Jewish home, the Jewish school, the Jewish theatre, the Jewish book, and everything Jewish.

Like Unto the Nations

Renaissance!—a single word without qualifications as to time and space, a mere word, yet it bears the seed from which will sprout a world, our Jewish world.

Renaissance!—a proud and mighty word but not new! It goes back to the prophets of old. It embodies the Messianic idea—rebirth!

Ideas are eternal. They merely change forms in the course of evolution. Renaissance—this word, in its purest Messianic connotation, has not yet come upon the scene.

After the retreat of clericalism and the collapse of the walls of the ghetto, our prison but also our fortress, Jewishness was too depressed and too weak for an immediate rebirth. It was out of breath for a while.

One diagnostician felt for its pulse and could not find it, or else he was slightly deaf and did not hear it, and so he concluded:

"Jewishness is dying!"

He felt sorry for it:

"Once it was so magnificient. It gave God to the world!"

Then he consoled himself:

"Jewishness does leave a wealthy heritage behind. Jewishness was great and dignified in its day. It has a claim upon the world's reverence."

Finally, he resigned himself to the inevitable:

"Nothing can exist forever. Religion (and Jewishness was for him nothing more) belongs to the past. Even Christianity, the younger and the stronger religion, is on the decline. Let us give Jewishness its due; let us sew for it a nice shroud; let us select for it a prominent spot in the mythological cemetery. Jehovah was, after all, mightier than Jupiter."

A second diagnostician approached Jewishness with more piety. He advised:

"Don't just bury it. Embalm it! Keep it petrified in its present form unto all eternity! Let it remain as an historic monument for archeologists —an eternal joy for them!"

This means, in other words, that the Jewish nation has abdicated. It has gone from the contemporary stage. What remains of Jewishness would make a fine tombstone to be put on this nation's grave.

There are, however, Jews who refuse to abdicate.

A nation does not die so easily.

Blood is thicker than water. The national instinct persists. It is at times befogged, silenced, deluged by worldly considerations, but then it reawakens more vigorous, more vociferous than ever.

Besides, where can a Jew go? Doors and gates are not wide open to receive him. The Gentile stomach is not so large and not so robust that it can digest more than a mere handful of select individuals. Rich bankers and politicians, famous scientists, singers, and violin-players can somehow be ingested and assimilated, but not all Jews.

If the Jewish masses are left behind, they exercise a magnetic attraction, drawing even the élite back into the Jewish orbit and preventing any easy escape.

The individuals who do not accept baptism to ease the path for their children and children's children therefore often arrive at the following conclusion:

"We who are within the Jewish fold cannot remain static. We too must move on. The stream of life goes forward and will carry us along. But not with all our baggage. We have too much baggage. It is so bulky and not nice at all. Let us reduce it to a minimum and let us make it more tidy-looking."

So one operation after another is performed. Surgeons cut into dead cells and not a drop of blood appears. Not a groan is heard. Perhaps there is a moaning of the divine spirit in some ruin or other, but nobody pays attention.

To tear out page after page from the Prayer-Book is so easy! Religious books are really most beautiful—on library shelves! Let us clean up the Jewish home and put in a Christmas tree. Then the home will look nice.

What remains of Jewishness belongs in the synagogue and can be left in care of the rabbi. But the rabbi must look like a decent human being! The pastor's costume is so becoming! The rabbi should wear one like it. The synagogue must be modernized. It must be renamed the temple. It must be stripped of its poor features, because poverty is always disgusting.

The prayers are therefore emasculated of poetry, sacrificial-ritual, and references to Zion as the land of Israel. They are translated from the Hebrew into the vernacular. They can no longer shock anyone. They are not even called prayers but merely Divine Services. Once a year ought to suffice for them.

It is true that such Divine Services fail to attract. They have lost something indefinable which did attract. Well, let organ-music be introduced. Perhaps a choir of girls will attract youth to the temple's portals. Furthermore, the intimate, heart-warming but rather unelaborate ancient melodies must be changed. They must resound as sonorously as in a church.

Besides, if they cannot resound on the Sabbath, let them peal on Sunday.

As long as something remains!

Judaism is thus cut to style, whipped into shape, perfumed, but still there is no real life. Older people pay lip-service out of a sense of reverence but youth keeps aloof. Reform Judaism is bankrupt.

A new physician appears on the scene. He acknowledges the failure of the reforms and prescribes:

"Don't touch! The soul has departed, the form has remained. Hold on to the form! The wine has been drunk or has evaporated. The barrel has remained. Hold on to the barrel! Pour in fresh wine! Fresh contents are easy to obtain! There is no dearth of wine-dealers. The forms change, but what of it? Formerly, Aristotle was the acknowledged authority, now it is Herbert Spencer, tomorrow it will be somebody else. Just hold on to the barrel. Look about for an empty and safe cellar, in which to store the barrel."

The barrel-idea is also an idea. But ideas have their vogue and then they cease to be in vogue.

The estranged, who are expelled from Europe or who return to us voluntarily because of pity for the poor tortured people or because of newly awakened reverence or because of homesickness, they bring us the news:

"You are a people!"

Well, we Jews have known this fact for a long time. There is no language richer in terms for race and people than the Hebrew. The estranged re-discoverers of the Jewish people do not stop at this point, however. They add:

"A people—but nothing more!"

They did not feel more and they did not see more, while away from us.

"A people and nothing more!"—a dangerous statement requiring careful inspection.

The Difference

A stranger, looking at our Jewish tradition with foreign eyes or at least through foreign spectacles, sees something uncanny. Unable to understand it, he calls it abnormal.

Goethe once said: "Where a concept is lacking, a word takes its place."

Abnormal may mean above normal as well as below normal. Genius and insanity are both abnormal. The atavistic criminal and the prophetic revolutionist are both abnormal.

Since biblical days it has been known that the Jews are not normal: "A people to live alone, a single people in the land, a single chosen people in the world."

The abnormal must be correctly evaluated. And one must be absolutely objective in all evaluations, even when it concerns the individual himself and his own nation.

To evaluate means to compare, but not for the purpose of equalizing or of fitting into a Procrustean bed, rather for the purpose of finding points of difference, diverging characteristics.

This is the method used by individuals. The higher the individual, the more often does he engage in introspection, and the more often does he ask himself: why? to what end?

He does not subordinate himself to any other individual; he does not ask anyone else for a justification or an endorsement of his existence; he does not base his *raison d'être* upon his usefulness to his peers or his similarity to others.

He engages in introspection because he wants to find himself; he wants to purify himself of inferior traits; he wants to cherish and develop his own originality; he wants to maintain his uniqueness; and he is ready to do battle and to sacrifice his last drop of blood for his right to live his own life.

Such a superior person, seeking to evaluate objectively, applies as a measure the summit to which he must strive in accordance with his nature, the goals towards which his ego must direct its efforts.

This summit is his guide; by this goal does he judge himself.

He is not bankrupt. His past supplies him the material with which to know himself. He does not liquidate his life. He does not judge and evaluate himself on the basis of his momentary status. His goal in the future, his striving toward it, his faith in it, are the justification for his present life.

The same principle holds for peoples.

If I inquire into my Jewishness, I do so for my own sake. I seek its goal in the future on the basis of the material in its creative past.

The present, with its formalism and its ossification, I leave out of account. The present is our decadence, our moment of decline.

Just as the judge of the individual man is his ideal of the man-to-come, so the judge of the individual nation is its ideal of its own national future, when its specific stream will flow into the sea of common humanity.

I confront my unique people with its ideal of its national future and I ask: Am I of greater value or of lesser value than others? I know that I am different.

My past tells me: Serve no other Gods save the one and only God.

Erect your temple in the midst of your land, in Jerusalem.

Thrice yearly shall you come to the temple to show yourself before God, to offer up your sacrifice, to thank him, to pray to him, and to serve him.

One people, one land, one temple, one law, one God.

Unity everywhere, in every breath and atom of the universe.

No temple and no altar may be erected at any other place and no sacrifices may be made elsewhere even to the one God—upon penalty of death.

The temple is, however, to serve all, all.

The stranger may come and pray. God will listen and accept the sacrifice. Whosoever calls in the name of the one God is numbered among his children. From Zion the law is to go out to all the peoples.

The Jewish national idea—a world-idea.

Do other peoples have it?

Do the Germans, French, English, Russians, and other European peoples have a national world-ideology, a national world-religion, or national world-ideals?

We do have German philosophy, meaning philosophic books written in German for Germans, but not a German philosophic idea for world-happiness.

There are French ideals, but for the French nation only: France is to be great, powerful, adored, and to bask in glory.

There are ideals for England: "I am to be the factory and the whole world my market."

Other nations have similar ideals, every one of the European nations.

They are so-called Christian nations, but they have neither produced Christianity nor have they been united by it. Christianity was either imposed upon them by force or they may have accepted it voluntarily. It did not spring from their brain. It did not sprout from their blood.

They are peoples who have been subjugated by the church. This superimposed religion, Christianity, swims about on the surface and does not penetrate into the core of their souls. It has no real relation to their daily existence. It is not a social experience. It is merely a faith. It is a key to open up a heaven after death and not a key with which to force open the portals of this life. It is an affair of the other world and does not apply to this earth and to earthly conduct. It is a negation of work and progress here and now.

Christianity is a creed and not an inner urge. It is a denial of this world, a severance from reality, an abdication, a means of redemption from life and not of salvation in life.

It is therefore carried aloft, like a cloak covering the surface of existence. Below this Christian covering, there dominate Roman law, Greek art, European technology.

To these four streams of culture, a fifth is added: the specific nationality, which justifies all crimes against other nationalities in the name of patriotism.

Hence, if a European nation seriously wants to liberate itself, it must first get rid of the clerical covering, the international church. If such a nation is to progress in this world, it must first renounce the superimposed heaven and the superimposed religion.

We Jews, on the other hand, a people without territory, without a common language, with an urge for culture, yes, even when deprived of culture, we as "a nation—and nothing more" would amount to nothing.

And how easy it is to go away from nothing!

Other Ways

The struggle between us and the others is not academic. It is real.

Only a superficial person can fail to see the connection between cultural eras and a world-ideology.

The world, seen through Jewish eyes, is an organic unity bound together by a common force. It is, therefore, a morally responsible world.

The world, seen through heathen eyes, consists of epileptic, accidental, mysterious, or revealed forces. These forces are not subject to a universal will and are therefore without any moral responsibility.

On the road from heathendom to Judaism, there is much debating and generalizing, until mankind conceives of gods and demi-gods, with the world as a battleground of conflicting divinities. The strongest of these is Jupiter. He emerges as the victor. Nevertheless, each of the other deities retains a voice; each interferes; each in his own time and place, in his own temple and on his special day, lays down the law and his own moral system.

The nearer one comes to Judaism, the more does idolatry disappear outwardly. The divine symbols, carved on wood or cut into stone or painted on walls and on canvas, are destroyed and reduced to dust. The world, however, continues to be ruled by hundreds of legal and moral codes. Not a single national philosophy except the Jewish has attained to unity in all aspects of life.

Not a single other nation submits at heart to the one and only God.

Compared to the Jewish concept of the world, all other philosophies are provincial, local, for domestic use only, restricted to home consumption.

Our slogan today, is therefore, renaissance!

Let me utter my word freely, let me work and create cultural values in harmony with my world-view. I, the Jew, gave you so much formerly, let me give you of myself once more.

The battle betweeen us is not restricted to any one place. It is a long time since we left the cradle of our national life. Willingly or unwillingly, we became a world-people. The conflict does not hence rage within any one boundary but is worldwide in scope.

We do not wage war against this people or that or against a coalition of several peoples. We face each other as Jews and Gentiles, Jewish will and Gentile will.

Jews, monotheistic by religion and monistic in their thinking, cannot mingle with others who have not yet attained this level of feeling and thinking. Jewishness cannot submit to a less advanced form of civilization. It must struggle for the right to create a world-culture according to its light.

Scholars, whose training lies outside of the Jewish orb, come to us and offer us gratuitous advice.

For a long time our mouths were shut and our hands tied. We could neither talk nor work. We were advised to go to others and to beg crumbs of others. We were told to assimilate. Why set up our own workshop?

If I have my own evaluation of good and evil, they advise me to change my standard of values.

If I fight for my concept of truth, they laugh at my so-called mission.

But the greatest danger to our people now accrues from two groups: those who are too rash in promising and those who succumb too easily to exaggerated pessimism.

The former told us: "Your home is open, tomorrow I'll give it to you!" And when the morrow came and the home was not opened up to us, many fled in despair from our midst, having lost their hope for salvation.

The latter tell us: "What you build in the diaspora is built on quicksand and water, the wind carries it away." Hence, many give up building and turn to foreign cultures and foreign values. When the foreign nationality insists that, as condition of admittance, you acknowledge that the

Messiah and Redeemer has already come, you ponder: "Perhaps it would be wiser to abdicate."

Conclusion

Now, I am not advocating that we shut ourselves up in a spiritual ghetto. On the contrary, we should get out of such a ghetto. But we should get out as Jews, with our own spiritual treasures. We should interchange, give and take, but not beg.

Ghetto is impotence. Cultural cross-fertilization is the only possibility for human development. Humanity must be the synthesis, the sum, the quintessence of all national cultural forms and philosophies.

(1904–1914)

AHAD HA'AM

Ahad Ha'Am, the exponent of Cultural Zionism, played a major role in the Jewish national movement of our era, and has been recognized as an independent thinker, a man of character, and an essayist with a lucid Hebrew style.

Asher Ginzberg, who became famous under the pen-name Ahad Ha'Am, was born in the Ukraine into a Hasidic family in 1856, and was educated in the traditional manner. Later he attended universities at Vienna, Berlin, and Breslau. Settling in Odessa in 1886, he became a leader of the Hoveve Zion. From 1908 to 1922 he resided in London, and there he participated in the negotiations leading to the Balfour Declaration (1917). In 1922 Ahad Ha'Am settled in Tel Aviv, where he died five years later.

Ahad Ha'Am taught that the nation is the people's "ego," i.e., its internal creative force, which is the sum total of its memory and will for survival. The will to live is an instinctive power, a mighty, irrational force of nature that stems from the unconscious areas of the soul. In order to survive the Jewish people must strengthen its national will. This can be done in two ways that complement each other: (1) by establishing colonies in *Eretz Isroel,* and (2) by strengthening the national spirit of the people, which finds expression in the national culture and destiny.

The Jewish national spirit, Ahad Ha'Am maintains, finds expression primarily in morality, not in religion. To him the religious beliefs and practices of Judaism are but the external garb of the intuitive and unique moral conviction of the Jewish people. To create suitable conditions for the survival of the Jewish spirit is the main concern of Ahad Ha'Am's thought. The Jewish spirit does not, for Ahad Ha'Am, depend on Judaism, but rather on our national ethics.

Ahad Ha'Am reformulated Jewish fundamental ideas and gave them a modern cut: "national will" instead of Providence; ethics instead of divine inspiration. He mercilessly dissected the servile face of the assimilated Jewish intelligentsia. His writings were stamped by a great moral personality for whom nothing but the truth and the right deed matter.

IMITATION AND ASSIMILATION

As early as the time of the Prophets, our ancestors learned to despise physical strength, and to honor only the power of the spirit. For this reason, they never allowed their own individuality to be effaced because of the superior physical strength of the persecutor. It was only in the face of some great *spiritual* force in the life of a foreign people that they could sink their own individuality and give themselves up entirely to that life. Knowing this, their leaders endeavored to cut them off entirely from the spiritual life of other nations, and not to allow the smallest opening for imitation. This policy of separation, apart from the fact that it caused many to leap over the barrier once for all, could not, in view of the position of our people among the nations, be carried out consistently. When the era of contact set in, and continued unbroken, there were constant proofs that the apprehensions of the patriots had been groundless, and their efforts at restriction unnecessary. The Jews have not merely a tendency to Imitation, but a genius for it. Whatever they imitate, they imitate well. Before long they succeed in appropriating for themselves the foreign spiritual force to which they have become subservient. Then their teachers show them how to use this force for their own ends, in order to reveal their own spirit; and so the self-effacement ceases, and the Imitation, turned into the channel of competition, gives added strength to the Hebrew self-consciousness.

Long before the Hellenists in Palestine tried to substitute Greek culture for Judaism, the Jews in Egypt had come into close contact with the Greeks, with their life, their spirit, and their philosophy: yet we do not find among them any pronounced movement towards Assimilation. On the contrary, they employed their Greek knowledge as an instrument for revealing the essential spirit of Judaism, for showing the world its beauty, and vindicating it against the proud philosophy of Greece. That is to say, starting from an Imitation which had its source in self-effacement before an alien spiritual force, they succeeded, by means of that Imitation, in making the force their own, and in passing from self-effacement to competition.

If those Elders, who translated the Bible into Greek for the benefit of

143

the Egyptian Jews, had also translated Plato into Hebrew for the benefit of the Jews in Palestine, in order to make the spiritual power of the Greeks a possession of our people on its own land and in its own language, then, we may well believe, the same process—the transition from self-effacement to competition—would have taken place in Palestine also; but in a still higher degree, and with consequences yet more important for the development of the inner spirit of Judaism. As a result there would have been no "traitorous enemies of the covenant" among our people, and perhaps there would have been no need of the Maccabees and all the spiritual history which had its ultimate cause in that period. Perhaps—who knows?—the whole history of the human race would have taken a totally different course.

But the Elders did not translate Plato into Hebrew. It was only at a much later date, in the period of Arabic culture, that the Greek spirit became a possession of our people in their own language—but not on their own land. And yet even then, though on foreign soil, self-effacement soon gave place to competition, and this form of Imitation had the most astonishing results. Language, literature, and religion, all renewed their youth; and each helped to reveal the inner spirit of Judaism through the medium of the new spiritual possession. To such an extent did this new spirit become identified with the Hebrew individuality that the thinkers of the period could not believe that it was foreign to them, and that Israel could ever have existed without it. They could not rest satisfied until they found an ancient legend to the effect that Socrates and Plato learned their philosophy from the Prophets, and that the whole of Greek philosophy was stolen from Jewish books which perished in the destruction of the Temple.

Since that time our history has again divided itself into two periods—a long period of complete separation, and a short period of complete self-effacement. But once more we are nearing the conviction that safety lies on neither of these ways, but on a third, which is midway between them: that is, the perfection of the national individuality by means of competitive Imitation.

Signs of this conviction are to be found not alone in the most recent years, since the day when Nationalism became the watchword of a party in Israel, but also much earlier. We find them on the theoretical side in the production of a literature, in European languages, dealing with the spirit of Judaism and its value; on the practical side, in a movement towards the reform of the externals of Judaism. This practical movement is, indeed, held by many, including some of the reformers themselves, to be a long step towards Assimilation. But they are wrong. When self-effacement has proceeded so far that those who practice it no longer feel any inner bond uniting them with their own past, and really wish to emancipate the community by means of complete assimilation with a foreign body, then they no longer feel even the necessity of raising their inheritance to that degree of perfection which, according to their ideas, it demands. On the contrary, they tend rather to leave it alone and allow it to perish of itself. Until that day comes, they imitate the customs of their ancestors to an extent determined by accident. It is a sort of artificial, momentary self-effacement, as though it were not they themselves who acted so, but the spirit of their ancestors had entered into them at that moment, and had acted as it had been accustomed to act of old.

Geiger expresses the opinion that a writer who writes in Hebrew at the present day does not express his own inner spirit, but lives for the time being in another world, the world of the Talmud and the Rabbis, and adopts their mode of thinking. This is true of most of our Western scholars, as is evident from their style, because in their case the link between their ancestral language and their own being is broken. But with the Hebrew writers of Northern Europe and Palestine, for whom Hebrew is still a part of their being, the case is just the reverse. When they write, the necessity of writing Hebrew springs from their innermost being; and they therefore strive to improve the language and bring it to a stage of perfection that will enable them to express their thoughts in it with freedom, just as their ancestors did.

When, therefore, we find Geiger and his school giving their whole lives and all their powers to the reform of another part of their inheritance, according to their own ideas; when we find them content to accept the language as it is, but not content to accept the religion as it is: we have here a decisive proof that it is on the religious side that their Hebrew individuality still lives. That individuality is not dead in them, but only stunted; and their real and true desire, whether or not they admit this to themselves and to others, is just this: "To reveal *their own* spirit or personality in those ways in which their model reveals *his.*"

Assimilation, then, is not a danger that the Jewish people must dread for the future. What it has to fear is being split up into fragments. The manner in which the Jews work for the perfection of their individuality depends everywhere on the character of that foreign spiritual force which is at work in their surroundings, and which arouses them to what we have called "competitive imitation." One cannot but fear, therefore, that their efforts may be dissipated in various directions, according as the "spiritual force" varies in different countries; so that in the end Israel will be no longer one people, but a number of separate tribes, as at the beginning of its history.

Such an apprehension may derive support from experience. The Jews of Northern Europe, for example, received their first lessons in Western culture from the Jews of Germany. Thus their central object of Imitation, before which they sank their own individuality, was not the "foreign spiritual force" at work in their surroundings, but that which they saw at work among their own people in Germany. They therefore imitated the German Jews slavishly, without regard to differences of place and condition, as though they also had been perfect Germans in every respect. But in course of time, when the Jews of Northern Europe had made "enlightenment" their own to a certain extent, and became conscious of their new-won strength, they passed from the stage of self-effacement to that of competition in relation to the Jews of Germany, and began to depart from their prototype, being influenced by the different character of the "spiritual force" in the countries in which they lived. Similarly, the Jews of France are even now a model for Imitation to the Jews in the East; but even in their case this state of things is only temporary, and will disappear when the Eastern Jews become conscious of their new strength. Thus, the more any section of our people adds to its spiritual strength, the more completely it becomes emancipated from the influence of that other section which it formerly imitated; and so the danger of being split up into fragments grows ever more serious.

But there is one escape—and one only—from this danger. Just as in the stage of growth the members of the community were welded into a single whole, despite their different individual characteristics, through the agency of one central individual; so also in the stage of dissipation the different sections of the people can be welded together, in spite of their different local characteristics, through the agency of a local centre, which will possess a strong attraction for all of them, not because of some accidental or temporary relation, but by virtue of its own right. Such a centre will claim a certain allegiance from each scattered section of the people. Each section will develop its own individuality along lines determined by imitation of its own surroundings; but all will find in this centre at once a purifying fire and a connecting link.

In the childhood of the Jewish people, when it was split up into separate tribes, the military prowess of David and the wise statesmanship of Solomon succeeded in creating for it a centre such as this, "whither the tribes went up, the tribes of the Lord." But to-day, in its old age, neither strength nor wisdom nor even wealth will avail to create such a centre anew. And so all those who desire to see the nation reunited will be compelled, in spite of themselves, to bow before historical necessity, and to turn eastwards, to the land which was our centre and our pattern in ancient days.[1]

NOTE

1. Here there is an allusion to the attempt of Baron Hirsch to create a Jewish national center in the Argentine—an attempt which at that time made a deep impression on the Jewish communities in Russia, and was regarded by many as the beginning of the national redemption.

CHAIM ZHITLOWSKY

Chaim Zhitlowsky was a philosopher, essayist, and orator—in Yiddish, Russian, and German—who played a major role in the Yiddish cultural movement in America. He was one of the foremost exponents of Jewish secularism and Yiddishism, and a founder of the Jewish Seymist party.

Zhitlowsky was born in a small town near Vitebsk in White Russia in 1865. His traditional Jewish education ended when he was thirteen. He entered a Russian Gymnasium (high school), where he absorbed the the ideas of the Russian Folk Revolutionaries, and at twenty-one he went to Petersburg, where he published his first book in Russian, *Thoughts on the Historical Destiny of the Jews.* In 1888 Zhitlowsky left Russia and settled in Switzerland, where he lived for about fifteen years. During that period he graduated from the University of Bern in 1892 with a Ph.D. in philosophy, and became a central figure among the Russian Folk Socialists, participating in debates and symposiums, and contributing to socialist periodicals.

In 1904 Zhitlowsky came to America, and four years later he settled in New York, where he established and edited the Yiddish magazine *Dos Neie Lebn,* which became the most important vehicle for his ideas, and for those of the Yiddishist intelligentsia. Zhitlowsky traveled the length and breadth of the United States and Canada, lecturing to ever larger audiences, who were spellbound by his oratory. He attracted many admirers, who looked up to him like Hasidim who revere a Rebbe. He died in 1943.

In his essays and lectures he expounded an ideology that routed the socialist assimilationists of his day; he was the architect of a secularist philosophy for agnostic Jews which is, in essence, still tenable.

THE NATIONAL POETIC REBIRTH
OF THE JEWISH RELIGION

Even if the branch called "religion" on the cultural tree of mankind should completely wither and fall down—a matter in which we cannot, by any means, believe—there would then still remain with mankind its most precious inheritance—those most noble and delicate emotions of which we are now speaking—and to the good aspects of the darkest religion (everything has *its* good side) we must add the fact that it taught the human soul to feel holiness and infinity.

Every religion has created factors that evoke the emotions of holiness in the soul of the believer. It has holy *persons,* partly supernatural—like its gods and angels, partly invented human ones—like its legendary heroes, partly historical figures that have actually lived, who through their lives and deaths expressed the truths of their faith. It has holy places—temples, mountains and valleys, holy springs and trees—so that the believer begins to have entirely different feelings when he steps into their proximity; it has holy *objects—tallith* and phylactories, scrolls of the Torah, icons, crosses, etc. It has holy *periods*—holidays, fasts— and also has holy *actions*—praying, bringing sacrifices, confessions, and the like.

All these sanctities—persons, places, objects, periods, and actions—act like a magnetic force on the soul of the truly religious person and transfer it into an emotional atmosphere which it is impossible to express in words.

The question now is: can all these sanctities evoke the same atmosphere in our feelings when we stop believing in their supernatural significance? Must modern man create entirely new sanctities in order that the emotion of holiness should shine forth in his breast?

We have had the opportunity more than once to demonstrate the fact that even such gods as have died, who have been forgotten and surrounded in an atmosphere of ritual impurity, were able to become resurrected in the paradise of human poetry. They could do so because, however covered with heavenly rapture a god or any religious conception may be, he or it has grown out of *human* needs and ideals, which must at all times be dear to the human heart. And when the supernatural covering wholly loses its religious spell, the purely human essence emerges even more clearly, and the signs and wonders, the ceremonies and rituals, become transformed into *poetic symbols,* which express a significant spiritual content. This spiritual *human* content evokes in man the same emotion of holiness as the old religious conception.

The poetic rebirth of religion evolves, cleans, and deepens the human kernel in all religious fantasies and transforms the supernatural elements into purely poetic symbols.

The movement in favor of a national poetic rebirth of Jewish religion —a movement which is now suffusing the air—must do the same with all old Jewish sanctities. It has to examine them all critically, reject those in which the human essence has been entirely consumed, either through supernatural craze or through chauvinistic malice; to purge those that still have a human essence, to deepen and bring out more clearly their human worth and their national significance. The *purified sanctities ought to become the foundation of a free-religious life for every Jew who wishes to identify himself with the destiny and needs, sufferings and hopes, of his people.*

The movement must, however, emerge from the beginning with the clear consciousness that it does not venture to create new supernatural worlds, or to pour a new devoutly religious force into the old Jewish molds. That is the task of the eternally creating religious spirit, and we, simple mortals, who think about the sufferings and joys of mankind and the Jewish people in the world, do not have the presumption to meddle with its affairs. Our task is: to shape in a national poetic fashion those molds of the old faith and leave of them only that content which can become the foundation of a humane spiritual world, a *Jewish*-humane atmosphere, in which every educated, progressively thinking, and nationally feeling Jew should be able to breathe.

Unconsciously, a large part of our generation is working on this. I shall cite a few examples of such an effort, in order that the reader should get a clear idea both of its significance and its method.

Let us begin with the holy personages of the Jewish religion.

We must, of course, leave out the Jewish universal God, the "Holy One of Israel" of Jewish religious *philosophy,* which has, for the time being, attained its highest level in Spinoza's pantheism. The universal deified universe belongs to the superhuman world and must remain for the modern religious person, even in its Spinozistic form, a "Living and Everlasting God" in the simplest sense of the word, a living, constantly acting divine power which cannot be transformed into a poetic symbol. God stands *above* the national-poetic rebirth, and it must leave Him alone: let Jewish theology concern itself with Him.

However, the God of Jewish legend, the God of Abraham, Isaac, and Jacob, the God of the Aggadah,[1] is a humanized God about whom many wonderfully beautiful poetic things are told. And all the narratives, from the Aggadah to the last Hasidic fantastic story, contains so much purely human beauty, are so rich in national poetic motifs (e.g., the sufferings and joys of the Divine Presence in exile), that even the soul of an atheistic Jew can be inspired by them, as soon as you rip off the religiously believing garment and let them shine in the divine nakedness of pure poetry. The same applies also to other supernatural personages of the Jewish legendary world—the angels, and the figure that is dearest to the Jewish heart—the figure of the Messiah, the son of David.

If we proceed to the *natural,* sacred personages—the invented ones like the Patriarchs and perhaps also Moses and Aaron, and the historical ones like David, Solomon, the Prophets—here, too, of course, the critical shears will have considerable work to do. It is very doubtful, e.g., if such a strange "saint" as King Solomon should be able to satisfy the requirements of the national-poetic canon. But however freely the shears may "weed," there will remain enough great men and saints, whose personalities can evoke in us the emotions of sanctity and infinity. The life, creativity, sufferings, and teachings of our Prophets, which affect *every* human soul no less than a chorale by Bach; the Maccabees, Bar Kochba,[2] and the Ten Martyrs who were killed by the Roman government: many of the so-called false Messiahs (e.g., Solomon Molcho)[3]—the whole great series of men of God and martyrs down to Gregory Gershuny[4]—what an infinite source of sacred humaneness.

Almost as rich in national poetic content as the Jewish sacred personages are the Jewish sacred *periods.* They too must be purified by critical research before their pure souls will be able to enter the paradise of national-poetic religion.

Take the first and most important Jewish holiday: Passover. According to the results of modern research, one must assume that the holiday is much older than the Jewish people; that it is a very old Semitic spring holiday, from the time that is lost in the thick mist of the past. The Jewish tradition, however, related the revival of nature to the revival of the Jewish people, to its deliverance from Egyptian slavery. Paring off all natural and historical improbabilities, the story tells us that a people that languished for generations in slavery, plucked up its courage and forcibly pried itself loose from its slavish yoke. It set forth into a desolate desert, suffered hunger and thirst, often stood at the brink of the abyss, was forced more than once to look death straight in the eyes, more than once became subservient and small, but, inspired by a forward propelling ideal, it nevertheless attained what it sought. It conquered the "Promised Land"!

If there really exists a "spirit of freedom" in the world whom we celebrate in our revolutionary songs, he certainly could have turned to the Jewish people with those ardently felt words which the Prophet Jeremiah puts into the lips of the Jewish God:

> I remember for thee the mercy of thy youth,
> The love of thine espousals
> You followed Me into the wilderness,
> To a desolate uncultivated land . . .
> Through a land of deserts and of pits
> Through a land of drought, and of the shadow of death,
> Through a land that no man passed through
> And where no man dwelt.

And this dazzlingly beautiful historical fact, the golden cradle of the Jewish people, is a great deal more than a historic event: it is a *poetic symbol* of the human struggle for freedom at all times, all generations, all human conditions. A symbol of that struggle, driven by a great ideal, that compels a person to cast behind him all the flesh pots of Egypt and to follow it "through deserts and dark pits, through drought, bearing the shadow of death," and to seek new, untrodden paths to go "through a land that no man passed through, and where no man dwelt . . ."

All of mankind might well celebrate the Jewish Passover—shall *we* forget about it?!

The example in regard to Passover will give the reader a clear idea of what we call "the humanization of Jewish religious sanctities." We shall, therefore, not dwell at length on all the Jewish Holy Days, and will content ourselves only with a few remarks about the most important of them. The great mass of *lyricism* that accumulates in our hearts when we think about them would be more suitable for editorials in the daily press on each particular holiday, and therefore no one will take it amiss if we suppress them here almost altogether.

Shabuoth, like Passover, had also been previously a pure nature holiday, or more correctly an *agricultural* holiday: the first *harvest time* of grain in the field. However, the Jewish tradition linked the holiday with the legend of *Matn Toyre*.[5] This legend is again one of the most beautiful human features by which the old Jewish religion is distinguished. Cleansed of the supernatural but grandly poetic covering, the legend tells us that a people that has just been liberated from slavery and ignorance in exile bestowed on itself "a law of life," a science, how people should live among themselves in social tranquility.

In its Torah the Jewish people not only achieved the highest stage of contemporary civilization; it outgrew the old civilization "from its shoulders and higher," and for years and years acquired the right to look down on it. At that time only the Jewish people stood at the height of the Torah of Moses, and the Torah of Moses was the Mount Sinai from which the Jewish prophets—Amos, Hosea, Micah, Isaiah, and Jeremiah—could spread out their eagle wings and rise to the highest heavens of the human ideal.

The "Torah of Moses," regardless of who its authors were, is an important historical document of human progress, and since the Jewish people designated a holiday for it, we can, with the clearest conscience, keep these days holy together with them. For us the "Torah" will be sacred because it is a symbol of *science in general,* because in it the people collected their entire treasure of knowledge and justice, and for the first time declared before mankind that the treasure of knowledge and justice is the *most sacred thing* a people possesses, about which a person should think day and night and transmit it as an inheritance to the coming generation.

Passover is the holiday of the revolutionary struggle for freedom; Shabuoth, the holiday of peaceful progress, of the ideas that are gradually being realized in life. Passover is based on revolutionary pessimism, for which the entire past is immersed in the darkness of Egypt and whose glances are fixed only on the Promised, Holy Land, which lies so very far away. Shabuoth offers the necessary optimistic balance. It shows that the struggle of mankind heretofore has not been in vain. After the wandering in the desert they settle in a land and eat its fruit and gather spiritual treasures which make life worthwhile.

After Shabuoth there come, in the series of Jewish holidays, Rosh

Hashanah, the Ten Days of Repentance, the Sabbath Hazon,[6] Yom Kippur. They are rather universal than national in character. The autumnal mood in nature is transformed in them to the autumnal mood of human life. Man's "sinfulness," his imperfection, his striving to give an account of himself ("spiritual stocktaking!") for the last year, his striving to improve himself, to wash away the dirt that had adhered around his soul, and the consciousness of death that lurks over each one of us—these are all such serious moments in the moral life of every person that the holidays have truly merited the name of *Yomim Neroim,* "the Days of Awe."

Sukkoth does not require a special explanation and defense. It is the "festival of ingathering," the holiday of gathering the fruits from the field, the conclusion of the agrarian economic year. In it man sanctifies his human work on the field for the sake of a human life in *this* world. The purely material activity to preserve the human body has been elevated here—as in all old religions, with full justice—to the level of religious act.

The Jewish religion terminates the holiday with the most happy day of the entire year—Simhath Torah. With this it expresses the thought— again with full justice—that the material existence of man is no more than a necessary condition for a higher *spiritual* life, for the joys of understanding and knowledge, of justice and beauty, which are embodied in one single word—*Torah.*

The eight days of Hanukkah must, in our opinion, be elevated almost to the same level and sanctity as Passover, because the content of Hanukkah is almost the same as that of Passover—the victorious struggle of the people for its freedom and independence. Purim, however, certainly does not deserve that such a fuss should be made about it. The most remarkable and most beautiful aspect of this is that the people itself, in the depths of its consciousness, always felt that Purim is actually no holiday at all.

The people are quite justified in treating the holiday with an ironic smile on their lips; when they permit their Purim players to make fun of the entire story.

No people can exhibit such a superhumanly brave, such a dreadfully tragic contest for freedom and independence as the Jews demonstrated in their struggle against the hundred-times-stronger enemy, the world-dominating Rome. Zionist or non-Zionist, whether one believes in the Jewish "state of the future" or not, every nationally minded Jew must feel the great national misfortune of that time, when the people lost its freedom and independence, and everyone, even the Jew who is not nationally minded, cannot deny that the generation which sacrificed itself so heroically for the freedom of the people, deserves forever an annual commemorative day to the sounds of the dirges and the sad melody of the *Eli Zion*.[7]

And last but not least! the most beautiful and best of the Jewish holy days we left for the end—the Sabbath, the sacred *social* holiday, in which for the first time, to a certain degree, there was realized the *right to rest* for the slave and worker—a right which is much more important than the famous "right to work" with which many Utopians hoped to solve the social question, and the Jewish people can be truly proud of the fact that the first seeds from which the modern socialist ideal sprouted were implanted in its prophetic literature and became realized, insofar as the justice of the period permitted it, in many of its social institutions.

One can see that the Jewish people does not need to be ashamed of its Holy Days. *Life,* human life in its most sublime moments, is sanctified in the Jewish Sabbaths and holidays. The sufferings and joys of an entire people that strive to what is "great" and "eternal" find a resounding echo in them. We say once again: they deserve that all mankind should celebrate them. Can it be that we, progressive Jews, will not take them to our hearts, not hold them sacred in faithful love?

The Jewish people has *one* sacred place, which has a very particular national poetic value. This is the *Holy Land,* Palestine, the home where the Jewish people was born, the place where the most important episodes of its history took place, the soil in which there rests the dust of its most beautiful heroes, the place where it created what was the greatest and most beautiful in its culture. This place is truly dear to the heart of every devout Jew and also of very many who are not religious.

Perhaps the Zionists make a mistake when they think that they can solve the Jewish problem with the colonization of Palestine and give the opportunity to the entire Jewish people to live a respectable free, rich, and secure life. This is, perhaps, an impossible Utopia. However, *this* is not important for the national-poetic rebirth of the Jewish religion. It is important that the Holy Land should forever remain a *shrine of the Jewish people.* However, for this it does not suffice that the *recollection* about Palestine should live in the people's memory, as some non-Zionist nationalists claim. If the land of our great past is truly a *holy* land for us, then our feeling can on no account become reconciled to the thought that our shrine should lie in strange hands, should lie so forsaken and desolate that even a Zionist-minded traveler could flee from there with a heart tormented by its ravaged condition. The national poetic rebirth of the Jewish religion imposes a sacred duty on every nationally minded

Jew, to redeem the land from strange hands—be it "publicly legalized" or privately legalized, chiefly, that it should pass into Jewish hands that should transform it into a paradise, into the most splendid place in the world, into a state that it deserves in accordance with our feeling of *love* and devotion to it.

(1909)

NOTES

1. The nonlegal, fictional, imaginative material in the Talmud and rabbinical literature, as differentiated from Halakhah, the legislative part of these writings.

2. Famous Jewish hero in Judea, 132–35 C.E., who led a rebellion against the Roman oppressors. He had as one of his supporters the Tanna (teacher included in the Mishnah) Rabbi Akiva.

3. Born 1501, a Christian and son of Marranos, Molcho returned to Judaism and led a movement, together with Reubeni, aiming at the restoration of a Jewish kingdom in Palestine. Molcho was burned at the stake in Mantua, Italy, in 1532.

4. Gregory Gershuny (1870–1908), a Jewish revolutionary in Czarist Russia, member of the Social Revolutionary party.

5. *Matn Toyre* = Granting of the Torah at Mt. Sinai.

6. The Sabbath preceding the fast of the ninth of Ab (on which the first chapter of Isaiah, beginning with the word *Hazon* ["vision"] is read).

7. *Eli Zion* (Hebrew, "Lament, O Zion"), lamentation arranged in alphabetical order, recited on the ninth of Ab. The traditional tune was used for one of Byron's "Hebrew Melodies."

MORRIS R. COHEN

Morris Raphael Cohen, the Russian Jewish immigrant boy who became one of the foremost American philosophers and one of the greatest teachers of our time—"a modern Socrates"—was born in 1880 in the city of Neswish, near Minsk, White Russia. He was brought to the United States in 1892, graduated from the College of the City of New York eight years later, and received his Ph.D. at Harvard in 1906.

Cohen taught philosophy at City College from 1912 to 1938, becoming famous for his use of Socratic irony, and at the University of Chicago until 1942. His influence, through his students and his works, has been far-reaching, and he is considered one of the most original American philosophers since William James.

Cohen's mother tongue was Yiddish, for which he always maintained a special love. He said he owed a great deal of his education to the Yiddish press. In the early 1920s Cohen became active in ORT (an abbreviation of the Russian name of the Society for the Promotion of Crafts and Agriculture Among the Jews), and in 1933 he organized the Conference on Jewish Relations, to which he dedicated himself during the last years of his life. He had a role in establishing the important quarterly *Jewish Social Studies,* and became one of the founders, and the first chairman, of the Research Institute on Peace and Postwar Problems of the American Jewish Committee. He died in 1947.

Piety as defined by Santayana—"reverence for the sources of one's being"—was for Cohen, as he says in the first paragraph of the following selection, a necessary corollary of the Socratic maxim "know thyself." If a Jew is to know himself, he must know the history of the Jewish people. Cohen rejected monotheism and all other forms of theism, for he was not able to reconcile the reality of evil with the idea of a benevolent and omnipotent God.

In his moving autobiography, *A Dreamer's Journey,* Cohen describes how in his later years he came to appreciate the role of ritual in human life.

> For each of us the symbolism of our childhood offers paths to peace and understanding that can never be wholly replaced by other symbolisms . . . and though I have never gone back to theologic supernaturalism, I have come to appreciate more than I once did the symbolism in which is celebrated the human need of trusting to the larger vision, according to which calamities come and go but the continuity of life and faith in its better possibilities survive. [p. 218]

RELIGION

The ideal of intellectual integrity compelled me and many others of my generation to reject superstitions that had been bound up with the practices of our Orthodox parents, but it did not prevent us from cherishing the spiritual values which they had found in those practices, and which many others have found in the practices of other older and younger religions. The struggle between Orthodoxy and active opposition to all religion seemed to me, like so many of the passionate struggles of life, to overlook possibilities and values which a more tolerant and rational outlook could find.

Indeed I marveled then, and have never ceased to marvel, at the fact that on matters where knowledge is readily demonstrable—such as cooking or chemistry—discussions show little of the heated mood of the zealot and fanatic, whereas, in matters on which it is much more difficult to arrive at the truth, such as questions of religion, we are inclined to be very sure of ourselves. Perhaps we try to make up by our vehemence for the lack of demonstrative evidence.

Of course, if you claim to be in possession of a special revelation, then you have a mortgage on the truth of the universe, the other fellow can have nothing true to tell you, and the thing to do is to hold on to your revealed truth with all the ardor that is in you. But then the other fellow is just as certain that he alone has all the truth and there is no use in any argumentation. But if you take your stand on human history and human reason, and recognize, for example, that the claim to the possession of a special revelation of the Jew is, as such, not a bit better than that of the Christian or the Mohammedan, or any of the ten thousand other claims, then, it seemed to me, you must grant that each possesses both truth and error.

Having once made up my mind that the whole truth of the matter did not lie with either side, I saw the religious problem of my own intellectual generation as a problem calling for creative thought rather than simple loyalty. "Before we can appropriate the religion of our ancestors," I wrote in an article on the religious question on the East Side, in June, 1902, "we must build it over again in our own hearts. This holds good not only of religion but of all the products of civilization. Whatever thou hast inherited from thy ancestors, earn in order to possess. Only that which we have worked out ourselves is truly ours."

Twenty years later I was still seeking for a way of uniting naturalism in science with piety towards that which has been revered as noble and sacred

161

in the spiritual history of man. Of all philosophers, it seemed to me that Spinoza had most clearly developed the rational and tolerant attitude to the values of religion for which I had been searching. In my addresses before the American Philosophical Association in 1922 on "The Intellectual Love of God," I undertook to defend the validity of the Spinozistic ideal, "amor Dei intellectualis," as a beacon that may illumine the problems of modern life and thought. Naturalism, for Spinoza, did not import that worldliness which wise men in all generations have recognized as a state of spiritual death. Nor did he conceive of love as a passive emotion. The quest for understanding. Spinoza saw, is an activity, often a breathless activity, that even apart from its practical consequences, is the most divine of human enterprises.

It is true that Spinoza rejects the idea of an anthropomorphic God who will respond to our flattering prayers, reward us for our unsuccessful efforts, and in general compensate us for the harshness of the natural order and the weaknesses of our reason. If, however, religion consists in humility (as a sense of infinite powers beyond our scope) charity of love (as a sense of the mystic potency in our fellow human beings), and spirituality (as a sense of the limitations of all that is merely material, actual or even attainable), then no one was more deeply religious than Spinoza.

And while Spinoza has little regard for the immortality which means the postponement of certain human gratifications to a period beyond our natural life, he does believe in the immortality which we achieve when we live in the eternal present or identify ourselves with those human values that the process of time can never adequately realize or destroy. He thus showed me the path to that serenity which follows a view of life fixed on those things that go on despite all the tragedies and depressions which frighten hysterical people. Above all, Spinoza made clear to me the vision that saves us from the worldliness that drowns out life. We are all like the waves tossed high up by the ocean and breaking on the sands of actuality. If we are to attain 'true human dignity, we need some sense of our continuity with the past and the future, a consciousness of ourselves not as temporary flies but as waves of a human ocean larger than our own lives and efforts.

Spinoza, like the other great religious teachers and the morally wise men of science, teaches the great lesson of humility—that there are always vast realms beyond our ken or control, and that the great blessing of inner peace is unattainable without a sense of the mystery of creation about us and a wisely cultivated resignation to our mortal but inevitable limitations.

These limitations men surmount only as they learn to subordinate their separate individualities to the interest of families, social or religious groups, nations, races, or that humanity whose life is the whole cosmic drama of which, as thinkers, we are spectators.

In the days of my first youthful revolt against the Jewish observances, I was inclined to regard cultus, prayer and ritual as of little importance in comparison with belief or faith. This was certainly the view that my teacher William James took of the matter. The conclusion he drew from this was that the religious experience of the great mass of people, who follow in the steps of great masters, is of little significance. My own studies of the great historic religions led me, however, to see that ritual, what men do on certain occasions, is a primary fact in human religious experience, and that the beliefs and emotions associated with ritual are more variable than ritual itself, as is shown by the diverse explanations and justifications of the Hebrew Sabbath and the Easter ceremonies. Indeed the character of the founders of the great religions, as we know it, is largely a product of tradition.

Men cling to sanctified phrases not only because of the insights they contain but even more because, through ritual and repetition, they have become redolent with the wine of human experience. For each of us the symbolism of our childhood offers paths to peace and understanding that can never be wholly replaced by other symbolisms. For me the ancient ceremonies that celebrate the coming and going of life, the wedding ceremony, the *b'rith,* and the funeral service, give an expression to the continuity of the spiritual tradition that is more eloquent than any phrases of my own creation. The ritual may be diluted by English and by modernisms, but the Hebraic God is still a potent symbol of the continuous life of which we individuals are waves. So it is, too, with the celebration of the eternal struggle for freedom, in the family service of the Passover.

Like vivid illustrations in the book of my life are the prayers of my parents, the services at their graves, the memory of an old man chanting funeral songs at the *Jahrzeit* of my dear friend Dr. Himwich, the unveiling of the monument to the beloved comrade of my life's journeys, and the celebration of the continuity of generations in the Passover services in the home of my parents and in the homes of my children. And though I have never gone back to theologic supernaturalism, I have come to appreciate more than I once did the symbolism in which is celebrated the human need of trusting to the larger vision, according to which calamities come and go but the continuity of life and faith in its better possibilities survive.

(1949)

IV
Judaism, Jewish Nationalism and Assimilation

Y. L. PERETZ

Yitzkhok Leibush Peretz, the father of modern Yiddish literature and perhaps its greatest personality, was a sophisticated, Westernized intellectual. He was born in Zamosc, Poland in 1852, and died in Warsaw in 1915.

Reared in the East European religious tradition, he early came in contact with modern learning, and later passed the examinations as an advocate. He began to write poetry in Hebrew, but later turned to Yiddish. In 1889 he settled in Warsaw, becoming an employee of the Jewish Communal Bureau—the Geminah—and continuing to work there to the end of his life. His home in Warsaw became the most important literary center of the East European Jewish intelligentsia.

Peretz, the innovator, the modernist, gave expression in his writings to the ferment that swept Jewish life at the end of the nineteenth century. He was a brilliant, versatile, and original artist and thinker, writing stories, poems, plays, and essays. In addition he was a leader of the Jewish cultural movement then at its height in Poland. "Peretz was"—in the words of the poet Jacob Glatstein—"the Reb Levi Yitschok[1] of the agnostics. He was their advocate. Through his marvelous Hasidic tales, he sought to give the agnostic merit, and to preserve Jewish life for him. . . . Esthetically and ethically we were lonely until Peretz linked us with the world, and demanded that the world listen to the Jewish voice that has something to tell the century of great anticipation."

Peretz, the subtle artist and profound thinker, was a deeply rooted Jew who distrusted the modern world, loved the Jewish tradition, and wished to conserve the moral values of Judaism. He has put his ineradicable imprint on Jewish literature and thought.

---

[1] Levi Yitschok (1740–1809), noted for his profound "Love of Israel," and particularly for the common people.

ADVICE TO THE ESTRANGED

Times Change

Two electric balls with opposite charges are suspended not far from each other on two separate threads in mid-air. They alternately attract and repel each other.

At one moment they rush towards each other with love and longing. They want to unite. The next moment they leap away from one another in disgust and hate, seeking to put the maximum distance between themselves.

Similar reactions are observable among peoples.

"There is a time for everything," says Solomon.

There are alternating periods of attraction, of pushing towards each other, and periods of retreat, of mutual repulsion.

There are alternating historical periods: thesis and antithesis.

In periods of attraction, general humanitarian feelings develop. Hearts spin the golden threads of common human ideals and weave the web of common human interests.

In periods of repulsion each people retreats into itself, seeks solitude, takes stock of its own spiritual resources, digs into the deepest layers of its soul for buried treasures, works on its own internal growth, develops its own specific traits, spins and weaves the garment of its own intimate national life.

Thesis and antithesis! What is the synthesis?

Humanity of the future, consisting of free, independent, and culturally differentiated peoples.

This future is remote. The historic process of mutual attraction and repulsion will last a long time. The cycles are speeding up but, even so, they are still of considerable duration and human life is brief, so very brief.

A human being, whose short life with its short memories is contained within a single moment of history, regards such a moment as eternal. If this period comes to an end during his lifetime and if he himself is incapable of changing his modes of thought and his habits of reacting, then this fossilized individual wants to prolong the existing historic moment by force. He cannot succeed! Human hands are too weak to arrest the wheel of time. Such a person, therefore, sits down, closes his eyes, and refuses to look at the changes that, despite his own will, take place all around him. He sits with folded hands and dreams the dream of his generation with its obsolete thesis.

This is the position in which you, assimilationists, find yourselves. Now it is rumored that you have at last awakened and opened your eyes. Now you want to work with us.

This is our triumph!

We have been aware for some time that the springtide in the relations between peoples is over and gone, and that winter is in the air. Evil winds are its harbingers. And so we have hastened home.

The gusts of winter will soon be in full blast and there is work for all hands. Walls must be sealed, the roof repaired, windows inspected, fuel stored, lights held in reserve, and—bread! We have been active for some time in our own workshop.

You remained in the houses of others; you tarried in the halls of strangers; you followed in the footsteps of foreigners.

You found their homes so bright, so rich, and our home so dark, so poor.

You, therefore, lived for them, worked for them, until they hinted to you that you were not welcome and that they did not need your help. You thereupon dispersed, in the hope that the fewer there were of you in one spot, the more likelihood was there of your being tolerated.

If two of you found yourself in the same place, one got away from the other. Two in one spot at one time might be more than the others would welcome. If one of you happened to look into a mirror and to see his own face there, he jumped aside, he did not recognize his own mask, he thought there was another person in his way.

But even the single individual was felt to be superfluous and no knives or forks were set for him at the table of the others. Coughing failed to attract their attention. Then you moved to one side, sat down in an obscure corner, closed your eyes, dreamed your day-dreams, and drowsed off.

Now you have awakened!

You want to come back! You want to work with us!

This is our triumph. But we, the victors, shall not put our foot on your necks; we shall not close our doors to you. There is no lack of work for you in our workshop. We shall admit you as one of us, but we shall watch you carefully. We shall make sure that you do not sow the wrong seed-mixture, that you do not spin and weave threads of diverse qualities, that you do not introduce into our midst foreign contraband.

With us this is now a time for spiritual accounting and stock-taking, for holy work; and all hands that participate must be clean.

Times change! Formerly there was jubilation when one of the estranged returned to our midst. We pointed to him with pride and we held him up for all to see.

We are no longer so poor!

If you want to take from us, we shall gladly let you have of our own, our warmth, our intimacy.

If you want to give to us, however, we should like to know what you are giving. Is it gold or is it spurious currency?

Times change!

Home-Coming

Are we correct in assuming that you are coming back because of home-sickness, because you have become conscious of your duties to the people of your origin, because you want to renew your severed bonds with your relatives, brothers and sisters, fathers and mothers? If you really want to return, then do so in all honesty. . . .

Come, see, hear, learn, study, and, until you have amassed knowledge of our ways, maintain silence! . . .

Don't come back to preach to us the ideas of others and to plant in our midst the culture of others. We say, all roads lead to the ideal man, but each people has its own specific road. You say, let us change roads, let us exchange cultural values? We want to develop our own hearth and worship at our altar in our own way. You ask us to throw out our own hearths and to borrow the fire of strangers for our altar.

We shall not stop up your loud mouths. But we should like to give you the following advice:

If you compare, do so honestly. If you talk of exchanging, then use honest weights and measures and place comparable goods on the two sides of the scale.

Take equivalents for your comparative evaluation! . . .

If you speak of superstitions, compare our *Kaddish* and our religious provisions for the souls of the dead with the methods in use among others.

Or take *Gehenna,* our post-mortem penal institution, with its maximum sentence of twelve months, and compare it with the eternal hell that others hold out as a possible prospect.

Perhaps, you don't like our Prayer-Book? Let us see what is in it.

"May awe of Thee, O God, come over all Thy works and fear of Thee over all that Thou hast created! May all join in unison to do Thy will with all their heart!"

These are the prayers of a Jew. Have you more beautiful prayers to offer?

What does a Jew ask for when he recites his daily prayers? Peace, and may there be no shedding of human blood! Justice, and may evil pass away like smoke and the rule of wantonness disappear from the earth!

Are your prayers better?

A Jew waits for Messiah to come and to redeem the world from fear and pain, from the cataclysmic conflicts between rich and poor. All shall enjoy the earth. This means, in popular imagination, that bread and clothes shall grow, ready-made, on trees.

Do you have more winged ideals?

Did you ever compare our folksongs with those of others? Or, our folktales with those, for example, of the Grimm Brothers? Do you find among us, as you do find among them, songs and tales of robber-heroes, sly deceivers, and seven-league boots?

You want to compare laws?

Do compare our Sabbath, our day of rest for all, God and man, lord and slave and cattle, with their religious equivalent, their Sunday. Do compare our ancient laws on how to treat strangers with the laws in force today, in your vaunted twentieth century, among the freest and most humanitarian peoples, whom you are holding up as models.

I have stressed those cultural items which you ask us to discard and which we rather select for further development, those cornerstones which we put down as a foundation for our cultural sanctuary, those sparks which we gather and fan into a brilliant fire.

Are you serious about an exchange? Will we not be getting the poorer bargain? . . .

A final bit of advice to all assimilationists:

If you want to talk to our people, talk with less arrogance!

Respect for an ancient people, yes, respect for the most ancient of peoples! No less than others was this people able to conquer and govern a land and defend it to the last drop of blood against the heroic armies of world-powers. Yes, it could do so better and more gloriously than all of them. And even afterwards, it produced a long, long chain of generations of warriors who continued to battle for holy convictions to the last drop of blood.

Respect for a people whose history is the only tragedy of world-wide, heroic proportions, a history of unceasing self-sacrifice and of extreme martyrdom for an idea!

No wonder that you, frivolous worldly individuals, left us: you deserted those who preach the joy of living and are forced to endure suffering and you escaped to those who preach suffering and live a life of joyous abandon. . . .

Like black ravens, you now come and croak to us of our decline, but you do not terrify us.

We heard your kind in Egypt, Persia, Assyria, Babylonia, Greece, Rome, and ever since. We are accustomed to such talk.

Worlds are not built or destroyed by talk like yours.

Preach what you will. The wind carries sound. But preach with respect!

If you do not want to suffer with our people, you need not do so. If you cannot love our people, it can get along without your love. But don't fail to respect it!

Bow your frivolous heads before the eternal warrior, the eternal people!

Bow your heads deep, deep, to the very ground!

SIMON DUBNOW

Simon Dubnow is the great Jewish historian and exponent of Diaspora Nationalism, or Autonomism, whose philosophy of Jewish existence offers some help in confronting the dilemma of living as a minority within the general majority culture.

Dubnow was born in White Russia on September 10, 1860, the last in a line of rabbis and scholars. He received a traditional Jewish education, but in his early youth became absorbed in the literature of the Haskalah as well as in general European culture. Like many of his contemporaries, the young Dubnow stood upon a platform of assimilation for the Russian Jews according to the Western European model, but the wave of pogroms that swept over the Jews in the wake of the assassination of Czar Alexander II in 1881 smashed all the hopes they had placed in emancipation and Russification. The trauma of the 1880s provoked Dubnow into beginning a lifelong study of Jewish history, which resulted in the three-volume *History of the Jews in Russia and Poland*. The monumental ten-volume *World History of the Jewish People,* a three-volume study of Hasidism, and a systematic philosophy of Jewish existence which was developed in a series of *Letters on Old and New Judaism* (the *Letters* are available in English under the title: *Nationalism and History,* Jewish Publication Society, 1958).

From 1890 until 1903 Dubnow lived in Odessa, from 1903 until 1906 in Vilna, from 1922 to 1933 in Berlin, and from 1933 in Riga, where he was murdered by the Nazis in 1941.

Dubnow's philosophy of Jewish existence remains relevant for our generation, and may be considered one of the best and most helpful guides in the search for identity on the part of Jewish youth in America.

THE DOCTRINE OF JEWISH NATIONALISM

What is the distinguishing mark of nationality? This question has up to most recent times aroused sharp controversy both in theory and in practice. I shall not dwell on the details of the controversy. I wish to underscore but one fact: the scientific definitions of the concept "nation" exhibit the same transition from the material to spiritual factors as the concrete historical development of nations. Philosophers of the old school looked upon nationality as the product of biological elements, climate and territory. Contemporary legal philosophers and political scientists frequently confuse the terms "nation" and "state." For them the typical nation is the uninational state and, where they find a multi-national state, they condemn the national minority to assimilation and fusion with the ruling majority (this opinion originated during the French Revolution and was for a long time widely accepted in jurisprudence). More liberal political theorists benevolently accord the right of cultural autonomy to national groups which do not have a state of their own but have not yet lost their territory and their language. Lately, however, the view has gained ground that a nation may be defined as a historical-cultural group which is conscious of itself as a nation even though it may have lost all or some of the external characteristics of nationality (state, territory or language), provided it possesses the determination to continue developing its own personality in the future. Objective criteria of nationality are giving way in the scientific definitions of the concept to subjective factors.

Theoretical sociologists and political scientists have arrived at the conclusion that subjective or spiritual factors are supreme in the development of the national type, while all the material factors are but stages leading to the highest point of this development, namely, the crystallization of a well-defined and conscious national individuality. In the same way in which spiritual affinity is a more important factor than blood relationship in families of higher cultural circles (there are numerous instances of families being broken up because of profound differences in ethical and spiritual aspirations among their members), so also in higher types of

177

national families the common spiritual aspirations are the unifying and cohesive forces.

What is the supreme moving force in the national struggles of our time for political freedom and communal autonomy, if not this desire of nations to preserve their spiritual possessions and to develop freely their historical personality? The German War of Liberation against Napoleon I at the beginning of the nineteenth century and similarly the subsequent struggle of the Italians against Austria were battles against the injection of foreign national culture into the national life of the Germans and Italians. In all liberation movements of oppressed peoples, in all uprisings against political tyranny, a strong sense of national self-preservation is manifested which claims for itself the right to free cultural development. Usually the shell of political or territorial independence is placed around this precious kernel—the freedom of the nation—in order to protect it. From time to time, however, a nation is forced to forego this protective shell of political autonomy and to remain content with social and cultural autonomy. In place of the external instruments of nationality, which it had to give up, it strengthens its inner resources, the consciousness of its identity, the collective will, and the common aspirations necessary for building up its autonomous organizations and institutions, its language, its educational system and its literature. If this struggle is carried on successfully over a long period, it is safe to predict that it will also succeed in the future, provided the utmost is done to increase and strengthen national unity.

After what has been said above it should be clear to all how greatly mistaken are those Jews and non-Jews who deny to the Jews of the Diaspora the right to call themselves a nation, only because they lack the specific external marks of a nationality which were taken from them or which became weakened during the nation's long history. Only he who completely fails to understand the nature of the national "ego" and of its development can refuse to accord nationality to this old historic community which, during the last 2,000 years, has been transformed from a simple nation into the very archetype of a nation, a nation in the purest and loftiest sense, which has attained the highest stage of nationality.

The rejection of Jewish nationalism among Jews stems from two opposing camps, the orthodox and the freethinkers. Since religion completely dominated all spheres of Jewish life for two thousand years, the mass of orthodox Jews accepted the idea that Judaism is not a nationality in the accepted sense but a religious community living according to sacred traditions, laws and commandments that encompass the life of the individual and the community. The mass of the people who do not understand the interdependence of historic events failed to see that all the ancient national values of the Jewish nation—the historical festivals, customs and usages, laws, social institutions, the whole system of self-administration retained in the Diaspora—all had been incorporated gradually and artificially into the sphere of religion. The national body became wrapped in the garb of religion so that . . . its true form was unrecognizable.

In essence the views of the orthodox may be formulated as follows: "Judaism is a religious nation, its members are held together by religious ordinances and practical commandments; whoever violates this religion removes himself from the national community." This view is not opposed to the concept of a spiritual or cultural nation. It is mistaken only in the sense that it confuses the concepts of "spiritual" and "cultural" with "religious." It is the result of a limited perspective characteristic of men who do not distinguish between fossilized tradition and living, creative development. Let the mass of the orthodox consider nationality and religion as one. for the time being, . . . let them be satisfied with this partial understanding as long as they cannot arrive at a full and complete understanding based on theoretical analysis and research. In the end they too will see the light. The observing and believing Jew will realize that there are many Jewish freethinkers who, while disregarding the religious laws and commandments, are nevertheless true and dedicated members of their people and that they not only remain within the fold of Judaism but strive with all their power to strengthen and exalt it. From this realization it is but one step to theoretical analysis and research. These Jews will then come to differentiate religion from nationality, and the scientific study of history will reveal to them how these concepts came to be confused. When that happens the movement of the secularization of the national idea, which has already begun among an important segment of the community in modern times, will gain ground among the broad strata of the people.

While the mass of old-type orthodox Jews sees itself in practice as a religious nation and resists assimilation in the surrounding nations by the force of its faith, the assimilationist intelligentsia, on the other hand (mostly freethinkers of the neo-orthodox of the West), sees in Judaism only a religious community, a union of synagogues which imposes no national duties or discipline whatsoever on its members. According to this view, the Jew can become a member of another nation and remain a member of the Mosaic faith. He is a German Jew, for example, in the same way that there are German Protestants or German Catholics. It follows logically from this premise that a freethinking or non-religious Jew must be excluded from the community of Jews of the Mosaic faith. This corollary is usually glossed over so that whatever remains of Jewish "unity" may not be disturbed. I shall discuss this doctrine, which was in vogue only a short time ago but has recently lost ground among its adherents, in greater detail in the following Letters. Here I only wish to point out that it contradicts both the traditional view of many past generations that the "religious nation" must be kept pure, and the scientific view of the non-assimilability of the spiritual or cultural nation. This kind of doctrine comes neither from religion nor from science. It is the invention of naive ideologues, or calculating opportunists, who seek to justify by means of this artificial doctrine their desire to assimilate into the foreign environment in order to benefit themselves and their children. This is but a repetition of the process of natural selection and of the weeding out of those weak elements of the nation which are unable to bear the pressure of the alien environment.

The natural tendency to strip the Jewish national idea of its religious cloak is liable to lead to still another extreme position. While the orthodox say: "The Jewish religion is the sole foundation of our nationality," the freethinkers can claim: "The Jewish religion is not at all a necessary condition of nationality; it can exist without it by virtue of the law of psychic heredity and cultural-historical factors." In practice this theory would make it possible to justify religious apostasy. A Jew could give up Judaism, embrace another religion, and still remain a Jew by nationality. Those who hold this view are guilty of a grave and dangerous error. By aspiring to secularism, by separating the national idea from religion, we aim only to negate the *supremacy* of religion, but not to eliminate it from the storehouse of national cultural treasures. If we wish to preserve Judaism as a cultural-historical type of nation, we must realize that the religion of Judaism is one of the integral foundations of national culture and that anyone who seeks to destroy it undermines the very basis of national existence. Between us and the orthodox Jews there is only this difference: they recognize a traditional Judaism the forms of which were set from the beginning for all eternity, while we believe in an evolutionary Judaism in which new and old forms are always being assumed or discarded and which adjusts itself unceasingly to new cultural conditions. Their main concern is holiness, ours is creative freedom. Here I may be asked: "And what of those who do not accept religion in general and the Jewish religion in particular?" This is a most important question and demands special attention.

Historical Judaism is not merely a religion, like Christianity or Islam. Judaism is a body of culture. Unique historical conditions which brought the life of the Jewish nation under the dominance of religion converted Judaism into an all-embracing world view which encompasses religious, ethical, social, messianic, political and philosophical elements. In each of these areas history has piled up layer upon layer. The Bible, the Talmud, Rabbinic Judaism, rationalist Jewish theology, Jewish mysticism are not merely chapters in Jewish religious teaching but also stages in the development of Judaism. Judaism is broad enough and variegated enough so that any man in Israel can draw from its source according to his spirit and outlook. The orthodox Jew accepts all the principles of religious faith and practice formed in the course of generations and rigidly set down in the codes of law and in the ordinances of the rabbis. The "reformed" Jew rejects the decisions of the rabbis and even the laws of the Talmud and accepts only the religious principles, laws and obligations of the Bible. Adherents of rationalist theology find satisfaction in the religious philosophy of the Middle Ages. The freethinking Jew who accepts only ethical teaching can find an exalted moral and social worldview in the teachings of the Hebrew Prophets. The ethical teachings of the Prophets can well become the "religion of the future," the moral doctrine of a free society. All those who base their religion on poetic content will find in the Bible and in medieval Jewish literature a source of poetry that fills the soul with magic splendor. Followers of mysticism will find a great treasure house in the kabbalah and to a greater degree in Hasidism, the "religion of the heart." Thus one may be a Jew according to the teaching of the Prophets or of the Talmud, according to Moses Maimonides or the *Shulhan Arukh,* according to Moses Mendelssohn or the Besht, according to Geiger or Samson Raphael Hirsch, as long as one does not reject entirely the national idea, which is not a matter of theory but a historical fact.[1]

---

[1] I believe that even Spinoza would not have turned away from his people if he and the Jews of Amsterdam had understood history well enough to realize that it was possible to be a natural Jew without retaining traditional religion. The seventeenth century was not yet advanced enough, however, to understand the secular Jewish national idea.

In the end those Jews to whom any form of religion is alien will prefer to remain within the Jewish fold rather than embrace another faith. The enlightened among us, who in the main tend toward rationalism and scientific positivism, will not betray the Covenant of Abraham out of conviction and submit to the yoke of another religion for the simple reason that, if the principles of the Jewish religion, which are so closely related to rationalism, do not suit them, the symbols and mysticism of Christianity surely will not do so. Diderot once said that the way of science leads from Christianity to Judaism and thence to philosophical Deism. In any event, a rationalist in search of ethical ideals will turn to the philosophy of life of the biblical prophets rather than to the other-worldly doctrine of the Gospels.

A non-believing Jew may be counted as an adherent of Judaism so long as he does not identify himself with any other faith that conforms to his philosophical views. He may also join the "dissidents," or *Konfessionslose,* who do not believe in any religion. In any case he cannot attach himself to another Church out of sincere conviction. Absence of faith takes the Jew out of the national community only if he believes in complete national assimilation. In practice, conversion to another faith, under conditions prevailing in the Diaspora, means also separation from the Jewish nation. If this may not apply to the apostate himself, it certainly does to his family, which has no choice but to assimilate with the non-Jewish environment in the national as well as the religious sense. A convert of this kind may consider himself in his innermost heart as a "Christian son of the Jewish nation"; in fact, however, the tie between the two is broken. This does not apply, of course, to the marranos of Spain who, under a Christian cloak, clung to Judaism and educated their children in its spirit. In general, a Jew may be a son of the Jewish faith potentially or actually, or he may be without any religion at all; but exit from Judaism by acceptance of the Christian religion means exit from the Jewish nation.

(1907)

SIMON DUBNOW

Simon Dubnow is the great Jewish historian and exponent of Diaspora Nationalism, or Autonomism, whose philosophy of Jewish existence offers some help in confronting the dilemma of living as a minority within the general majority culture.

Dubnow was born in White Russia on September 10, 1860, the last in a line of rabbis and scholars. He received a traditional Jewish education, but in his early youth became absorbed in the literature of the Haskalah as well as in general European culture. Like many of his contemporaries, the young Dubnow stood upon a platform of assimilation for the Russian Jews according to the Western European model, but the wave of pogroms that swept over the Jews in the wake of the assassination of Czar Alexander II in 1881 smashed all the hopes they had placed in emancipation and Russification. The trauma of the 1880s provoked Dubnow into beginning a lifelong study of Jewish history, which resulted in the three-volume *History of the Jews in Russia and Poland.* The monumental ten-volume *World History of the Jewish People,* a three-volume study of Hasidism, and a systematic philosophy of Jewish existence which was developed in a series of *Letters on Old and New Judaism* (the *Letters* are available in English under the title: *Nationalism and History,* Jewish Publication Society, 1958).

From 1890 until 1903 Dubnow lived in Odessa, from 1903 until 1906 in Vilna, from 1922 to 1933 in Berlin, and from 1933 in Riga, where he was murdered by the Nazis in 1941.

Dubnow's philosophy of Jewish existence remains relevant for our generation, and may be considered one of the best and most helpful guides in the search for identity on the part of Jewish youth in America.

183

THE SECRET OF SURVIVAL,
AND THE LAW OF SURVIVAL

Our Future: The Manifest and the Hidden

A revolution came to the western world that was both political and cultural, the period of liberation—emancipation—or the striving for liberation. In most states the external wall isolating Jews from Gentiles was demolished and Jews for their part tore down the internal wall which their fathers had built.

They laid down their weapons, the national "fences" in their religion. They leave the camp, enter the alien environment, and absorb alien principles into their spirit. The emancipated Jew exchanges his national freedom for civic freedom. To a certain extent he is forced to this in line with the statement heard in the National Assembly in Paris during the great Revolution: "Give all the rights to the Jews as men, but give them nothing as sons of a specific nation!" This formulation by Clermont-Tonnerre, a partisan of emancipation, became the cornerstone of the emancipation structure in all countries. The emancipators demanded clearly: "Since citizenship has been introduced we must dissolve all national institutions: autonomous administration of the communities (except in religious affairs), schools that are not like the general state-schools, the use of Hebrew or Yiddish in the life of the community, etc." Thus emancipation liberates the Jew from both his bondage and his Judaism at one and the same time. It seems as if the dreaded end of Israel has come; limb after limb is swept into the stream and swallowed up in the abyss of the Gentile world.

Then the tempest comes from the north and the wheel turns back. The hatred against the eternal people that appeared to have subsided rises again. The war is renewed, in a cultural form in western Europe and in a savage form in the East. The Jewish masses who did not lay down their old weapons meet their enemies with the well-tested strategy of their fathers. But those who already have acquiesced in the environment and remain naked and without national armor—what about them?

The answer is heard in all corners of the Diaspora, one answer consisting of two parts: (1) return to national Judaism in a form appropriate

185

to modern humanitarian culture; (2) return to Eretz Yisrael in order
to build a pure national culture. Once more a period of construction
succeeds a period of destruction. But there is no peace among the builders
nor is there faith in the hearts of many of their number. Those who call
for an ingathering of the exiled in the land of Israel despair of spiritual
salvation in the lands of the Diaspora and sentence all the dispersed of
Israel to national death; and the spiritual nationalists do not believe in
a miraculous ingathering of the exiled through the new "messianic" idea.
Voices rise to proclaim either the "end of the nation," or the "revival
of Israel," and they deafen the ears and confuse the minds.

There is one remedy for the faint-hearted and for those who cling
to vain illusions—detailed and thorough study of the law of survival
of the Jewish people. This law will come and smite the faces of those
who despair of the spiritual revival and say to them: "You view only
the limited range of modern history and are frightened of what you see.
You imagine that there never was a period like this before in Jewish
history—a period of assimilation and wholesale conversions. You are
wrong. In just the same way the sword of the Diaspora wrought havoc
in Alexandria and Syria "in front of the Temple" (despite the influence
of the center in Judea), in the lands under Moslem rule in the eastern
Caliphate, in Arab and Christian Spain— yet with all this the law of
survival never ceased to pursue its work. Apart from this, are you not
also my witnesses yourselves, you members of a generation that saw the
withering of assimilation and the growth of the national idea in all its
many shades? Your parents saw groups of Jews who denied their Jewish
nationality in order to receive civic freedom—while you have seen myriads
of Jews fighting for both civic and national freedom in the Diaspora centers and raising the banner on which was inscribed: "National Rights!"
They have not yet won the struggle, but do you not see the "way of the
spirit," the trend toward building up the nation, not toward tearing it
down and destroying it? What is this if not a phenomenon often repeated
in our history: in the hour of danger, the enduring elements win out
over the disruptive elements; the national force accumulated in the past
triumphs over the destructive force and restores the national group to its
position. Out of the depths of the Jewish soul the gigantic force of the
past bursts into the open and combines with the forces of the nation that
are currently active and leads them to the cleared path, the path of life.

If this is so, one might ask, is not everything predetermined and don't
we merely have to place our trust in the favors of history? Must we have

complete faith in the survival of the Jewish nation despite all the frightening spectacles that pass before us?

Yes and no. If faith in the survival of Judaism is not just a vague belief, but a conclusion derived from the knowledge of all causes and effects in our history; if the understanding of the secret of survival flows from the understanding of the law of survival, from a knowledge of the conditions on which it depends, then this faith is tied to action, to practical commandments, although not those derived from the *Shulhan Arukh.* The principles of the national commandments are known: perennial struggle for communal autonomy—autonomy of the cells that make up the body of the nation—in a form that is appropriate to the conditions of the time; a struggle for national education at home and in schools established for this purpose—education in the ancient national language and the vernacular languages developed in the Diaspora which unite the entire people or large sections of it; a struggle for the cultivation of all basic national possessions and their adaptation to universal culture without damaging their own individuality. The believers who declare themselves free from such practical commandments harbor a dead faith in their hearts, and they will not awake to the national revival. We demand a living, active, and effective faith that stirs the will to life and does not lull it to sleep. Perserverance in the "will to survive"—this is the goal of our labors.

But the faint-hearted object even to this "refined faith" that depends on knowledge and understanding, and assert: "We doubt that the will to a national life in the Diaspora will endure. National feeling is decreasing under the impact of the alien environments; the Jewish community will be swept into the midst of the life of the ruling nations, and the national will—the basis of our survival—will be weakened accordingly. The Jewish nationality is approaching its end in the Diaspora; only *in* the land of Israel, in a national environment, can we remain alive, or, at least *by means of* the land of Israel and its influence on the Diaspora."

To objections of this kind I answer: If you do not believe that the will to a national life in the Diaspora will endure (that is in something that is borne out by the events and experience of thousands of years), how can you believe that the will to revive the land of Israel can be strengthened to the degree required for a tremendous ingathering of the exiled—unparalleled since the time of the destruction of the Second Temple—or even for a center small in quantity but great in quality, for the creation of a center in Eretz Yisrael that would spread its influence over the Diaspora? If the source of the will in the Diaspora is destroyed, where will the revival come from? And if you say: "We are satisfied with a partial ingathering of the exiled, while the rest perish in the desert of the nations," are you not decreeing the destruction of the majority of the Jewish people? If our ancestors had entertained such notions, Israel would already have ceased to exist. Your error stems from the fact that you base your conclusions on a theoretical and not on a historical analogy.

History teaches us to believe that the national will must endure everywhere and to carry on by the power of this faith. National faith and activity are two sides of one coin, and if the image is rubbed off one side, the reverse side will also be effaced. Only after we realize that the national will can endure in all the lands of our dispersion and that it can give strength to the national centers, can we believe that from it as the source, there will come forth a striving to build a cultural center for a part of the Jewish people in Eretz Yisrael; then we can also work toward the end that this center will be established and will influence appreciably the lands of the Diaspora as a shining example of pure national culture, free of alien admixtures. But far be it from us to put all our hopes upon this influence alone and to divert our attention from the overwhelming majority of our people. As long as Zionism continues to pursue the path of the "negation of the Diaspora" (which embraces also the cultural possessions of the Diaspora which have become active national forces, like the spoken vernacular, etc.), it is bound to destroy with one hand what it builds with the other. "Hatred of the *galuth,*" rooted in the hearts of many in order to honor "love for Zion," is dangerous. Love that springs from hatred generally is suspect, but especially so if the hatred is directed against a powerful historical phenomenon that is part of our very being and that, under the historical conditions in which we find ourselves, cannot be severed from the body of the nation without wounding its soul.

From all this we conclude that there is great danger in the "serenity of the righteous," and the quietism of those who believe that Israel exists through a miracle, whether they be adherents of the "mission" idea or mummies of *Wissenschaft des Judentums* who had not tasted of its elixir of life. They are those who are afflicted with the plague of assimilation and preach "sweet sermons" on the immortality of the soul just as it is leaving the body and those who proclaim: "Let the Jewish nationality die and long live Judaism!" But danger may also come from those who reject completely the existence of the Jewish nationality in the Diaspora, who direct their efforts only toward the goal of exodus and "redemption," and who out of despair are prepared to condemn all the Jews in the Diaspora, that is, the entire people, to death by assimilation. We share neither the serenity of the "believers" nor the troubled spirit of the deniers. We demand a faith as closely linked to action as fire is to coal. Our history (living, not mummified, history) teaches us what to do and what to believe, and it says: "You are sons (*banim*) of your people in the measure that you are its builders (*bonim*), to the degree that you combine faith with action and fight with dedication for the survival of our nation and for its inner autonomy in all the lands in which it is dispersed."

AHAD HA'AM

Ahad Ha'Am, the exponent of Cultural Zionism, played a major role in the Jewish national movement of our era, and has been recognized as an independent thinker, a man of character, and an essayist with a lucid Hebrew style.

Asher Ginzberg, who became famous under the pen-name Ahad Ha'Am, was born in the Ukraine into a Hasidic family in 1856, and was educated in the traditional manner. Later he attended universities at Vienna, Berlin, and Breslau. Settling in Odessa in 1886, he became a leader of the Hoveve Zion. From 1908 to 1922 he resided in London, and there he participated in the negotiations leading to the Balfour Declaration (1917). In 1922 Ahad Ha'Am settled in Tel Aviv, where he died five years later.

Ahad Ha'Am taught that the nation is the people's "ego," i.e., its internal creative force, which is the sum total of its memory and will for survival. The will to live is an instinctive power, a mighty, irrational force of nature that stems from the unconscious areas of the soul. In order to survive the Jewish people must strengthen its national will. This can be done in two ways that complement each other: (1) by establishing colonies in *Eretz Isroel,* and (2) by strengthening the national spirit of the people, which finds expression in the national culture and destiny.

The Jewish national spirit, Ahad Ha'Am maintains, finds expression primarily in morality, not in religion. To him the religious beliefs and practices of Judaism are but the external garb of the intuitive and unique moral conviction of the Jewish people. To create suitable conditions for the survival of the Jewish spirit is the main concern of Ahad Ha'Am's thought. The Jewish spirit does not, for Ahad Ha'Am, depend on Judaism, but rather on our national ethics.

Ahad Ha'Am reformulated Jewish fundamental ideas and gave them a modern cut: "national will" instead of Providence; ethics instead of divine inspiration. He mercilessly dissected the servile face of the assimilated Jewish intelligentsia. His writings were stamped by a great moral personality for whom nothing but the truth and the right deed matter.

191

JUDAISM AND JEWISH NATIONALISM

To M. SHENKIN (Jaffa). *London, Feb.* 14*th,* 1908.

. . . Of course Paul Nathan and the other members of the *Hilfsverein* think that "the only bond that unites Jews is religion." The strange thing is that you and your colleagues never realised this till now. But perhaps it is not so strange after all, because I see now that you do not even understand your western Zionist friends, with whom you have worked at eight Congresses. Almost all the Zionist leaders here are of the same opinion as Nathan and his people. That is how you have educated them. You have been too busy with politics to have time to notice in the course of ten years that their whole conception of Zionism differs profoundly from ours. Consequently we have to choose between two alternatives. One is to part company with the western Jews and make up our minds to wait until we are strong enough to establish a school system without any help from any of them, Zionist or non-Zionist. In that case the school system will of course be what we want it to be. The other alternative is to persuade ourselves that it is better to have good schools in Palestine, even if the pupils wear caps in class and there is no Higher Criticism, than to sit with folded arms and wait for some miraculous increase in our resources. You may be surprised, but I must tell you quite frankly that I prefer the second alternative. When we had to deal with the *Alliance* and its teachers, who saw no use at all in Hebrew education, we were bound to oppose them tooth and nail, and to regard their system of education as worse than none at all. But the present-day western Jews, who want an "orthodox" Hebrew education, are not so dangerous. If the pupils acquire a thorough knowledge of the Hebrew language, the Bible and the Talmud (even on orthodox lines), and an adequate knowledge of Jewish history, and if at the same time they get a good general education, Palestine will be very much better off from the cultural point of view, even if their ideas do not agree with ours. Such material will be much more amenable to our influence than the Palestine Jews are now. And even if we assume that they will stick to their orthodoxy, what of it? Do you expect all the Jews to become free-thinkers? I only wish we might have a real people in Palestine, even if it were all orthodox—not in the uncouth fashion of *Halukah* people, but decent civilized men like the Christian Englishmen whom I meet here. I should be very happy if I could hope to live to fight against orthodoxy of that type in Palestine.

. . . Certainly I should prefer our cultural work in Palestine to develop on my lines; but because that is out of the question, I cannot therefore abandon the work altogether. What we need in Palestine is more and more knowledge and education, no matter how much religion goes with them. When we become the cultural power in the land, and have sufficient influence, we shall be a long step nearer the attainment of our aims, even if you and I and a few others (for we must recognise that the great majority is not on our side) are dissatisfied. But for my own part I am inclined to think that national education (in our sense) will win in the end. The western Jews will not succeed, try as they may, in turning out only "Jews by religion," and gradually the national element will conquer the religious.

If the High School cannot continue to exist unless caps are worn in class and the Higher Criticism is excluded, I do not think that this should be made a question of principle. My son, who is studying in the *Yeshivah* [Talmudical College] in Odessa, told me when he first went there that it was the custom to wear caps for the Talmud lesson, and that he had decided to wear his cap for all the lessons, so as not to have to put it on specially for that one. Both of us laughed over this, and I confess it did not occur to me that he was being false to the cause of culture. . . .

ALBERT EINSTEIN

Albert Einstein, the great physicist, mathematician, and humanitarian, was not only an intellectual giant, but a conscious Jew and an active supporter of Zionism.

Einstein was born in Ulm, Germany in 1879, and was educated in Switzerland. After receiving his degree he was appointed an instructor at Bern University. Later he was a professor at Zurich and Prague. In 1914 Einstein became professor of physics at Berlin University, where he remained until the rise of Nazism in 1933. He then settled in Princeton, New Jersey, where he died in 1955.

After the death of Chaim Weizmann (1952), the first President of Israel, Einstein refused an invitation to stand for election as President of Israel. He was deeply interested in Israeli scientific institutions, especially the Hebrew University, of which he was a trustee, and to which he donated the manuscripts of his theory of relativity.

When he returned to Germany in 1914 he became conscious of his Jewishness. His interest may have been aroused by his warm sympathy with East European Jews who, during the war and the postwar period, fled to Germany, craving the assistance of their fellow Jews. He became a Zionist, being repelled by the assimilated German Jews. Einstein the humanitarian believed that concern for man himself and his fate should always form the chief interest of all technical endeavor.

Although Einstein's greatness was achieved in science and mathematics, his writings on humanistic and Jewish topics contain many noble expressions of human feeling, and penetrating insights. Here are some:

Never do anything against conscience, even if the state demands it. My religion consists of a humble admiration of the illimitable superior spirit who reveals himself in the slight details we are able to perceive with our frail and feeble minds. That deeply emotional conviction of the presence of a superior reasoning power, which is revealed in the incomprehensible universe, forms my idea of God. I believe in Spinoza's God, who reveals himself in the orderly harmony of what exists, not in a God who concerns himself with fates and actions of human beings.

195

JEWISH IDEALS

Striving after knowledge for its own sake, a love for justice that borders on fanaticism, and a striving for personal independence—these are the themes of the tradition of the Jewish people which make me feel that belonging to it is a gift of fate.

Those who rage today against the ideals of reason and individual freedom and seek to accomplish this spiritless state-slavery by means of brutal violence, justly see their implacable opponents in us. History has imposed a difficult struggle upon us. However, as long as we remain devoted servants of truth, justice, and freedom, we shall not only persist as one of the oldest of living nations but also create, as hitherto in productive work, values which contribute toward the ennoblement of mankind.

Is There a Jewish World-Outlook?

In my opinion there is no Jewish world-outlook in the philosophic sense. Judaism seems to me to be concerned almost exclusively with the moral attitude in life and for life. Judaism seems to me rather the essence of the attitude to life prevailing among Jewish people than the essence of the laws established in the Torah and interpreted in the Talmud. The Torah and the Talmud are for me only the most important evidence for the dominance of the Jewish view of life in earlier times.

The essence of the Jewish view of life seems to me to be: affimation of the life of all creation. Life of the individual only has meaning in the service of the beautification and ennoblement of the life of all living beings. Life is sacred, i.e., the highest value on which all other values depend. The sanctity of superindividual life involves the veneration of all that is spiritual, a particularly characteristic feature of the Jewish tradition.

Judaism is not a creed. The Jewish God is only a negation of superstition, an imaginary result of its elimination. It is also an attempt to base the moral law on fear, a regrettable, discreditable venture. Nevertheless it seems to me that the strong moral tradition in the Jewish people has

197

largely liberated itself from this fear. It is also evident that "Service of God" was equated with "Service for the Living." For this the best elements of the Jewish people, particularly the Prophets and Jesus, struggled indefatigably.

Thus Judaism is not a transcendental religion; it has only to do with the life experienced by us and which is to a certain degree palpable, and with nothing else. It therefore seems questionable to me whether it can be named a "religion" in the familiar sense of the word, especially since no "faith" is demanded from the Jew but sanctification of life in the superpersonal sense.

There inheres, however, something else in Jewish tradition which is revealed so splendidly in many psalms, namely, a kind intoxicated joy and wonder at the beauty and sublimity of this world of which man can attain only a feeble notion. It is the feeling from which also real research derives its spiritual strength, which, however, seems to manifest itself also in the singing of birds. To connect this feeling with the idea of God seems a childish irrationality.

Is what has been said characteristic for Judaism? Does it also live elsewhere under a different name? In a *pure* form it does not exist anywhere, not in Judaism either, where much worship of the letter obscures the pure doctrine. However, I see nevertheless in Judaism one of its most vital and purest manifestations. This applies particularly to the principle of the sanctification of life.

It is characteristic that in the Commandment of the sanctification of the Sabbath the animals were expressly included, that is how strongly the demand for the solidarity of the living as an ideal was felt. The demand for the solidarity of all mankind comes to expression even much more strongly, and it is no accident that the socialist demands emanated for the most part from the Jews.

To what extent the consciousness of the sanctity of life is vital in the life of the Jewish people, is very beautifully illustrated by a short comment which Walter Rathenau[1] made to me once in conversation: "If a Jew says he is going hunting for pleasure, he lies." One cannot give more simple expression to the consciousness of the sanctity of life that dwells in the Jewish people.

---

[1] Walther Rathenau (1867–1922), German Jewish industrialist and statesman, who was assassinated by German anti-Semites.

ISRAEL ZINBERG

Israel Zinberg is the author of the nine-volume monumental *History of Jewish Literature*—the first attempt to describe Jewish literary creativity from the Middle Ages until the end of the nineteenth century. He lived most of his life in Petersburg, later renamed Leningrad, working as a chemical engineer in the daytime, devoting his leisure hours to the writing of his magnum opus.

Zinberg was born in a village in Volhynia, Ukraine, in 1873, and was given a thorough Jewish education. His father inculcated in him a deep love for Hebrew literature, with which Zinberg remained enamored throughout his life. His higher education he received in Karlsruhe, Germany, where he graduated as a chemical engineer, and in Basel, Switzerland, where he received his Ph.D. in philosophy. In 1898 he settled in Petersburg, becoming the chief of a chemical laboratory in a large concern.

In the Petersburg Jewish community Zinberg became an important figure among the Jewish intelligentsia, and a prolific writer contributing studies on Jewish literature, culture, history, and thought to Russo-Jewish, Yiddish, and Hebrew magazines. Together with the historians Simon Dubnow and Saul Ginzburg, he established, in 1912, the monthly Yiddish magazine *Die Yiddishe Velt*. After the October Revolution in 1917 Zinberg published most of his writings abroad—in Poland, and in the United States.

The first four volumes of his great *History* Zinberg wrote in Russian; later he rewrote and thoroughly reworked them into Yiddish. The additional five volumes he composed in Yiddish. All the nine volumes— except the additional one that was found after the Second World War, and published by Brandeis University— were published in Vilna, Poland, in the years 1929–37.

Zinberg was arrested by the Soviet government at the end of 1938, being banished to a concentration camp. When he reached Vladivostok he became ill, and he died in the camp hospital in 1939.

TWO PHILOSOPHIES IN JEWISH LIFE

The Maskilim[1] were completely unable to understand the historic role of Hasidism in Jewish folk-life. It was typical of these exponents of enlightenment that they could not distinguish between their own sympathies and interests and those of the people as a whole. They had not yet learned the fundamental truth that the intelligentsia is not the people, and that it is the duty of the intelligentsia to serve the people and become its mentor. Thus, fighting and speaking only in behalf of their own cause, the Maskilim represented no one but the Jewish intelligentsia. They were spiritual aristocrats preoccupied with their own purely personal interests, displaying not the slightest concern for the interests and needs of the people, let alone its independence.

That this was so is evident from the attitude of the intelligentsia toward the language of the Jewish masses. The intellectuals regarded the "Jargon"[2] as an object of shame. To speak "Jargon," wrote Judah Leib Gordon,[3] "is like promenading on Nevsky Prospect[4] dressed in rags."

Since the educated class of Jews knew the "Holy Tongue," the Maskilim conducted their Haskalah program in Hebrew. When this effort succeeded, especially among the intelligent segment of the Jewish populace, and there came into being a significant number of Jews who had received a European-style education and understood the language of the country, they began creating a Russian Jewish literature for this new class.

The great body of Jewish common people, however, who knew neither Hebrew nor Russian, were abandoned. The intelligentsia were not concerned with the spiritual needs of the masses; they regarded the common folk as the embodiment of fanaticism and ignorance, and maintained that any means was permissible in combating them.

Anyone who is familiar with the cultural history of Russian Jewry in the second half of the nineteenth century knows how eagerly the Maskilim jumped on the Russification bandwagon. They turned their backs on Jewry as soon as they got their university degrees; some of them even converted to Christianity.

In the 1870's however, just after the Odessa pogrom, the more serious exponents of enlightenment began to ponder the Jewish plight. Peretz Smolenskin[5] propounded his nationalist philosophy and severely criticized the "Berlin Haskalah." His bold propagandistic writings, albeit convincing, succeeded mainly in arousing opposition. But what this talented writer could not achieve was achieved by the pogroms of the 1880s.

The pogroms were a watershed event in the history of Russian Jewry. The Jewish intellectual suddenly began to sense the complete emptiness of his spiritual life. His past was dead; his ideals and his faith had been mercilessly dissolved; his idols had all been shattered. A great void had been created, and there was nothing with which to fill it.

The same Judah Leib Gordon who had dreamed of a "complete and rapid Russification" now bitterly described the bankruptcy of his ideals:

> Of all my dreams nothing is left.
> And after the great catastrophe and ravages,
> I fell from heaven to earth.
>   (1882)

"The rings of time had fallen apart," and the Jewish intellectual did not know how to join them together again, how to unite past and present with the mysterious future. The old world of his ancestors, unable to withstand the onslaught of the new epoch, had vanished forever.

Thus the edifice built by the Haskalah generation turned out to be a very weak structure, destroyed by cruel reality. With nothing left but the remains of the broken tablets and some crumbs of disappointed hopes, it was necessary to build another edifice, and this time on entirely new foundations. Now there was a need for dedicated, determined "builders" who believed fervently in their "obligation" to build.

Transition periods are usually not conducive to the development of such integrated, creative personalities. Breaking with the old gods, experiencing the dissolution of so many hopes, illusions, and expectations—these are costly sacrifices. The best energies of the time were expended on the work of demolition and criticism. The typical Jewish intellectual began to feel empty, dejected, disoriented. Even in the literature we do not find whole, fully integrated personalities, but only a sense of longing and searching. The strong Jew, because he was absent in reality, becomes the object of hope, an ideal.

Our writers of the transition period diligently studied the Jewish intellectual's "intellectual slip," his "inner rift" and "sickness of heart." They try to contrast him with a well-balanced, whole man who stands erect and lives in full harmony with himself; doing so, they turn their attention not to the present but to the recent past, not to the exponents of European culture but to representatives of the unique world of Hasidism, the very world that was so ridiculed by the Maskilim of the earlier epoch.

These writers—Peretz, Feierberg,[6] Berdichevsy,[7] and others—argue as follows: Even granting that the world of Hasidism cannot satisfy the present-day Jew, nonetheless it possesses something impressive and compelling. The world of Hasidism offers exactly what the present-day Jew is seeking so passionately: equilibrium, a harmonious unity of self.

The Hasid's world-view is narrow and circumscribed; he lives in the realm of imagination, not in the real world. But in this realm he leads a full life. He is a whole personality, intimately bound to the past and, perforce, to the future as well. Uneducated and profoundly superstitious, he possesses an inner sanctum that blends his thoughts, his feelings, and his will into one harmonious whole. thus rendering him a person of remarkable spiritual beauty.

It is no accident, then, that a poignant longing for the harmonious human personality, and a muted protest against the senseless, cruel conditions of life, which crush the human being, suffocating and disfiguring him, runs through all of Peretz's creativity like a red thread. Nor is it an accident that Berdichevsky, the enthusiast of Hasidism, was a devoted follower of Friedrich Nietzsche, who also longed for the advent of a harmonious, strong, creative, beautiful individual.

After the Khmelnitsky massacres[8] in 1648 the people yearned for a miracle, craved with passionate longing for a redeemer who should lead the Jews out of the "Vale of Tears" and bring them into the Holy Land.[9] But after the pogroms of the 1880s the people, permeated by fear, did not have even this consolation. The two centuries had not remained without a trace in the Jewish isolated ghetto, although the belief in miracles had somewhat weakened. Then there appeared Maskilim "Penitents," [10] who wished, on a rational, natural basis, to realize a miracle and transfer the suffering Jews to Eretz Yisroel without the help of a Messiah. Naturally such simple mortals as the Maskilim-"Penitents" were incapable of giving reality to this miracle. That is why their good intentions gave such slender results. But instead of the "Penitents" there suddenly appeared a man, necessarily outside the ghetto, who had a very vague understanding of living Jewry, a man of tremendous willpower and broad imagination; a man who was a remarkable combination of medieval fanatic and educated European, of exalted dreamer and first-rate agitator. This was *Theodor Herzl* (1806–1904).

This man believed in miracles. He believed that determination can create miracles; that you can conquer a land for the people even without an army, a navy, finances, and that you can transfer the homeless, scattered people into this land. This great and beautiful personality flared up like a meteor, glowed briefly and intensely, and was consumed. But he did not vanish without a trace.

Herzl's opposite and persistent opponent is Ahad Ha'Am. He is a man with a strong and profound intellect, a man who is not ready to take anything for granted until he can analyze it with his cold, analytical mind. Ahad Ha'Am knows that Jewish history represents a long chain of persecutions and harassments, of terrible sufferings and disgraceful tortures. And now the Zionists appear and say: "We have to rally all Jews, establish our own state, just as the Bulgarians or the Serbs did."

Ahad Ha'Am then asks: "Let us imagine that at last we will accomplish our goal and succeed in establishing a Jewish state. Can such an achievement satisfy us? Have we suffered so much in the course of several thousand years for this—to be rewarded at the end of our suffering with a tiny state that will be a plaything in the hands of the great powers?" Ahad Ha'Am cannot acquiesce in the thought that the finale of the great tragedy, which is unmatched in world history, will be a puny state. In the incalculable suffering of the Jewish people one must look for a deep meaning. Ahad Ha'Am thinks that he has found that meaning.

The Jewish people has a mission. Jews are the carriers of a great "national ideal" that will redeem the world. This "national ideal" is the "national idea" of our prophets—the victory of absolute justice throughout the world. But in order for this idea of justice to vanquish the hostile forces, it must rally the Jewish people behind it. According to Ahad Ha'Am, the prophets imposed this great task upon the shoulders of a small people. In this way, the ideal of "absolute justice," which is still the ideal of the future, becomes the "national ideal" of the Jewish people.

But, Ahad Ha'Am laments, we are a people living in modern times who concluded, after many disappointments, that we will have no tranquility in the Diaspora, and we no longer possess the moral heroism of our grandfathers. We are no longer certain of their tough, firm faith as the possessors of the "truth." We have only retained the negative consciousness that we exist because we cannot do otherwise, because the national instinct has not withered in us. But one cannot live by a negative consciousness. The national consciousness is the cause of our perseverance, while our tormented heart yearns passionately for a goal, for a purpose in our terrible existence.

For this reason the *Goles* [exile] oppresses us much more harshly than our grandfathers. We do not possess a national ideal for whose sake we are ready and able to endure miseries and calamities; therefore, the rebirth of the national, spiritual ideal is a question of life and death for us. But a vital idea, a great national ideal, cannot be brought to life in the Diaspora. In alien lands the people's vigor languishes, because it is severed from the source of its normal growth, and cannot reach the outside in order to develop freely.

"The spirit of our people is in need of freedom," Ahad Ha'Am wrote in the preface to his *At the Crossroads*—the free development can only take place in the historic soil of the land of our ancestors. There the spirit can be roused from its long sleep, get the strength to revitalize the national ideal, and fashion it in a manner that is in consonance with our needs. This ideal should become the basis for the scattered people. The ideal should protect it against moral decay. The ideal should strengthen it, in order that the people may quietly and consciously suffer to the end, and be unmistakenly aware of why it is suffering.

The mission of the Jewish people, Ahad Ha'Am believes, consists in becoming a "super-people," a "People of Prophets" that personifies the highest type of ethics, and becomes the faithful carrier of high moral duties. The people does not consider whether this is detrimental or beneficial for mankind. This is done for the sake of the existence of a higher type, "Absolute justice is the spiritual trust of the superman who does not tolerate any restrictions even when it is at the expense of the happiness of the majority."

Ahad Ha'Am regards the Prophets as the true fighters for such "absolute justice," and he considers the Prophet the "superman" who sets himself a motto in life that "the world may go under, but justice should be victorious"—but this is far from the ideal of a Jewish Prophet. The Prophets could never comprehend how one can fight for justice, not for the sake of people, but for the sake of justice, as an abstraction only. Such a person they would have considered an immoral, unjust, and harmful individual. Such a person, who brings suffering and evil for the "majority," only for the sake of the principle of an individual—such a person is not a Jewish Prophet. The Prophets fought against oppression and oppressors. They protected the weak, the poor, the helpless ones.

For the sake of an abstract idea Ahad Ha'Am completely forgot the living, actual personality. He forgot that ethical truths are rendered meaningful and full of content only when they are tied to human needs. The idea of justice is a reflection of social relations, of a social life. Man, not the abstraction, which is a product of man—man is the measure of ethical truths. The one who suppresses in himself what is human is not the carrier of higher justice, but rather it is the one who always bears in his mind the human being, and is capable of being permeated with man's sufferings and anguish.

Ahad Ha'Am's strong intellect fell into a cobweb of scholasticism. He can by no means release himself from the slavery of the "dead letter." In his intellectual socio-ethical system man is not the center, but rather the autonomous moral principle. The clouds of an abstraction cannot provide man a terrestrial heaven.

In the 1860s and 1870s the anti-Semites in Russia continually argued that the Jews are not a productive element. They are only engaged in business. All the Russian liberals and even Jewish publicists maintained the same thing, the latter fighting for civil rights on behalf of Jews. Only in the 1880s did they change their minds, becoming convinced that the greater part of the Jewish people in Russia consists of toiling men. They discovered a Jewish proletariat, poor and squalid, but nevertheless a proletariat.

This fact had an impact parallel with other factors in that disillusioned "transition period" in Jewish life impelling a segment of the Jewish intelligentsia to "go to the people"—this time to their own people.

A new democratic philosophy makes its appearance in the arena of Jewish life; this time not an exalted and mystical philosophy like Hasidism, but a realistic and rational one based on modern knowledge. The role played by this democratic intelligentsia in Jewish folk-life is truly a gigantic one. It rouses consciousness, strengthens the feeling of protest, teaches the dejected folk-masses to fight for human living conditions, and to fight against violence and exploitation. The practical activity of this intelligentsia consists in the struggle for the emancipation of the individual from the chains of capitalism, against economic slavery, and against the illegitimate social and political institutions that are closely linked with the capitalist system.

But this intelligentsia helps, on the one hand, in the liberation and normal development of the human personality, and, on the other hand, it imposes new claims upon that same personality. The left faction of the active Jewish intelligentsia removes the backward, relieves the Jewish common man from his old traditions, obliterates his beliefs and customs, and tears the threads binding him to the past. But this intelligentsia does not replenish his soul with a new spiritual content. In place of the old *Shulhan Arukh*[11] it gives the people a new, more modern, more rationalistic, but not less barren and one-sided one. In place of the democratic, "medieval religion of the heart," there was created a democratic but cerebral hair-splitting "religion." They try to convey to the common man that the only true "Credo" is the dogmatic idea that "every ideology is determined by the character of the means of production." Everything that is not in consonance with this "Credo" is considered heretical, "unreasonable."

The economic factor that played a dominant role under primitive conditions in human history, really reflected the ideology and the psychology of primitive man. But as human life became more complex, with the growth of human consciousness and the development of culture—then, in place of one universal factor in historic life, there arrived a multifaceted and mutual sway of factors that are closely linked, and define the historic destiny of humanity.

But the Jewish toiler is being served as dogma that the martyrological historic process is closely linked with economic causes, as the only ones that determine the course of history. According to this dogma the best criterion, when evaluating social phenomena, is not the interests of the human personality, but the interests of a definite group, of a certain class with its "class psychology," "class ideology," and "class consciousness." The entire spiritual wealth of humanity, everything that has been achieved through brilliance and work; the beauty and the poetry of life are considered not from the vantage point of the interests of an individual but— the interests of a class. The diverse phenomena in life, the entire internal, rich, spiritual world of man with its complex range of emotions and sentiments—all of this they want to put into the Procrustean bed of "class consciousness."

The proletarian personality is proclaimed as the only one capable of being completely permeated by the "ideology of the future." The truth is that this personality manifests more narrowness and one-sidedness, uniformity and aridity.

It is no accident that the Jewish writers, even those who know very well the life of the Jewish toiling masses, whenever these writers wish to portray a harmonious figure—they do not seek it in contemporary life, but rather in the past, in unique Hasidic life. The reason for this phenomenon does not lie in the fact that our writers particularly love the world of romanticism, or because they are "conservative and reactionary," as that faction would label them. The real cause lies deeper. The harmoniousness of the Hasidic world attracts our writers, just as Gleb Uspensky[12] was attracted by the world of the Russian peasants. There a struggle for bread and spiritual personality is going on. For the very same reason the Jewish writer is attracted to the Hasidic world.

The Jewish writers know, as Uspensky knew, that the harmoniousness and equilibrium of the world they are describing is not permanent. They are also aware of the naive ignorance pervading that world. They comprehend very well that the harmoniousness of today's conscious personality cannot abide in the old theological edifice based on mysticism and superstition. They understand that a new structure must be erected upon a foundation of knowledge. In this edifice there must be a fusion of the "two philosophies in Jewish life," the democratic "religion of the heart" with its cult of the human personality, and the bright light of intelligence, truth, and human, this-worldly justice.

This edifice, similar to the old one, must unconditionally bear a national stamp. In the awakening of man's consciousness in the struggle for individualism, and the free manifestation of human endowments, the idea of national awareness plays a very great role. But this national principle will no longer require that man should renounce freedom and knowledge. His task is, in the name of the rights of the individual, to be on guard in behalf of the proudly proclaimed motto: each nationality has a right to live and freely develop its powers, not harming thereby the right of other nationalities. Such an edifice can be built only by an intelligentsia outside classes. In order to avoid a misinterpretation it must be said that this intelligentsia cannot ignore class contrasts and class interests, which put their deep stamp on the social development of society. It is not its task to engage in the Utopian plan of concealing these contrasts. Its function is to guard the interests of the toiling masses, whenever the human personality is being crippled, whenever precious human powers are devoured by the insatiable idol of profits.

The intelligentsia should carry out this mission not in behalf of class interests, or in behalf of "absolute justice," but rather in behalf of the bruised, bleeding, vilified, and tormented, living, suffering human being. Because man is above all classes, because man is the highest truth in the world, he is the highest measure for all social, national, political, and cultural problems.

The active Jewish intelligentsia must take into consideration the components of human psychology and ideology that are a result of class and national interests. It cannot deny their existence, and it must reckon with the antagonisms and disparities between these interests. But the "national autonomy"[13] and social organization of the future—all of these must not be regarded as a goal for their own sake, but rather as a means of helping to release the individual from a national and economic burden, from the heavy chains that impede the growth and the building of the versatile, harmoniously developed human personality.

(1938?)

NOTES

1. Adherents of the Haskalah, i.e., the Jewish Enlightenment.

2. "Jargon," a derogatory appellation applied to Yiddish by the Maskilim.

3. Judah Leib Gordon (1830–92), Hebrew poet and leading figure among the Maskilim.

4. "Nevsky Prospect," one of the main boulevards in St. Petersburg (Leningrad).

5. Peretz Smolenskin (1842–85), Hebrew writer who, after the 1881 pogroms, joined the Hibbat Zion movement and advocated immigration to Palestine.

6. M. Z. Feierberg (1874–99), Russian Hebrew writer who expressed the struggle of East European Jewish youth disappointed in Haskalah and yet unable to remain within the bounds of traditional Judaism.

7. M. J. Berdichevsky (Bin-Gorion) (1865–1921), Hebrew novelist and thinker who urged that Hebrew literature draw its inspiration from life and nature and thereby heal the rift in the soul of the younger generation struggling between Judaism and humanism.

8. Bogdan Chmielnicki (Khmelnitsky) (1593–1657), Cossack leader who annihilated hundreds of Jewish communities and murdered hundreds of thousands of Jews in the Ukraine and Poland.

9. Zinberg is here referring to the Messianic movement of Sabbatai Zevi (1626–76).

10. "Penitent" in Hebrew is *Baal-Teshuvah,* i.e., "returnee," one who renounces his former mode of living and "returns" to the old way.

11. *Shulhan Arukh* = the code of laws governing the life of an Orthodox Jew.

12. G. I. Uspensky (1840–1902), Russian novelist who began his career as an extreme populist.

13. "National Autonomy" is the concept of Jewish "national rights" for the self-governing Jewish community in Russia which was adopted by most Jewish groupings.

J. W. LATSKY-BERTOLDY

J. W. Latsky-Bertoldy was born in Kiev, Ukraine, in 1881, and died in Tel Aviv in 1940. He was a thinker, a dedicated leader, a student of Jewish history in search of a synthesis between the transitory and permanent strands in Jewish existence, between the mystical attachment to Judaism, on the one hand, and the devotion to the Jewish land, on the other.

Latsky-Bertoldy received his Jewish and general education in Riga, Latvia. In 1901, while studying at Berlin University, he founded, together with Nachman Syrkin, the Socialist Zionist Heruth group. Later he became an exponent of the Socialist Territorialist ideology and an activist in that movement. For a number of years he lived in Petersburg, and devoted his energies to the ORT.

After the March Revolution in Russia (1917), he founded, together with N. Shtif and others, the Folks party. In 1918 he became minister for Jewish affairs in the Ukraine. In the decade 1925–35 Latsky-Bertoldy lived in Riga, where he edited the pro-Zionist Yiddish daily *Dos Folk*. When the Fascists took over the Latvian government, he left the country and settled in *Eretz Isroel*. Here he contributed to Hebrew dailies and periodicals, writing on political, literary, and artistic topics.

Latsky-Bertoldy was not a prolific writer, but what he wrote—focusing on the rift between the two currents in Jewish life: the religious and the secular—was polished, original, flashing with profound thoughts of enduring value.

JEWISHNESS AND JEWS; OR,
ON JEWISH HERESY

The way people say it: The Torah is more important than anything else; but I would say: Jews are holy and more important. (Talmudic maxim)

This is the history of the enslavement of Jewish thought by the creators of the Talmud, who are the ancestors of all sorts of rabbis in the Jewish world. They lacked valor, so they self-confidently interpreted the words of our Prophets, and instead of creating a people, they created a faction with one opinion—a sectarian Judaist organization. And these creators of our Jewishness could not have done it differently, for they took it upon themselves to create a spiritual *Eretz Yisroel* in place of the destroyed homeland. Instead of an earthly Jerusalem they gave the people a heavenly Jerusalem. And the spiritual country, Judaism, had to be as firm and secure as the true earth of Judea. No individual opinion or spirit was allowed to upset the spiritual edifice: only up to a certain limit was the Jew permitted to think and to feel. The body was circumscribed by the Sabbath, but the soul was restricted by all the days of the week. In a spiritual homeland, to digress from the collective opinion, to exceed the appointed limit, was tantamount to a disavowal of the people, the betrayal of the nation. And upon the altar of spiritual patriotism they had to make human sacrifices—these were the martyrs of free thought. . . .

And because the Jewish exile is the fountainhead of Jewish rabbinism, Jewish heresy is linked with Jewish redemption.

It is hard to understand the power that is possessed by the rabbinic *shtreiml*,[1] and that is why it is so easy to ridicule it; but can the Maskil [enlightened person] hope and expect to vanquish it? Not with criticism and satire, i.e., with pure *theoretical* reason, because the rabbinic *shtreiml* is sustained by Jewish troubles, and whoever wants to subdue Jewish rabbinism must defeat the Jewish exile, and that is not so easy. The problem of Jewish free thought becomes the problem of a free Jewish people—the question of *knowledge* is transformed into a question of *deeds.*

Our Maskilim did not understand the problem, and that is why they all became penitents. I know, we are living in queer times. Even enlightened Jews will answer my query: So what, all right, we can get along without free Jewish thought and without a free Jewish land. It is not my intention to engage in polemics with them; my aim is only to illustrate one thought, to clarify the relation of Jewish heresy to the Jewish problem. Incidentally, I should like to remark that it does not pay to get involved in a debate with these modern rabbis; they are making a living from the ancient rabbis, who are the true and original creators of our heaven-oriented Jewishness.

And these old rabbis argue constantly that the Torah is more important than anything else, while we, modern heretics, affirm that Jews are more important and we do not care that the commandments will be abrogated as long as . . . , and here we should bear in mind that the commandments are a religious commentary on our national freedom, a mental image, a symbol, and a parable of our independent life, and this parable can only be abrogated in its object, in a Jewish country. In the great historical debate that is going on in Jewish life, in the strife between Torah and Jews, between rabbinism and the mundane, godliness and secularism, all Jewish thinkers must choose one of two roads: either a mystical union with the Jewish religion or a living attachment to a Jewish land.

For only in a Jewish land will Jewish heresy be able to shake off its national sin. Science and morality, theoretical and practical reason, cannot live at peace in the Diaspora—free thought must become a sin for us, and conversely, the enslaved thought, the sin against the holy spirit, becomes transformed among us into a good deed.

Let us recall Uriel Acosta, Baruch Spinoza, and Solomon Maimon. We boast about them to the world. But for us they are like Hanukkah candles that you must not use. . . . We banished them from our communities, we closed our hearts and minds to them, and, to our misfortune, we were *compelled* to do it. Is it possible for holy communities to get along with free thought? Could we watch nonchalantly how this world is being turned into a God, this gloomy world, this vale of tears, where we have suffered so much, and where we are still suffering so much? . . . We and the world—two truculent enemies—a weak and a strong one—could we permit them to take away our only consolation and the sweet vengeance of belittling "this world"? Was it possible for free thought to grow in our world? And what a free thought! Uriel Acosta repudiated "Reward and Punishment" and he prophesied about naturalistic religion; Spinoza deified nature; and Solomon Maimon assembled

the whole world into the human spirit and thereby he transformed man
into God—were such teachings appropriate for the Jewish world and for
our powerless people?

They were pure and therefore tragic Maskilim (enlightened people),
who because of their ideas had to sacrifice the Jews, and being freethinkers among a rabbinic people, they disavowed their people by their
very existence. In this lay their personal tragedy and at the same time
the tragedy of our culture. Thus, the fate of Jewish thought is linked
with the fate of the Jewish people. And a hint, a symbol of their similar
fortune, has been left to us by Jewish history, which brought into existence at the same time Spinozism and the Sabbataï Zevi movement, the
freedom movement of Jewish thought and the freedom movement of
the Jewish people, as if it—Jewish history—thereby hinted that the victory of Spinoza can only be made possible by a victory of Sabbataï Zevi,
that pantheism—earthly divinity— can only stay alive among an earthly
people. This is not just a conclusion one reaches by a theoretical premise; rather, we find traces of this lesson in Jewish history. The heretical
criticism leveled against Jewish rabbinism brought Spinoza up to the
Jewish State ideal when the great freethinker stumbled on the national
goal of the great mystic. "If the spirit of Jewish religion," he writes in
his *Theologico-Political Tractate,* "had not emasculated their minds,
they might even, if occasion offered, raise up their Kingdom again, and
God may again elect them." And that is the implicit moral in the entire
third chapter of the *Theologico-Political Tractate,* where Spinoza is
attempting, with the help of a thousand arguments, to prove that Jewish
prophecy is not an exceptional phenomenon, and that all nations had
prophets, and that that is not the cause of Jewish chosenness. "The eternal Election of the Jews," Spinoza says, "perhaps consists in the fact that
they will return to their State." Only now can we comprehend the meaning of this utterance. This implies the *theoretical* revelation of the political Jewish nation, as the Sabbataï Zevi movement was the *practical*
revelation of the Jewish nation. This means the recognition of the Jewish
national-political ideology that was erased from the people's memory
by the Judaist philosophy, and this is, perhaps, the most profound thought
in Spinoza's criticism of Jewish rabbinism: against the mystical-religious
Chosen People ideal of the rabbis he delineated, in precisely defined ideas
—in laconic language—the Chosen People ideal of the social Jewish
State.

History also gave us a second hint in this respect. Is it not characteristic that the defenders of Jewish spirituality, of the rabbinic-spiritual essence of the Jewish people, have not ceased to shout with one voice, that both Spinozism and the Sabbataï Zevi movement were—Heaven preserve us!—wicked afflictions for the Jewish people? Blind "rabbinic" reason and a ludicrous rage guided, in the nineteenth century, the pen of Professor Heinrich Graetz, when he wrote about both of these movements. The anti-national rabbinic ideology dulled his mind and heart to such a degree that he pronounced the wide and deep Sabbataï Zevi movement, which embraced all Jewish communities from East and West, as simply a Kabalistic fraud! Now, if the enlightened Professor Graetz, who is absolutely convinced that the *Zohar* is full of nonsense, had lived in those days, then Jewish history would have looked quite different.

To be sure, if Spinoza had known something about German "Science of Judaism," he would not have been a heretic, and would have thought and lived quite differently! Both movements faced, among the Jewish people, one enemy and one destiny: rabbinic learning vanquished them. Redemption remained a fantasy: Jews remained a Kingdom of Priests, a rabbinic nation, and the rabbis had to excommunicate the heretic. Should Spinoza have renounced his own free thought, and should he have helped to build the young rabbinic community of Amsterdam? Should he have thought *disgustingly* in order to act *beautifully?* But *could* such a genius surrender? The contradiction between Spinoza's heresy and the collective Jewish faith could not have been avoided, and again repudiating rabbinism, it inevitably dragged along with it the second sin, the rejection of the rabbinic nation: it was a tragic conflict, and Spinoza left the Jewish community.

Those who uphold the spiritual character of the Jewish people repel thereby all the free and great intellects of the Jewish people, because a spiritual people requires a definite collective faith. Assimilation becomes, therefore, a cultural necessity, and you will not subdue it with ethnic words. Spinoza had to seek friends in the Dutch state and he found them there. Solomon Maimon ran away from the Polish and Lithuanian Jewish settlement and from the West European communities; Boerne and Heine felt themselves confined among Jews in the ghetto, so they attached themselves to the German nation. Marx and Lassalle found secular nations for themselves and their activities. The same thing happened with Lord Beaconsfield, who, in his fantastic novel *David Alroy,*[2] described with genuinely prophetic pathos the tragic struggle of the mundane and rabbinic factions in the Jewish liberation movement. Bagdad or Jerusalem, a secular state or a spiritual center—these are the two contrasts that Beaconsfield sensed and realized in Jewish national life. His secular nation he found among the British.

The contradiction between free thought and Jewish collective life lies in the rabbinic spiritual essence, in the religious character of the Jewish people in the Diaspora, and with reforms, with assimilationist adjustments and ethnic interpretations, we will not accomplish anything.

And that is why the focus of today's secular Jewish philosophy must be looked for somewhere else. The question is not about the nature of Judaism, but rather about the nature and roles of Jews. Not the history of our rabbis and scribes, but the history of our masses, is our main concern today. Now, really, what is prior and more important: Torah or Israel? Those who are satisfied with a philosophy of Judaism ask only whether this or that is correct in the Torah, and whether science is in harmony with Judaism or not. And when these Judaist philosophers are filled with creative power, they continue spinning Judaist thread and they show us the gems and the light of Judaism. However, if they conclude that Judaism is obsolete and stagnant, then the question emerges whether they should not drop out of Judaism altogether. For the very reason that the Torah is for them more important than anything else, they waver between Jewishness and apostasy. But with the critical Jewish heretic the question about the nature of Judaism is not at all the primary question, and certainly not at all a question of the People's survival; it is only a scientific problem, which has importance as a theoretical question that can wait for an answer. For its chief heresy lies in the fact that he disparages in general the previous role of Judaism as the essence, the beginning and end, of the Jewish People. Israel and the Torah are, after all, not identical, for actually Israel created the Torah and not the other way around. True, we see constantly that nations disappear and their ideas survive, i.e., that their culture has *actually* become more important than they. But against this fact the Jewish heretic points out another, fact: the survival of the Jewish people. Jews survived—perhaps because "Jews came first." The people is sovereign and does not live for the sake of ideals, for the ideals live because of it and due to its physical and spiritual powers. And the sovereign people recognizes that, after all, it is not worth living because of the merits of the ancestors, for the sake of historical ideals, for the greatest heritage may sometimes become depleted, if not because of its diminished significance, then because of its effect on the life of the people. Thus the heretic reaches the conclusion that the mundane people of the soil is more important than the "People of the Book," at any rate, more important than the religious Judaist organization that was created by the Talmudists.

In the well-known poem by Yehuda Leib Gordon, "Zedekiah in Prison," the unfortunate Jewish king pleads with God,

> What injustice have I committed? I have fought with my people for freedom? Have I thereby committed any sin? I did not bow my head to Jeremiah the Prophet? This dejected man with the soft heart, who advised us to live as slaves, and had but one remedy for our distress: we should all study the Torah, everybody, from the fieldworkers to the rulers, should become students; the heroes should discard their shields and bows and arrows—and should wrap themselves up in scrolls and fight with pens?! Oh. I can visualize with my spirit the sad future: the Torah will remain, but the *State* will perish, the people will be learned, but the people will be harassed, crushed as dust and ashes.

Therein you see the problem of the secular versus the rabbinic Jewish nation in classic form, and therein consists the historic problem of free Jewish thought. Jewish heresy is linked with Jewish redemption, and Jewish redemption needs Jewish heresy. "If the spirit of the Jewish religion had not emasculated their minds, the Jews might even raise up their Kingdom again, and God may again elect them."

(Petersburg, 1913)

NOTES

1. Fur hat, symbol of a rabbi's prestige among Orthodox Jews.
2. David Alroy (12th cent.), leader of a pseudo-messianic movement in Kurdistan. The character in the novel *The Wondrous Tale of Alroy* (1833) by Benjamin Disraeli (Lord Beaconsfield) is largely fictional, since he is there depicted as a conqueror.

ABRAHAM GOLOMB

Abraham Golomb, who is now living in Los Angeles, California, belongs to the small band of Jewish thinkers and educators, who have been attempting to reevaluate all Jewish ideologies in the light of the traumatic Jewish experiences of our epoch. He is a Yiddishist nonconformist who cannot be pigeonholed; he is inspired by a passionate love of Israel, and a deep faith in Eternal Israel. He is a secularist who has blazed his own trail in contemporary Jewish thought.

Golomb was born in the Vilna province of Lithuania in 1888, and received both a traditional and modern Jewish education. In the years 1922–31 Golomb was the dean of the Jewish Teachers Seminary in Vilna, which played a central role in the Yiddish secular-school movement in Poland between the two world wars. In 1932 Golomb went to Israel, where he taught for a number of years. At the end of the thirties he was invited to Winnipeg, Canada, where he became the director of the I. L. Peretz Day School. After having worked there for six years he settled in Mexico City as principal of the Jewish Day School. Here he labored for twenty years, expanding the school, and putting the stamp of his personality and philosophy upon Jewish education in Mexico. Since 1964 he has been living in Los Angeles.

At present Golomb occupies an important position in Jewish intellectual life. A pioneer in the Yiddish secular-school movement he has not only expounded its philosophy but also created the tools for its implementation —preparing the textbooks, the curriculum, the educational materials for the classroom.

FROM SECULAR
TO INTEGRAL JEWISHNESS

The Secular Origin of Religion Among Jews

European nations adopted their religion as "adults," when they already had a culture, a religion. And so there existed two separate currents among them—their previous folkways and the current of culture of the new religion that they "imported" and adopted. We are not concerned here with the manner in which the two currents merged. However, among Jews the whole period, through its long history, there was and remained only one current. Their folk-culture becomes the religion. At first it began as the secular folkways. Later it becomes sanctified as religion. Thus it was from the beginning. The way of life becomes tradition, and the tradition becomes religion. All the commandments of the Torah were originally customs, mores, purely secular traditions. The Jews were a people before they received the Torah with all its commandments. Abraham, says the Talmud, fulfilled all the commandments. It is told about our grandfather Jacob that he said, "I lived with Laban and observed the 613 commandments." In reverse order it is not a legend, but historical truth: the way of life of Abraham, of the Patriarchs, their entire folk conduct and way of life, became divine. The folk mores unfolded, increased, became different, and so the religious codification changed. However, the Pentateuch always says: "Command the Children of Israel," "Speak to the Children of Israel," always announced, commanded. The Jewish God, however, always bade the Jews do what was previously accepted by the folk. Until the Talmud ceased using the term *mitzve* (commandment entirely and substituted for it the word *Halakhah*, which means way, custom, mores. And they went so far that God does not command or announce, but He must, with all due respect to Him, sit down and learn the Halakhah, the mores of the people.[1]

We learn a number of things here: the divine is identical with the folkways, the ethnic Jewish is also religious. And secondly, the terms *secular* and *religious* merely express a difference in age; the recent, the new is secular; what is generations old, rooted in the folkways, that is religious.

The Catholic religion is not identical with Polishness, Frenchness, or Italianness. Whatever is ethnic, the national, is distinct everywhere, separated from religion. However, *Yiddishkeit* and Jewish religion have been identical until the most recent times. Moreover, Jews did not use the word *religion* at all. *Yiddishkeit* sufficed. And *Yiddishkeit* comprised the entire Jewish cultural way of life, both the old and ancient, canonized as religion, and also the younger, secular one, which was not yet canonized as religion.

Who is a Jew?—every person who identifies his way of life with that of the Jewish people, with the cultural traditions that prevail in life, in the mores of the Jewish folk masses. It is not a question of definite dogmas that one should recognize, and with which one can become a Jew—it is not a question of one definite momentary process, procedure. In order to become a Jew, one must get used and become accustomed to the traditional way of life of the Jewish people. It is also not a question of religion: just as one can be a Catholic and not be a Pole or a Frenchman, one can also be an adherent of Jewish religion and not be a Jew. The Khazars[2] were Jews by religion; however, as a people they were different, not Jews. The procedure of conversion to Judaism does not make a person into a Jew. It means merely opening the door of Jewishness. Already the Talmud said, "Converts for Israel are hard as a scab." The convert only registered, so to speak, as a Jew, but he did not yet accept Jewishness, he did not yet get used to Jewishness.

What, then, is Jewishness? Jewishness is the sum total of folkway traditions that live in the culture of the Jewish folk masses and originate from perennial Jewish mores. Jewishness is the quantity of long-accustomed, cultural life mores that have their origin in the history of the Jewish people.

What then is a people? A people is a product of history. A group which in the course of many generations of separate, independent life, consciously and even more unconsciously, developed an independent way of life, its own cultural forms, traditions, beliefs, folklore and linguistic forms. All these elements are organically bound up with particular spiritual, psychic inclinations and qualities of character, and it can culminate in particular physical, organic traits of form and organism. Peoples differ now by their particular intellectual traits and character more than by their cultural way of life, which has tendencies to level out. History has greater power than geography. Traits which have developed through many generations of history are more fixed in us than norms of place.

Thus it is also among all organisms, plants, and animals; in one place different organisms live, as they have developed in their history.

Jewish Religion Cannot Be Static

Among nations whose religion is not bound up with their peoplehood, religion can assume a permanent form once and for all. God is eternal and His religion does not change as He does not chage. The case is different among Jews, among whom religion is identical with peoplehood. And peoplehood is the life of a people. Life is not static. A people is a collective organism, and like everything that is organic, the Jewish people also continue to grow, to wither, to adopt, and to reject.

Elements of the way of life change, concepts change. It is true, gradually, piecemeal, slowly, but it must not remain static. What is static is like a dead mummy, like fossils of extinct organisms. Jewishness cannot assume a permanent form. So, too, the Jewish religion cannot assume a permanent form forever. In the Jewish Bible there do not exist any elements of private reward and punishment, of resurrection of the dead. These are elements that have arisen later. Laws of the Torah have been annulled (for example, money became a substitute for an eye for an eye). New laws have been added, added and dropped, as is always the case with living organisms.

Just as Moses did not understand what Rabbi Akiva[3] studied (according to a profound Aggadah in the Talmud), so Rabbi Akiva would perhaps have been unable to understand the Jewishness of a Rema[4] and even of Rabbi Solomon Ibn Gabirol[5] and the like. However, it must always be a "Halakhah, according to Moses on Sinai"—it must remain part of an eternal chain. The largest tree grows out of a tiny seed that an earlier tree has left. This is life!

The First Breakthrough in the Course of History

This course in Jewish history was established chiefly in the Jewish organization in Babylon, although a foundation for the existence of a secular religious people without the element of political statehood had already been laid previously. Not a state with a lofty dynasty will preserve the existence of the Jewish people, but intellectual independence in organized collectives, with religious peoplehood as its basis. However, its existence for future ages was established only in Babylon. Other peoples did not survive in dispersion. Their peoplehood endured with the power of states. Once they lost the state, they also lost their ethnicity.

Jews lost their faith in the state before they went into exile. "Some [trust] in chariots, and some in horses but we—in the name of God" (Ps. 20:8).

In a previous study I endeavored to prove that already the great mourner of the first Destruction of the Temple—Jeremiah—helped to construct the organized autonomy without a state in Babylon (in my book *Eternal Ways of the Eternal People*). And that is how things were until the French Revolution. It is an accepted fact that the French Revolution emancipated the Jews, gave them equal rights. This is not entirely correct. A formula was accepted at that time: "All right for Jews as citizens, but no rights whatever for Jews as a people." This means that for personal, individual rights Jews had to renounce their separate Jewish peoplehood. The Jews did this gladly. In the Sanhedrin which Napoleon assembled (1806), the Jewish notables announced publicly and officially that they no longer belong to the Jewish universal people, they are nothing but Frenchmen, together with all citizens, only that their religion is a Jewish one. Just as there can be Frenchmen of Catholic, of Protestant faith, so there can also be Frenchmen of Jewish faith. Several decades later Jews in Germany made a similar official announcement. "Jews of Mosaic faith." Mosaic religion is substituted for the religion of Christ. Why, however, was the old traditional expression "Jewish religion" superseded? Why was an entirely new term, *Mosaic faith,* used? First, they saw in this a parallel: the religion of Christ or Moses. Second, it was more pleasant not to mention the word *Jewish,* which can serve as a reminder, evoke associations with the Jewish people, from which they wished to sever themselves. Third, Jewishness or Jewish religion possessed a great many ingredients of a way of life not mentioned in the Torah of Moses. Therefore, "Mosaic faith" is far less connected with the Jewish people. Fourth, Moses is also accepted among Christians, so that the fusion, the assimilation, is easier.

What should be our attitude to this behavior on the part of the Jews? I am not a judge to pass judgment on historical processes. The principal thing, however, is that the *reidentification* of Jewishness toward Frenchness among Jews separated religious and secular Jewishness into two separate domains for the first time in history. Religion as a static fixed service to God can remain. However, the secular-folkish, the dynamic, what separates Jews from other Frenchmen in their way of life—all this is rejected. Hence the term *Mosaic faith* is better than the old *Jewish faith.* And as a result, the saying of the Talmud has been confirmed that the existence of the Jewish people lies not in the fixed written religion, but necessarily in the unfixed and undefined oral Jewishness (folk *Yid-dishkeit*), ("the Holy One, blessed be He, did not make a covenant with Israel except for the sake of the Oral Torah," *Gitin* 60:2). Jews exist; that is, Frenchmen who are descended from Jews. However, a Jewish people with a Jewish folk culture, organized society, language, literature, politics, this no longer exists. The same thing was repeated in Germany and later in Italy. Until the emancipation, the Diaspora was a collectivity. The Jewish individual lived his entire life only among Jews, only in a traditional manner. After the emancipation the Diaspora became an individual one, for each Jew in his private life. The community of Jews as a collectivity was dissolved. Each Jew separately obtained the opportunity of entering non-Jewish society directly. The only attachment to the Jewish people remained exclusively the religion of the synagogue. Secular Jewishness was discarded. Together with secular, noncanonized Jewishness the people declines purely physically: the number of Jews becomes smaller, the average age grows higher and higher, the number of births does not cover the number of deaths. The process of decline can last many generations. It is a Jewishness that maintains itself only in synagogues, it does not grow and does not change any more. It is a fossil Jewishness. It is remembered longer. Who remembers? The descendants of Jews, and even more, the anti-Semites remember.

One must also admit that the undefined, mysterious spiritual traits persist in the descendants of Jews; mostly without they themselves being conscious of them.

Can One Be a Secular Jew While Rejecting Everything Religious?

It is almost an accepted fact that secular Jews "must" not carry out anything that is sanctified in a religious sense among Jews. Secular Jews or, as they were previously called, "national-radical" Jews, must withdraw from everything that religious Jews do and perform. If not, it is hypocritical, and a national-radical Jew must not be hypocritical.

However, truly, such a division of Jewishness into religious separately and secular separately is not entirely possible: it has frequently been repeated that Jewishness does not consist of two particular currents—secular way of life and culture by itself and religion—again by itself, as is the case among other peoples that have taken over their religion, adopted from a foreign source, from a foreign people. As has already been said, Jewishness and Jewish religion are one current, one cultural way of life, which continues with alterations through the whole of Jewish history. The difference between secular Jewishness and religious is only in age: all mores which are religiously sanctified today were originally secular. Only in time, after long generations, were the mores adopted by all parts of the people and sanctified as religion, as though proclaimed by God. The people adopt and God sanctifies what pertains to the folk. Many elements of contemporary secular Jewishness will certainly, in time, in generations hence, become recognized as religiously sacred. To remain a secular Jew and reject all that is religious, just the same as if a person should forget his entire development until he has grown up through amnesia. Normally a living tree has old branches and young buds that are continually growing. Secular and religious elements are like young buds and old branches. Merely religious Jewishness is like petrified fossils, dead embalmed religion. Mererly secular Jewishness is like young fresh leaves, except that they are severed from the tree.

And as for hypocrisy, it depends on the perception, how one responds to, how one understands and what one puts in, how one explains the content to oneself. For instance, a Christian asked why there is a *mezuzah* on our door. It was explained to him: it is an ancient Jewish custom and the custom helps us to identify ourselves with our people. Why do we not eat pork? Because our grandmother and great-grandmother did not eat it. Secular Jews sometimes laugh at me because I go to synagogue on Yom Kippur. I answer: If it is a folly to you, I would rather be a fool together with all the Jews and with Jewish generations than be an isolated wise man. Secular Jewishness may (and should!) introduce its explanations and motives, its forms and formulations, into the folkway traditions, but it must not reject any folkway mores because they stem from religion. Jewish holidays until now have frequently changed their motivation and content, and so secular Jews also now introduce into the holidays, for example, *their* content, but on no account should they reject them.

(1971)

NOTES

1. It is an Aggadah that God Himself studies the Torah.

2. A Turkish or Finnish tribe which was powerful from about 200 A.D. to 950, at first in the Caucasus, later in southeastern Russia. In the eighth century many of them embraced the Jewish religion.

3. One of the greatest Tannaim (scholars) of the Mishnah, who lived from ca. 40 to ca. 137 C.E.

4. Initials of Rabbi Moshe Iserles, a famous rabbi and authority on the *Shulhan Arukh,* who lived in Poland in the sixteenth century.

5. Lived from 1021 to 1070, great Jewish poet and philosopher during the Golden Age of the Jews in Spain.

V

Israel and the Diaspora

HAYIM GREENBERG

Hayim Greenberg, the Labor Zionist spokesman, theoretician, and journalist, was a rare sort of a leader who impressed everyone with his artistic sensitivity, his broad view of things, his eloquence and wisdom. An East European by birth and education, whose knowledge of our ancient and modern Jewish culture was profound, and his love of it abiding, he was, at the same time, in love with the culture of Russia and the West.

Hayim Greenberg was born in Bessarabia, Russia, in 1889. He was an autodidact who at an early age mastered Hebrew, Yiddish, and Russian literature. In 1910–11 he lived in Odessa and became a contributor to Hebrew and Russian-Jewish periodicals. He gained wide fame as a Zionist lecturer, and his Zionism had a special appeal to intellectuals, for it was articulated in universalist accents and substantiated on solid philosophical foundations.

After the October Revolution Greenberg left Soviet Russia in 1921 and lived for several years (1921–24) in Berlin, where he edited *Haolam,* the official organ of the World Zionist Organization. In 1924 he came to New York, where he lived to the end of his life. Here he attained the peak of his creativity. As editor of the Yiddish weekly *Yidisher Kemfer* and the English monthly *Jewish Frontier,* he became one of the foremost essayists, orators, and scholars, and his death, in 1953, was mourned by all segments of the American Jewish community.

THE ETERNITY OF ISRAEL

The time has come, perhaps, that we should stop using expressions which have no meaning for us, expressions which are charged with content for others, but do not mean the same thing for us. For instance, there is the ancient phrase *netzach Israel lo yeshaker*—the eternity of Israel will not deceive. These four words contain an extraordinary wealth of implications. They express profound faith and an entire conception of the universe, when they are uttered by a truly believing traditional Jew. Should such a Jew ask himself, whence his certainty that no matter what happens to Jews, there will remain Jews till the end of all generations, he would have a ready answer. The eternity of Israel is for him a law of nature having the same force that physical laws have for persons thinking in scientific terms. Just try to persuade a physicist that after X years the law of gravitation will cease to operate, that we will simply wake up one fine morning and discover that there is no more gravitation. He will quite rightly inform you that either you have gone insane or that you have never understood what gravitation was. The same holds true for the believing traditional Jew. How is it conceivable that Jews should cease to exist? It is no more possible than a second deluge after God regretted the first one and pledged His word of honor never again to afflict the world with this particular punishment. How is it conceivable that Jews should at some time cease to exist? And what of the Guardian of Israel who neither sleeps nor dozes off? And what about the heavenly Prince of the People whose duty it is to remain ever on guard over them? God has made a covenant with Israel, and God is not one to break agreements or to default on covenants. How then is it conceivable that the world should survive, but without Jews? Go to! If this is the way you think, you are likely to come up with the notion that the earth will remain, but that the sun and the moon and the stars shall cease to shine and become cold and dead splinters in space.

This is how every believing traditional Jew thinks, and he is justified in thinking so. The phrase "the eternity of Israel will not deceive" is for him not a mere rhetorical exclamation, but a conception of the way of the world.

233

But what do these words mean when we hear them from one of "our sort," from Jews whose attitude toward traditional Judaism is purely literary, or esthetic, or culturally historical? They know that there had been other "people's eternities" in history that came to an end. Then why should not the "eternity" of the Jewish people come to an end under certain conditions? Do they believe in a heavenly *Sar Ha'oomah*—Prince of the People? Do they also believe that if it were not for the existence of Jews, God might reconsider the whole bother He had taken in creating the world? I recall how some twelve or fourteen years ago, when Bialik, of blessed memory, was on his way to visit the United States, he sent from the ship a radiogram of greeting to American Jewry, and he concluded his message with the verse: "And may the God of Zion and Jerusalem aid you." What did these few words mean to Bialik, if they meant anything at all? I didn't know then and I don't know now. I will leave it to Bialik's biographers and researchers in Bialikiana to decide whether he was a believer. From long conversations I had with him in Berlin and in Leipzig years ago, I obtained the impression that he did not possess the intellectual arrogance to believe in God. But he most certainly could not have believed in a God who favored one particular people and had a special attitude toward one particular land where He felt more "at home" than in other parts of the universe. I do not think that anyone in our generation hated rhetoric as much as Bialik, yet in this case, as in some others, he "stumbled" and employed a phrase just so—for its high style or simply to be folksy.

Some days ago we had a little gathering in New York to mark the occasion of the appearance of Jacob Leschinsky's book about Jews in the Soviet Union. It was not a particularly gay occasion. Leschinsky's conscientious work aroused some melancholy thoughts. But there too I heard it repeated—and not by ordinary speechifiers, but by persons who generally have something of value to say—the old maxim about the eternity of Israel. Never worry, also in the Soviet Union Jews will survive as such. Something will flare up, some tremor will animate them, if not today then tomorrow, if not under a dictatorship then under a libertarian socialist regime which is bound some day to replace the dictatorship. No conditions were specified, no proofs or logical conclusions were cited, only the verse about the eternity of Israel was quoted and this verse was expected to produce the effect of convincing arguments—the eternity of Israel will not deceive.

At this gathering I recalled that some days earlier I had read Cecil

Roth's essay on the same subject in the journal *Jewish Social Studies*. The Anglo-Jewish historian was courageous enough to say some brutally frank words about the delusion that history has issued us some kind of insurance policy that we will continue to exist forever. According to Roth, this principle about the eternity of Israel has already "deceived" on several occasions. He offers some statistics. At the time of the rise of Christianity, there lived about two and a half million Jews in Eretz Israel. (Other historians cite a still higher figure.) But at that time substantial numbers of Jews already lived in dispersion. One ancient report indicates that during the time of Emperor Claudius, in the first century of the Christian era, nearly seven million Jews lived in the area of the Roman Empire. To this number should be added at least one million more who lived in Mesopotamia, Persia and some other areas. We will be close to the truth if we say that during the beginning of the Christian era, there were some eight million Jews. Yet during the so-called Dark Ages of the medieval era there remained only between one and one and a half million Jews, on the basis of more or less reliable sources. Where did the others vanish to? We know that the total population of the then known world decreased during these centuries. Great numbers of Jews perished as a result of persecution and massacres, but this does not explain how eight million were reduced to one or one and a half million. Roth is inclined to assume that most of the Jews disappeared through assimilation during these centuries. Mass assimilation also occurred in other eras. Roth reminds us that most of the Jews of Portugal were converted to Christianity at the end of the 15th century. And passing over to modern England, where Jews returned some 300 years ago, Roth asks how many English Jews can today trace their descent from forebears who settled in Great Britain after the Revolution. Very few indeed. The majority of present day Jews in England are descendants of immigrants from Eastern Europe, especially from Russia, who came at the end of the 19th and in the beginning of the 20th centuries. The 'genuine" English Jews have become largely assimilated through conversion, intermarriage, or by a process of unnoticed disappearance. Were Jews not to have assimilated in great masses at certain times, there would today be about 200 million Jews in the world, according to Roth's calculations.

Naturally, Roth cannot draw a straight line of progression for Jewish assimiliation, and one can cite many arguments against his generalization that extinction is, so to speak, the law of our existence. Were this law to operate everywhere and at all times, then of the one and a half million

Jews who lived in the seventeenth century there should have remained no more than a couple of hundred thousand in our day. How did it happen that despite all the sharply dipping statistical graphs, there suddenly appeared on the scene some eight million Jews in the 19th century, and sixteen or more million Jews in our day? [As the reader will see at the end of this essay, it was written in 1941, before the Nazis and their accomplices exterminated one third of the Jews in the world; but this does not invalidate the overall reasoning of this essay today. Ed.] Cecil Roth also does not distinguish sufficiently sharply between Jews who became assimilated to their host nation and those who were converted by force. When large numbers of Jews are confronted with the choice of conversion or physical annihilation, conversion or exile, and they submit to conversion and later mix with the surrounding population and are lost as an entity, this does not prove that we wish to assimilate or that we are incapable of resisting the pressures of other cultures or other modes of living. The great Jewish increase in the 19th century demonstrates that when we are not persecuted—or less persecuted—we are, *under certain circumstances* not at all anxious to lose our identity. The case of Portugal therefore proves nothing. Nor does the case of Spain when toward the end of the 15th century large numbers of Jews became converted to Catholicism, at least outwardly, in order to avoid being exiled. The case of England, where Jews have become assimilated not out of fear but out of a desire to do so, is much more convincing. A similar process took place in Italy. In Germany, too, Hitler would have found only a handful of Jews, had there not been a constant influx of Jews from Eastern Europe to Germany in recent generations. Had it not been for this influx, which in time also became Germanized, there would now be even more quarter and eighth Jews in Germany than there are.

What then are we to conclude? Is geography a factor? Are we to conclude that eastern Jews don't assimilate while western Jews do? But East and West are not only geographical but also historical concepts. In a certain sense we may say that the present day East will be tomorrow what the West is today, that capitalist-liberal civilization, the weakening of church authority among Christians and of religious traditions and inhibitions among Jews will transform East into West. In his study, Leschinsky has demonstrated still another factor: that also in a socialist or a pseudo-socialist society, such as the Soviet Union is today, Jews are subject to the same assimiliating forces that operate on them in a liberal-capitalist

society. Of what avail then are verses from the Scriptures, artificially in-
duced spasms of chosenness, diaspora autonomism, all sorts of secular
nationalisms, cultural autonomies, Yiddishist romanticism, Hebraist senti-
mentality and all sort of theo-less theologies, when the main thing is lacking—that special mentality which alone transforms a minority into a kind
of exclusive aristocratic club whose members do not mingle with the rest
of the public. But such a mentality cannot be created artificially if it no
longer exists. It cannot be created by means of a theory or of a formula.
I recall that many years ago a Hebrew writer (Echad Harabanim Hamar-
gishim) said that he had no qualms about sending a single believing
Jew into the biggest city overseas or into a desert as long as he carried
with him his phylacteries in his hands and the Scriptures in his pocket. If
only he will not be physically destroyed, such a Jew will remain one. But
where are the phylacteries and where is the volume of Scriptures which
speak to the modern Jew the way they spoke to Jews of former generations? (Were this author still alive, I would suggest to him that he give
his wanderer a volume of the *Shulhan Arukh*—the code of laws governing everyday behavior—instead of the Scriptures which are now so uni-
versally accepted.) And I believe it was Gershenson[1] who declared that
the true destruction in Jewish history was not that of the Temple, but the
religious bankruptcy of the past couple of generations; the atrophy of
religious tradition and faith as a constant effective force. Without such a
total separate and vital religious culture, the Jew becomes ever more
simply a member of a minority group, and minority groups, unless they
cling to some irredentist movement, or they live in the midst of a people
of very low culture, in the natural course of events tend to become lost
in the majority, and even when they remain separate they lose their own
distinctive cultural identities. I frequently think that we modern Jews (or
Jews who had been "modern" in past eras in terms of their times) have
passed into the condition of a minority group. Of the truly pious ghetto
Jews it was impossible to say that they were a minority group. Ambas-
sadors and consuls representing their countries in foreign lands do not
constitute minorities and do not assimilate. The classical *Galut* Jew felt
like an ambassador or a consul of his kingdom of religion. His home and
his family were largely "extra-territorial." But we have lost this "extra-
territoriality" and I hardly believe that there is anything else to take its
place, except *a territory.*

The eternity of Israel will not deceive. Yes, within the context of a com-

---

[1] M. O. Gershenson (1869–1925) was a Russian-Jewish philosopher and critic.

plete Jewish culture for which the modern Jew is no longer fit, of which he has been completely emptied. Without it, the phrase remains a rhetorical exclamation, irrespective of whether the surrounding social framework is liberal-capitalist, or Soviet or even a higher type of socialism. Israel without the God of Israel can survive only in Eretz Israel (in the Eretz Israel as we know it today or in another version of it still to come). Without it, Jews become simply a minority without any element of eternity involved, like so many other non-Jewish splintered minorities. What do those other minorities do? They do not simply lie down and die. But they realize more or less clearly what the end will be—and they do not take it tragically.

The Diaspora Jew of our time must therefore accustom himself to one of two choices: either he must learn not to feel tragically about the question of existence or non-existence, survival or non-survival, or he must learn to look at the situation earnestly and realistically: if it is impossible to live as Jews extra-territorially, then one must begin to live as Jews territorially.

* * *

I just reread the foregoing few lines and felt displeased. Such banality. This formula is as old as the hills. I personally used this formula when I was still a youngster. But what is one to do? I know many Jews today, intelligent people, some of them even sophisticated and "well-travelled," who have heard this formula countless times and have still not grasped it fully.

* * *

Yes, one Jewish man tried to console me. "What?" he asked. "You don't believe in the eternity of Israel? Then it is you who are a utopian and live in a world of fantasy. Only one who has faith in the world, in mankind, in decency, can deny the eternity of Israel. But the world is moving to ever greater evil, and in the future we will be hated even more than now. Hatred for us will be the curtain that will keep us separate. You cannot assimilate with people who wish to murder you. According to you a time when Jew and non-Jew will be like cooing doves is right around the corner, and you promise us the kiss of death. But don't you worry. The world does not consist of doves of peace and it is in the nature of a *goy* to be an anti-Semite from childhood. They will see to it that we do not become extinct."

I did not answer this man. But if this is to be the face of *netzach Israel,* the eternity of Israel, then I am prepared to renounce it for myself and for my posterity and—without authorization—also for all Jews.

(1941)

HAYIM GREENBERG

Hayim Greenberg, the Labor Zionist spokesman, theoretician, and journalist, was a rare sort of a leader who impressed everyone with his artistic sensitivity, his broad view of things, his eloquence and wisdom. An East European by birth and education, whose knowledge of our ancient and modern Jewish culture was profound, and his love of it abiding, he was, at the same time, in love with the culture of Russia and the West.

Hayim Greenberg was born in Bessarabia, Russia, in 1889. He was an autodidact who at an early age mastered Hebrew, Yiddish, and Russian literature. In 1910–11 he lived in Odessa and became a contributor to Hebrew and Russian-Jewish periodicals. He gained wide fame as a Zionist lecturer, and his Zionism had a special appeal to intellectuals, for it was articulated in universalist accents and substantiated on solid philosophical foundations.

After the October Revolution Greenberg left Soviet Russia in 1921 and lived for several years (1921–24) in Berlin, where he edited *Haolam,* the official organ of the World Zionist Organization. In 1924 he came to New York, where he lived to the end of his life. Here he attained the peak of his creativity. As editor of the Yiddish weekly *Yidisher Kemfer* and the English monthly *Jewish Frontier,* he became one of the foremost essayists, orators, and scholars, and his death, in 1953, was mourned by all segments of the American Jewish community.

THE FUTURE OF AMERICAN JEWRY

Some eight centuries ago we produced a man who was a great authority on law and a great philosophic thinker. Responding to the need of his time, he wrote "The Guide of the Perplexed." Were we to have a Maimonides today, he would have to write another kind of book, a Guide of the Non-Perplexed. For the trouble with the modern Jew—and I am not referring here to the surviving spiritual remnant of authentically pious, rooted Jews who live only calendarically in modern times, but have little relationship to it—is that he is shockingly untroubled and finds himself, at least consciously, in no spiritual dilemma. I do not know whether this type of Jew of whom I now speak is an atheist: most likely he never took the time or trouble to analyze this question and to formulate an answer for himself. I need hardly say that I am not hankering after atheists, though I am inclined to believe that a tragic or melancholy atheist, one with "an ache in his heart"—and not the type of cheerful vulgar atheist who is perfectly content to believe that there is no God, for it is more convenient this way—is essentially and potentially closer to genuine religious life than most inert "believers." I am therefore not overwhelmed when I read that, statistically, synagogue attendance has increased here or there, or that new congregations are established. Among Jews, as also among some American Christians where Protestant family traditions persist, belonging to a congregation is conventionally approved as a sign of social solidity and respectability. Among Jews there operates the added incentive to express in some way one's belonging to the community, a measure of nostalgia and pious respect for parents and a dim fear of making the total break. But in most cases the specific religious impulse is both weak and unsure.

Can such elements (which have a visible tendency to increase) be converted, or reconverted to religious Judaism? Should this be possible it would present a very serious pedagogical problem. And, pedagogically speaking, it would be very difficult—if at all possible—to transform one into a religious Jew if he is not a religious human being.

I would not wish to be misunderstood. Anti-religiousness, or what is much more common, religious indifference, naturally is not a specific

Jewish trait. It is the result of a number of developments and mental changes which have taken place (and are still taking place) during recent generations. Let me point out some of them.

A) Religion has been discredited in certain segments of modern society because it tried to provide answers to some questions that are not in its province. To the extent that religion pretends to be a kind of science which solves problems which can only be studied experimentally, it must fail. Though *science* in itself is not and cannot be anti-religious, *scientists* of a certain type have become enemies of religion. Religion aroused their distaste with pretensions to which it was not entitled. A formulated or unformulated conviction thus became prevalent among many that religion as such is the enemy of clear and dependable knowledge, instead of the more logical conclusion that certain claims of some religions, developed in specific eras of religious evolution are anti-scientific. But true religion is agnostic when it is true to its own nature. I use the term "agnostic" in its strict etymological sense. Religion is "uninformed" in all those areas where research by means of the application of strict logical rules and experimental techniques are called for. Even in questions which would appear to be the natural province of religion, such as the existence of God, free will, immortality, etc., religion cannot provide rational answers. The role of religion is altogether different: it arouses and cultivates a specific ethic-poetic orientation toward the world, life and destiny, and it cultivates an attitude of confidence in the basis of existence and its intentions. Religion is neither able nor called upon to explain the mystery of life. But it stresses, by means of its specific and largely artistic means, the existence of mystery, veneration of it as well as confidence in it. God, as the prophet Isaiah expressed it, is an *el mistater,* a God who seeks concealment.

B) Religion has lost its one-time influence and prominence among many people because it (or rather the institutions which represented it publicly) was too long and too frequently . . . anti-religious: because religion allowed itself to be dominated by powerful social classes for their own anti-social, and consequently anti-religious purposes.

C) Technological progress of recent generations and the great ultilitarian benefits which resulted from scientific achievements and discoveries have created a widespread illusion that man is fundamentally not dependent on powers outside himself or above himself, that science is capable of solving all problems and contradictions of human existence without exception, and that therefore religion is no longer "necessary," that it is "useless." The conception that man is "something created," that all he possesses or is potentially capable of acquiring is "borrowed" or received as a gift, that he is essentially poor and helpless and destined to remain so, this conception has been weakened and watered down by the above-mentioned illusion. This is particularly apparent among the masses of the West and in "awakening Asia," but also many genuine and even prominent scientists belong, in this regard, to the type of mass man.

D) A new climate of "scientism" has engulfed millions who have no direct relation or access to science. In this climate people are carried away by materialist conceptions because matter in all its forms is the chief theme with which science can and should deal. This enthusiasm contributed in no small degree to the dulling and weakening of intuitive faculties without which it is impossible to consider the world metaphysically or religiously. It is impossible for one person to arouse esthetic elation in another with his beauty, if he is to be regarded too long or permanently only from an anatomic-physiological standpoint.

An anatomist or physiologist in love is a psychological impossibility, to the extent that he is exclusively a physioligst or an anatomist and is no longer capable of considering another person from a synthetically intuitive standpoint. This obsession with matter leads many to doubt or to despair about the reality of psychic existence. Among the more sensitive this reaches a mood which a European author once characteristically described with the text of a skeptic's prayer: "Oh, God—if there is a God; save my soul—if there is a soul; if I am I; and if 'I' has an existence."

E) The life of great masses in a metropolitan, industrial civilization with its tempo and extreme concentration on economic interests deprived modern man of his capacity (and opportunities) for altruistic contemplation, for that type of contemplation of the world and of the self which leads man to wonder and amazement. For a man who lacks this contemplation, the world and all that happens in it becomes trivial and triviality is the opposite and the enemy of religion, just as it is the enemy of art which sees sense and the eternally solemn in everything. In the rushing tempo of his life, modern man lacks the time (psychological as well as chronological time), or does not set aside the time for disinterested contemplation.

I have touched only on a few circumstances in the condition of modern man which deprive him of the capacity for religion. I am not sure that I described them exactly, or that these are the most important ones. But they should provide a general description of the condition of modern man and of his spiritual image. And I do not believe that in this area there exists any basic difference between modern man in general and the modern Jew. If this condition is indeed as I see it, then it is a morbid condition and this morbidity applies also to Jews. And this is what I meant when I said above that one cannot be a religious Jew if one is not fundamentally a religious man.

For this reason I can ignore theological, ceremonial or other differences which today distinguish the three types of institutional Jewish religion in America. The essence of the matter is elsewhere. All three trends suffer the same lack which afflicts the entire contemporary world: genuine and direct religious experience. This lack cannot be concealed with the chilly "dignity" of the Reform Temple, nor with the respectful but distant attitude to tradition of Conservative Judaism, nor also with the petrified loyalty of Orthodox Jewry to inherited religious forms which no longer contain the profound and rooted content of such a short time ago. The intrusion of nationalism and Zionism into what we define as religious life is no doubt a positive social fact which should not be underestimated, but it cannot lead to religious resurgence in Jewry. The evolution taking place in the state of Israel is, for the time being at least, a factor leading to secularization rather than to a revival of Jewish religiosity, despite the fact that Orthodoxy wields dictatorial influence in certain institutional areas of life in Israel.

It would be erroneous to conclude from what I said thus far that I am calling for some new kind of "Reform" in Jewry in the accepted sense of the term. Jews have gained little from the Reform movement in Germany and later in America. Criticize the Protestant Reform movement as we may —and indeed it bore within itself a religious sanction for capitalism, the germs of extreme nationalism and an idolatrous attitude toward the State and its authority, and also a sanction for race hatred—it aimed not to dilute but to intensify the religious life of the individual. Protestantism did not come to make the life of the individual more comfortable or morally easier and less responsible. On the contrary, it introduced greater strictness than Catholicism did in many areas of life. Its demands were more stringent. The Jewish Reform movement relieved its followers of the heavy "ballast" or commandments, but it did not demand more profound and personalized religious experience. It did not lead to increased spiritual tension. It is no accident that Reform Jews, in contrast to Protestant reformers, did not produce even one more or less prominent mystic. What I have in mind here are not reforms in the sense of the so-called Liberal Jewry, nor the decent but tragically earth-bound modifications "in the spirit of the time" of Conservative Jewry, but something similar to that which Hasidism once upon a time introduced into our life.

Hasidism did not reform Judaism—it reformed the Jews. Hasidism did not repudiate a single one of the 613 commandments, it did not do away with even one of the strictures of the *Shulhan Arukh*. It did not undertake to introduce any changes into Jewish theology (insofar as Judaism has a systematic theology) or ritual. It added nothing and detracted nothing. But it introduced new spirit into that which existed and was not traditionally hallowed. It introduced *kavanah* (intention) and *d'vekut* (cleaving) into the mechanics of religious life. Hasidism's reform consisted in providing or returning to its followers the capacity for experiencing and beholding the miracle in the everyday, in the normal lawful order of things, the capacity for marveling and being entranced. Hasidism did not revise the prayer book, but to the act of praying it imparted new dimensions and a lyricism which is perhaps the sole convincing justification for praying.

Religious life throughout the world now requires a revitalization through a new kind of Hasidism (I employ this term because I have no other), and this is perhaps especially true of Jewish religious life. Without such a revitalization religion is becoming ever more flat and horizontal, whereas its true mission is to be vertical.

I would not undertake to prove that such a "reform" is possible in our time. Such a basic reform of religious man, of modern man in general and of the modern Jew, is essentially a process of sanctification, a reawakening of intuitive forces, of the visionary and artistic capacities in man. And this requires that man should be less organized, more of a spiritual "vagabond," and that within the framework of society there should be room also for community. More time is also needed. I am convinced that without a removal of the obstacles which stand in the way of what I called contemplation, without a curing of that specific blindness that affects so many people as a result of their fixation on the material and on those problems of the material which can be experimentally solved, there is no room for authentic religious life, and naturally also not for authentic Jewish religious life.

(1951)

MAURICE SAMUEL

Maurice Samuel was a Jewish scholar and writer who thought and wrote in English but was at the same time embedded in Yiddish and Hebrew literature; a life-long Zionist and an affirmer—not a negator—of the Diaspora; an American novelist and essayist, and the ambassador of Yiddish culture to the Americanized Jews.

Samuel was born in Romania in 1895, and was brought to England at the age of five. He studied at Manchester University, where Chaim Weizmann became one of his teachers and friends. In 1914 Samuel migrated to the United States, and after America entered the First World War, he served in the army in France.

At the end of the Versailles Peace Conference Samuel went to Poland, where he familiarized himself with the intellectual currents in Jewish secular and religious life, and with the flourishing Yiddish literature which Polish Jewry was then producing.

Samuel published twenty-five books. In addition, he translated a number of books from Yiddish and Hebrew. As a linguist with a sensitive ear for the peculiarities of each tongue, Samuel knew that language is not only a means of communication, but is also the reservoir of a people's experience, ethos, joys, and sorrows. That is why two of his enduring books are on the Yiddish classical writers Sholem Aleichem and Y. L. Peretz. *The World of Sholem Aleichem,* which appeared in 1943, was awarded a prize by the city of New York; *The Prince of the Ghetto* (on Y. L. Peretz), which was published in 1948, won the acclaim of American as well as Yiddish critics.

To the end of his life in 1972, Samuel remained a balanced Jewish humanist who saw gleams of light in the non-Jewish world, particularly among the Anglo-Saxons. He believed that being Jewish-centered, one is also world-centered. "My people is my instrument for cooperating with mankind, my channel to humanity. . . . Love of humanity, when not implemented by love of a people, is usually gushy and diffused sentimentalism."

THE LONG WAY ROUND

American Jewry must address itself to the retrieval or re-creation of such a Judaism as will move a part of it—the most intense part—to voluntary self-transference to Israel. And while some of us believe this to be possible, others here, and the vast majority of articulate Israelis say: "It will never come to pass. Tomorrow you will be gone. You will be washed away by assimiliation. Your spiritual hopes are at best self-delusion, and very probably they are pitiable devices for the concealment of your moral bankruptcy."

A curious feature of this categoric negation of possibility, noted by many, is the participation of the American negativists in our affirmative educational activities. This is a true *m'ma nafshach* (the Talmudic protest "you-can't-have-it-both-ways"). The inconsistency does them honor; they can't stop fighting even when they think that all is lost. But while it does them honor it does us no good. For if there is any chance at all of our succeeding they are diminishing it; they take away with one hand more than they give with the other.

The participation of the Israelis in the debate is another matter. While they wrongly protest against our interfering in their affairs, they are rightly interfering in ours. For I consider it our business to speak frankly about conditions in Israel, and the business of Israelis to speak frankly about conditions here. *We* may have a totally erroneous picture of their life, and *they* of ours. That is not the issue. The issues are the propriety of interference (within certain limits, of course) and the accuracy of the pictures we have of one another. I shall not discuss here—it belongs to another series of important problems—the unity of world Jewry which actually demands the interchange of information and advice between Israel and the *Golah*. I shall discuss the accuracy of the picture which the Israelis have of us. I shall also bear in mind that they have for it the backing of a number of American Jews; but I shall also ask the reader to bear in mind that here is a minority report, and over there it is a majority—almost a unanimous—view.

It is proper to add that the Israeli position is, even if based on error, not inconsistent. We might protest to them, as to the local pessimists: "You are only making things worse." Both the Israelis and local pessimists can rightly answer from that point of view: "We do not want Israel to be deluded by false hopes." But the Israelis are not working *with us* on the spot, and the local pessimists are. The Israelis are not putting their energies into what they consider a futility (i.e. Jewish education in America), throwing good money after bad; the local pessimists are. The local pessimists teach Judaism, and keep shouting: "We're wasting our time! It won't take!"

There is however one respect of the Israeli attitude which must give us pause. If the Israelis believe that Judaism in America is doomed to rapid extinction, the kind of propaganda which they will conduct here for the State of Israel will be either of the purely philantropic kind, or else an appeal to purely psychological reflexes, chiefly mob pride without spiritual content. I exclude the appeal to fear, which some Israelis have tried, and have now given up as "bad strategy."

Except for what we say about ourselves, and what their emissaries who have been here tell them about us, Israelis rely for their ideas about us on historic and recent analogy. They and we know that Jewries in the *Golah* have always had a term; they and we know that the sociological instruments which enabled historic Jewries to develop identities and values do not exist for us. So the diagnosis by analogy is gloomy.

With regard to on-the-spot diagnosis there is, as we have seen, disagreement. It is my optimistic view that the pessimists here color their on-the-spot diagnosis with the generalizations of diagonsis by analogy. Again, it is the specific American scene which must be examined, in its specific time. And one important generalization must be modified: it is true that we do not have "the sociological instruments which enabled historic Jewries to survive, etc." But those historic Jewries did not have a Jewish State in the making as part of their spiritual environment. This enormous advantage is weakened, but not destroyed, by the vociferous pessimism of the Israelis regarding our future in America; the advantage will be greatly strengthened when, with the passing of the harassments and constrictions of Israeli life, the interchanges between Israel and America will lose some of their tensions

How helpful is the diagnosis by historic analogy? There have been immense Jewries of the *Golah;* none of them has endured. They dissolved, like Alexandrian Jewry; they failed under oppression, like Babylonian

Jewry; they were destroyed, like Spanish and East European Jewry. Why should American Jewry fare better? But note, first: none of those brilliant Jewries (and most of them had humble numerical and spiritual beginnings) passed away without leaving a great contribution to Jewish history; and second, the position of American Jewry is such that its destruction in the near future simply cannot enter our calculations, for the conditions making that possible would mean the destruction of mankind.

But, runs the argument, those other Jewries had instruments of survival which we of American Jewry have not. They had, above all, the enclosed life, the separate language (Yiddish, or the varieties of Yiddish —so to speak—like Ladino, Judeo-Aramaic, and Judeo-Arabic), and the intensely religious climate. That is correct; it constitutes the core of the argument. The other Jewries, however, had not the instrument of a reborn Jewish State to focus their will and sharpen their faculties. They had *faith* that God would recreate the Jewish land; we who have not the faith have the proof. Proof may be weaker than faith, and seeing not as good as believing, but they are not to be ignored.

However this contrast be evaluated, there is no ground for saying that at present American Jewry is on the decline. Its weak Judaism was weaker yesterday, and weaker still the day before. There is every sign that at least tomorrow it will be stronger. I mean, of course, American-born Jewry, not the immigrant Jewry which brought over enough Jewish capital for its own lifetime. The pessimists are thinking of the day after tomorrow. But their forecast, I repeat, is conjecture. It is not provable, and in my opinion not probable, that this Jewry of five million will disappear within a century or so and create no memorable Jewish values.

The strongest argument of pessimism is drawn of course from the data of assimilation. Assimilation, or as I prefer to call it here, dissolution, has three principal stages: indifference, imitation, and revolt. The first and second interact; so do the second and third. Final dissolution is reached in intermarriage and the complete forgetting. Conscious revolt against being Jewish is the least important form numerically, though it is not negligible; and whether of the right or left, whether bourgeois-intellectualist and bourgeois-careerist, or leftist-intellectualist and leftist-moral-political, it is the least manageable because it is most immediately a response to world conditions we cannot influence. But the other two interacting forms are more manageable, although they too, of course, are part responses to external conditions.

Even the pessimists on the spot admit that momentarily indifferentism to being Jewish is receding. The cause for this change is usually sought in the tremendous events of the last twenty years, the two apocalypses of Hitler and the Jewish State. My belief is that a cyclic process independent of these has been a factor of equal or greater importance. I refer to the settling down of American Jewry, the passing of the son-of-immigrants phase (helped by the passing away of the immigrants themselves), the integration of the Jewish with the general community of America, the recoil from initial uneasiness and from ignorance of the meaning of America. To this must be added the infiltration of the subconscious Jewish folk mind by the significant phenomenon of which I have written earlier—the revelation that the Anglo-Saxon tradition has an active, affirmative attitude toward the concept of the Jewish Return, and that America has played a Providential role in rescuing the Jewish people from extinction.

A word, incidentally, in explanation of what may strike some readers as a cynical parenthesis: "helped by the passing away of the immigrants themselves." The presence of the older generation delayed the integration of the younger. In retrospect, with the solemnity of loss at play on the mind and heart, the younger generation had a deeper appreciation of the worth of its progenitors. It has often happened that an embarrassing generation must disappear before it is understood.

Dissolution, the final stage of intermarriage and disappearance, almost always follows on imitative assimilation; and therefore every manifestation of the imitative, the "aping" of non-Jewish ways, is looked on as the beginning of the inevitable end. This is a mistake to which nearly all of us subscribe, and I was guilty of it myself when I should have known better from my reading Ahad HaAm thirty years ago.

Imitation does not necessarily lead to dissolution. It can lead to the reassertion of the self in a new form. I was wholly mistaken in regarding the Reform Judaism of thirty years ago (as I did in *I, The Jew*) as the prelude to dissolution; we have seen it, since then, take a Zionist or pro-Zionist turn in which other affirmations are now included. The YMHA's and Jewish Centers which thirty and forty years ago looked like—and were—imitations of the YMCA's have shifted their ground considerably in the direction of Judaization. (Professor Baron points out that actually the first YMHA preceded the first YMCA. Perhaps one ought to say that both institutions emerged on non-Jewish ground.) The Jewish summer camps or rather summer camps of Jewish children, which began as purely secular, non-cultural enterprises, are sprinkled now with consciously

Jewish-educational institutions. The summer "institutes" for adults, now becoming so popular that Bnai Brith has opened a special department to promote and service them, have a queer resemblance to Catholic retreats. They serve Judaism. For the present they do not take in more than a couple of thousand a year—I am quite certain that they will take in tens of thousands before a decade has passed. The parochial school movement is spreading—this again is an "imitative" reaction, as far as form is concerned.

Here is what Ahad HaAm, writing sixty years ago, had to say on the subject of imitation, applying it to European Jewry:

> We are coming to recognize that salvation (of Judaism) . . . lies along a third road . . . that of the enrichment of our national individuality by means of imitation of the competitive kind.
>
> If self-effacement had reached the stage of indifference to the maintainance of any link with the past, and of a genuine desire to be absorbed in the foreign life, there would no longer be any incentive to adapt the inherited tradition to modern requirements; the natural course would be to leave it severely alone till it vanished of itself, meanwhile carrying it on for a time without change, out of mere force of habit and respect for the past. (*Imitation and Assimilation,* translated by Leon Simon).

We must be careful to emphasize Ahad HaAm's proviso: "Imitation of the *competitive* kind." When a Jew tries to get into a non-Jewish golf club by suppressing his Jewish affiliation, that is imitation of the defeatist kind. But suppose Jews set up a golf club of their own, is that competitive or defeatist? One cannot tell except by the final issue. Incidental values may or may not develop there. Thus our Centers and YMHA's hold out considerable Jewish promise (I repeat, *promise*). And when we set up educational summer "retreats" for adults, that is definitely creative imitation of the competitive kind.

Nearly always the beginnings fill us with uneasiness, and rightly so, for we cannot always tell what variety of imitation is being initiated. To accept or to condemn wholesale is unwise, to distinguish in the early stages between the imitative and competitive is often difficult; and to transform the defeatist-imitative into the competitive and creative-imitative sometimes involves disruptive disputes. As an Ilustration of the last—and this is not my personal view alone—the imitative non-Jewish nationalism which associated itself with Zionism is, or should be, transitional, yielding to the Jewish nationalism which is very different from that of the modern nations. Many of us believe that Jewish nationalism should compete with non-Jewish nationalism by reverting to ethical, religious and universalist concepts which have been the continuing ideals of Jewish peoplehood; the effort to promote this reversion has created a good deal of rancor.

The will to be Jewish is here, the skill is not. Optimists emphasize the presence of the will, pessimists the absence of the skill. The ones believe that the first will create the second; the others believe that the absence of the second will stifle the first. The extremists among the pessimists also deny that the will exists; and those who say—as Israelis do—that there is only one true Judaism, that which means self-transplantation to Israel, are the last word in pessimism, for as far as they are concerned there is no Judaism at all in America.

Debates between optimists and pessimists are almost purposeless. Can I, an optimist, hope to lighten the heart of a single pessimist? Probably not; but if I can strengthen the will of an optimist here and there, I shall have achieved something. And the most heartening feature of the picture I have before me is this: the instruments of American Jewry described in the last section are *grass roots creations*. No great diaspora figures like a Rambam or Rabbenu Tam gave us these institutions which we are beginning to use for the development of our "skills" as Jews. They sprang up among "small" groups, they emerged tentatively, they spread without fanfares. They are still imperfect in form, insufficient in number; and great masses of Jews (a majority? probably not) are still outside the effects of the—shall we call it,—sub-renaissance. Yet the feel of American-born Jewry is not what it was forty years ago, when I arrived here, and still less what it was sixty years ago, from all accounts; and though it gropes and blunders, and lacks the teachers, American-born Jewry is today not wholly without implements of its own creation (I have left out the synagogues and temples simply because these are not of its own creation). Call these implements, if you like, the first flint artifacts. But do not deny their existence, and do not assert categorically that we shall not progress beyond them.

For, to repeat the crucial argument, progress will be impeded and perhaps entirely arrested if the pessimism of Israel regarding our failure continues to block its educational cooperation. If discourse from here cannot dispel that pessimism, it must be done over there by self-conversion;

and the first step toward such self-conversion must be an act of self-denial— there must be no more misrepresentation of those of us who see the long way round as the only way home. It is not out of coolness, and not out of failure of vision, that we talk of American Jewry having to find itself before it can find its contingents for Israel; these two phenomena are simply functions of each other and it is impossible to develop them separately.

Again I must return to Ahad HaAm, to give him the closing words, written in 1903 and 1904 (and what intellectual courage it needed to write thus when we had so little in the land). But let me preface that quotation by something already quoted from Mr. Ben-Gurion: "No one can know at this time whether *Kibbutz Galuyot* means the ingathering of the entire Jewish people, or the majority of it, or a part of it." Here is Ahad HaAm's summary of his views:

> Palestine will become our spiritual center only when the Jews are a majority of the population and own most of the land. . . . I am told every day that I am exclusively "spiritual," and that my ideal is to establish in Palestine a "heavenly Jerusalem" where unpractical idealists will sit and bask in the radiance of the "divine presence." This is a lie, invented long ago by my opponents, which has gained currency. If that were really my ideal, I should not have given so much time and energy to the practical work of Palestinian colonization, nor should I have made a study, as I have done to the best of my ability, of the methods of agricultural settlement in Palestine.
>
> The truth is that one single word has led to all the misunderstanding. I have always said that Zionism is a "spiritual movement," and some have inferred from this that I ignore the practical aspect altogether, and that the whole thing, from the settlers to the civilization which they will in time create, is to be the very quintessence of spirituality. Actually I called Zionism a "spiritual" movement only in relation to its end and purpose: that is to say, Zionism cannot put an end to the material Jewish problem, because not all the Jews can migrate to Palestine, and therefore the object of our movement is only to create for our people a national center, the influence of which *on the diaspora* will be spiritual only, in the sense that it will strengthen their morale, increase their sense of unity, and provide a suitable content for their life as Jews. But it

is obvious that a national center cannot come into existence, and
cannot create a new type of life, if it is purely spiritual. It most ob-
viously include all the elements necessary to a nation, from agricultural laborers and craftsmen to the purest intellectuals." (*Letters of
Ahad HaAm,* translated by Leon Simon).

(1954)

HORACE M. KALLEN

Horace Meyer Kallen, the exponent of cultural pluralism, was an eminent American philosopher who formulated a secularist rationale for Jewish humanists. In the course of seventy years he manifested creativity in both Jewish and American cultures.

Kallen was born in Germany in 1882. His father, an Orthodox rabbi, brought him, at the age of five, to Boston, where he received his general and Jewish education. He graduated with a Ph.D. in philosophy from Harvard University, where he had become the favorite student of the philosopher William James. He also studied at Oxford University and at the Sorbonne, and taught at Princeton, Wisconsin, and the New School for Social Research. Kallen died in 1974.

Among Kallen's numerous books are *The Book of Job as a Greek Tragedy, Judaism at Bay, Culture and Democracy in the United States, Secularism Is the Will of God, Art and Freedom,* and others on a wide range of intellectual interests and learning.

As a pragmatist Kallen evaluated Jewishness not in terms of definitions or historical correctness, but rather in its consequences for a stronger and richer Jewish life. He was of the opinion that Judaism comprises not *a* view of life, but *views* of life—views in the plural. Each grouping in Jewish life—Orthodox, Conservative, Reform, Zionist, Bundist, Yiddishist, or Hebraist—may, according to Kallen, emphasize in the texture of Jewishness whatever is pertinent for its struggles and ideals. All intellectual currents in American Jewry, all religious and secular philosophies, have their *raison d'être* in maintaining a meaningful Jewish continuity.

In his appearances at Jewish education conferences, Kallen never tired of stressing that Jewish education, if it is to be relevant for the young, not only has to be a record of the past, but must include Hebrew *and* Yiddish, Israel *and* the Diaspora, Zionism *and* all other movements and achievements of Jews.

WHAT PRICE "JEWISH LIVING"?

It is now more than a quarter of a century since I published in the *Menorah Journal,* a study calling attention, among other things, to the processes I have referred to, to their dynamic, and to its implications for "Jewish living." I called this inquiry *Can Judaism Survive in the United States?,* and some years later reprinted it, with revisions, as Chapter XV of a group of essays regarding the relations between Judaism and modernity, under the general title, *Judaism at Bay.* Summing up the changes of the quarter of a century of Jewish living in America that the essays envisaged, I wrote:

> . . . Judaism has been alienated from the Jewish people. Its upkeep is today the concern of a class above a certain income level, and by and large this class is concerned only to the point of supplying the cost of the plant and of the "spiritual leader" through whose professional expertness they may discharge their religious obligations. . . . They practice Judaism by proxy. . . . *Gabbaim* and *rabbanim* to the contrary notwithstanding, the Jewish way of life is no longer a religious way of life. Judaism is no longer identical with Jewishness, and Jewishness is no longer identical with Judaism. Jewishness—I prefer to say—Hebraism—is a focus of modernity. It is the Jewish way of life become necessarily secular, humanist, scientific, conditioned to the industrial economy, without having ceased to be livingly Jewish. Judaism will have to be reintegrated with this secular, cultural form of community which is Jewishness if Judaism is to survive

Since these lines were written, all mankind has lived in crises, one following another with no respite in sight. Humanity has suffered contamination and assault from communist, fascist, nazi, and falangist totalitarianism. It has been a perplexed witness of the betrayal unto death of the League of Nations. It has lived through a global economic de-

259

pression. It has been wilfully plunged into a second world war among whose results are: loosening the British colonial empire into a commonwealth of equal nations whose new members threaten each other with war; upsetting British rule in the Near East; thrusting upon the United States the British preeminence among free nations; Communist Russia's advancing its bid for global empire by every means of force and fraud. Mankind has seen this taking place within the framework of a United Nations Organization designed to keep peace just and secure, and against the background of the organization's Universal Declaration of Human Rights, intended to reaffirm, now specifically and in detail, the propositions of the democratic idea which as the American Declaration of Independence, embody the fighting faith of the democratic revolution. These are the propositions of the global religion, of that one faith which the entire miscellany of mankind can freely share. They are the battle cry of freedom wherever humans confront totalitarian tyranny, in hot war or in cold. Nevertheless, the peoples of the world saw such a tyranny impose dominion on its neighbors little and big, west and east. They also saw its bid for rule contained in a few places. They also saw the Jewish communities of Palestine counter mortal danger by reconstituting themselves as the State of Israel and betting their survival on strengthening and protection from peoples committed to the democratic idea.

Their wager is, of course, ultimately every Jew's wager. Jews, throughout this entire period, had been chosen by the foes of human liberty everywhere to be its avatars and scapegoats. Antisemitism has been inherent to totalitarianism, whatever its mode, whoever its missioners. In the concentration camps of the Nazis and the Communists, in the Warsaw Ghetto, on the Moslem deserts and on Palestinian sands, and in the refugee camps of their reluctant helpers, upward of six millions of them had been martyred to death in obscenity and abomination. Alone the free Jews of the United States of America had stood, as they continue to stand, sure redeemers to these lost; and the Americans had redirected their entire communal economy in order to meet the exigency, distorting the structures and dislocating the functions of its institutions, straining its strategy, tactic, and logistic to a point where liabilities are being felt to outbalance moral and cultural as well as material assets. Now American Jews are again in one of their recurrent moods of self-scrutiny and self-justification. "Research" is on the march among them. Communal organizations and establishment are having themselves surveyed and appraised by "social scientists." The self-acquiescent "Jewish intelligentzia" are joined by

marginal intellectuals of Jewish parentage sweating to reconsider what
"Jew" means to them and to redefine their personal relations with that
meaning in terms of faith, works, and "belongingness"; in terms, if you
prefer, of responsibility for future "Jewish living," hence for Jewish
survival.

"Research" is being grasped as a magic key opening the door of the
Jewish future in the United States. Is it survival or extinction? "Survival" is currently a term as blindly controversial as in former years
"congress," "assembly," used to be. There are Judaists who see no
good in survival and turn to research yearning that it guarantee the so
desirable release from the burdens of being a Jew by some infallible
demonstration that, even though Jewishness, like the old soldier in the
song, will never die, it will nevertheless, like General MacArthur in
public life, fade away. There are the "survivalists" who count on research to reveal for them an eternal ground for "Jewish living" and an
unalterable structure to erect on this ground. Both are turning to social
science for the gratification of their irreconcilable desires. They want a
scientifically established "law" to guarantee that what they fear but cannot themselves overcome will perish, and what they desire but cannot
themselves produce, will nevertheless surely come to them. If their frame
of reference is also theological, they shape the ends for Providence and
count on its omnipotence to shape the means for them.

Thus all are able with a good conscience to rationalize habitual inertia
and drift, to avoid both choice between alternative actions and orchestra-
tion of them, and to call it relying on the laws of nature or of nature's
God. They are apt entirely to disregard the fact, if they know it at all,
that their reliance on "research" is itself a choice of means to an end
they desire, and that it is first and last an act of faith on which they bet
their Jewish lives. They refuse to heed that no known suicide has ever
relied on fate or fortune to kill him, but must needs have taken his own
life according to plan by the ways and means he has himself devised
and implemented. They ignore the event that survival is an ongoing struggle against both fate and fortune, that it has no guarantees, that its means
and ends commingle, and that it requires of the struggler resistance to
natural necessity and divine providence, perhaps even more than reliance
on them. Resistance and reliance, when and how and with what to direct
them, are equally choices, and are either blind risks, or reasoned, cal-
culated ones. Such risks are the primal subject matter of the social sciences, and their statistical averages and "laws" are but their composites

or summations. Let those choices change, and change in the "laws" will also occur.

Thus, neither the survival nor the extinction of the American Jewish community follows inevitably from the nature of things or the will of God. Nor does it follow inevitably from the community's own will to survive or perish. But that will is a necessary precondition, whereas the others are contingent. On the record, man's arts and sciences are his achievements in altering the nature of things; his religions, with their prayers and sacrifices, their confessions and vows, and all their other rites and ceremonies, are his methods of influencing the will of God. The human enterprise is the knowledgeable determination to harness fate and fortune to the service of human living, either unto life more abundant or unto death. Jewish living is one unit of this ongoing determination, with its own singular compenetrations of works and ways. Where this determination holds, it can invoke "research" to explore the matter, means, and methods best suited to living on and growing, or to dying out. Jewish living *in toto* will consist in using those for both ends or choosing them for either.

The question *Can Judaism Survive?* was, and continues, an inquiry into matter, means, and methods. Most answers to it seem to me to have been devised either as special pleas for, or as rationalizations of, some one Judaist interest abstracted from the aggregation of diversified ones which together give the words "Jewish" and "Jew" their concrete meanings. Occasionally, findings appear which derive from an objective conspectus of the aggregation.

Within the past year, there has come to my attention one such conspectus which seems to me of prime importance. It is called *Agenda for American Jews.* Its author is Eli Ginzberg, a Jewish intellectual of the younger generation, who, continuing integrally a Jew, has orchestrated his cultural heritage of Jewishness with his occupational interests as an economic scientist of unusual eminence in his chosen field. Reading his *Agenda* was a heartening experience to a mind confirmed in its disillusions by more than a quarter of a century of disappointing scientific observations and organizational effort. While I find myself doubtful of Professor Ginzberg's hierarchy of values in American Jewish living, I find myself giving ready assent to his appraisals of its leaderships, its matters, its means, and its methods; to the techniques of inquiry wherewith he comes to his judgments, and to his suggestions how Jewish living in our country might be brought to greater excellence and abundance.

In the twenty-five years since the publication of *Can Judaism Survive in the United States?*, the problems and prospects there called attention to have reached a critical poignancy. English has become basic to the vernacular of the American Jewish community. Secularization has moved apace and brought new institutions and functions. The rabbinate has itself secularized, and Zionist and other secular organizations draw leaders from its members. The number and variety of Jews by profession, clerical and secular, has increased, and with them the alienation of Judaism from the Jewish generality, who in many ways pay more for its upkeep but care less, leaving decisions regarding the collection and disbursement of funds, and the ends for which they are disbursed, to fewer and fewer people, mostly professional Jews who care less and less about Jewish living as a whole. And so on. When read in the context of the global crises of which World War I was the first, Eli Ginzberg's *Agenda* makes me feel, *plus ça change, plus c'est la même chose.*

I feel the same regarding what must needs be done to redirect and repattern this change-without-alternation, to turn it into a truly *different* process. It is to educate and reeducate. As I have reiterated so often, survival is education, education is survival; and Eli Ginzberg's *Agenda* brings another, and a very significant, confirmation of this truism. The first and last condition of Jewish living is Jewish education, but education with its entire economy of plant, program, and personnel so reorganized as to enable the growing child and grown adult to acept the realities of the Jewish condition "in good cheer and without illusion," to enable him to live positively and freely as Jew, "vindicating the integrity of his Jewish being according to the democratic rule of equal liberty for all men, proclaiming that liberty 'to all the land all the inhabitants thereof.' "

That is, if the Jewish education of American Jews is to succeed in preserving Jewish living, it would need to be transformed from indoctrination in a Judaism only, confined to religious schools and ending for non-professional Jews at *Bar Mitzvah*. It would need to be shaped as an inquiry into the values of the entire Jewish cultural heritage, and as such extended to the secular educational establishments. It would need everywhere to be fused with the humanities of the liberal education. It would need to convert the records of the Jewish past from inert remembrances to contemplate into living roots of future growth owning a dynamic relevancy to the dangers, the problems, and the tasks wherewith the changes and chances of the time confront the Jewish present.

In this way, it might convert the centrifugal trends of contemporary Jewish living into an expanding spiral process in which a cultural enclave and its leaders endeavor, with some success, to realize, *e pluribus unum,* the democratic idea in American Jewishness.

But who will risk the hazards from such a revolution in Jewish education to the *status quo* of Jewish living?

(1952)

VI
Languages and Literatures

H. LEIVICK

Leivick Halpern, the poet and dramatist, deeply impressed his generation not only with his great artistic gifts, with his unique, original Yiddish poetry, but also with his committed, ethical personality, which reacted to every injustice perpetrated either by the radical "left" or by the reactionary "right."

Leivick Halpern, who assumed the pen-name H. Leivick, was born in 1888 to a poor family in Ihumen, province of Minsk, White Russia, where he studied to become a rabbi, and later joined the Bund, a Jewish socialist organization. In 1906 he was arrested and imprisoned for four years, then was banished to Siberia for life. At the end of 1913 he escaped and reached New York, where he resided until his death in 1962.

Leivick's cycle of Siberian poems established his reputation as one of the greatest representatives of modern Yiddish poetry. His poetic drama *Der Golem,* based on the medieval legend of the Maharal (1525–1609) and his Golem, aroused a tremendous furor in Jewish communities throughout the world. Leivick was a prolific artist who produced—in addition to his poetry—many plays and essays.

Redemption, the poignant enigmas of human existence, the individual's tragic dichotomies and dilemmas, constitute the leitmotifs of Leivick's poetry. He is the poet of our conscience, which cannot acquiesce in the absurdity of the soul's and body's torments, but feels that there is meaning to human suffering.

YIDDISH LITERATURE:
GUARDIAN OF OUR PEOPLE'S WHOLENESS

Our Yiddish literature gives the Jewish writer and the Jewish reader a feeling, when it seems to him that he has aroused the interest of only ten Jews, an experience, that he is writing for the whole people, which is scattered throughout the world. The same feeling is also experienced by the Hebrew writer. By no means can this be said about the Jewish writer who writes in a non-Jewish language, even when he writes on Jewish themes. The latter feels that he is writing for a group of Jews, not for the people; the former, wherever they are, are always in the spiritual homelike atmosphere of the people; they carry with them the homelike atmosphere no matter where they are.

I am beginning with such a simple, elementary formulation, and I am intentionally avoiding philosophical complexities. We are today in the position of a hungry person who knows very well that his hunger can be quenched first of all by plain bread.

About Yiddish and Yiddish literature we even wrote numerous songs, and songs are not written about a language and literature unless you revere them, and you are on the alert because of the danger that lurks over them. Our vigilance is the result of our love for our people, which has, with the help of Yiddish, undergone dire epochs. And when we bear in mind our last horrible epoch—the gas-chamber epoch—we may say justly that Yiddish and Yiddish literature have, together with other vigilant efforts, remained on the high level of their calling to guard the creative impulse of our people's wholeness. The more bloody pieces that were wrested from this wholeness, the more distressingly did we caress and sanctify the wounded Jewish body.

Yiddish literature sprung from the depths of our people, from its everyday and historical tragedy, from the people's will to live and to struggle for its life; this literature is today, more than ever, bound up with its entire being to our people's exploded roots. The roots are so blasted that we can literally see the internal bleeding veins.

Suffice it to think about the stirring reticence of the Jewish writers who themselves lay under Hitler's bloody sword and had to be silent. Only under the bloody sword did Jewish poets sense their vocation and their sacred mission, and their Jewish song ascended from the pent-up silence in the bunkers, from the concentration camps, and later from the anxieties of the remnants of the survivors. Some of them are sitting here today with us in this hall, here in New York—it is not a trifling matter in such a time to see them right here near us—may they be blessed! What was their lucky sign, the light of their lucky star? It was their dedication to the sacred mission of being Jewish writers. With the sounds of their language upon their lips, millions of martyrs went to their death.

Yiddish literature has thereby solemnly concluded an eternal covenant also with the millions of those who perished, and they, too, became a part of our people's wholeness.

Suffice it to think about Yiddish literature in most countries outside the Hitler crematorium; how it, not being able to come to their aid, has by auto-suggestion gotten to the depths of despair, and guilty conscience, in order to express in some way its solidarity with those who were gassed and burned. It is sufficient to reflect upon this in order to sense the Love of Israel that today permeates Yiddish literature, a love that, to our great sorrow, most American Jews pass by, they pass by with boorish and clogged-up hearts.

What is the real essence of the wholeness idea about which I am speaking? It is the thought and the feeling that our people, which is scattered throughout the world, is one fateful body which could not and would not permit itself to be torn apart. The meaning of our people's existence, its historic personality, its Messianic and redemption-idea— whether it is personified as today in the wonderful rise of Israel in Tel Aviv, or it is expressed in the countries of the world in a martyrdom- acquiescence to suffer for being a Jew—this meaning cannot be compre- hended without the idea of an absolute Jewish wholeness. No part of our people, wherever it may reside and no matter how strong its desire to incorporate itself into a non-Jewish social system, culture, or language— it must not cease to be concerned as to how good or bad its incorpora- tion will affect our people's organism as a whole. Its concern cannot be manifested except through a true, brotherly, free contact, through a full national cooperation with the whole body of our people by being a full partner in its ubiquitous destiny, in its indivisible culture and litera- ture. If it does not do it, it causes a rupture in the living folk-organism, a wound. The wound must affect the part. And the part inevitably will thus begin to wither and shrivel.

This wholeness idea was, in previous generations, supported absolutely by the Jewish religious organization. In contemporary generations the religious exclusiveness has, among most of our people, been transformed into a secular one. Secular culture and literature, both in Yiddish and Hebrew, have become the more active and energetic transmitters of the wholeness-idea. They emerged from it.

In this respect—and this is the most important aspect—Yiddish and Hebrew were not, and need not be, and I hope will not be, in belligerent opposition to each other. They are historically mated. Both of them are deeply anchored, and for the good, in our history, and in our traditional symbolism. The more the better!—This is by the way.

Whether literature has a mission or not is but hair-splitting. Nothing lives in our world without a mission. Yiddish literature surely emerged as a result of a summoned mission. And the mission was: the previous historic-spiritual forces of our people are being weakened, the people's wholeness is being weakened, the people's wholeness is in danger—now, you new force, come and become one of the protectors and strengtheners of our people's organism.

I need not tell you how painfully traumatic, but also how wonderful, was the path of Yiddish literature. You know it well yourselves, and I think that you know well how poignantly our literature came close today to the point of tragedy. Its tragedy is the tragedy of our people, which today faces one of the greatest tests in its history: either to be antagonistically torn in three separate parts—*Eretz Yisroel,* America, and Soviet Russia—or exert all our efforts in order to strengthen more the spiritual wholeness of our people by a truly honest, free, mutually national .partnership.

Now arises an inevitable voice saying thus: Why torture yourself with a dream about Yiddish literature, which should be one of the chief transmitters of the people's wholeness? Are you blind to what is going on around you? In America Yiddish is experiencing the acutest crisis. There is no new generation of continuity for it. Yiddish is dropping out of the mouths of most American Jews. Yiddish and Yiddish literature are poised in a vacuum without a Jewish way of life, without a traditional home. In *Eretz Yisroel* life is being built on the foundation of Hebrew, and in Soviet Russia—there Yiddish literature is altogether severed from us. And it is not a question only of literature. The entire unique Jewish set of problems, and the very thought of our own Jewish configuration and fatefulness, of a literature whose foundation should be an all-Jewish intimate partnership, all of this is not being accepted by the Soviet Russian Jewish writers. How then can you think about wholeness?

This voice I hear more than once within me, and around me, so that I do not intend to run away from it, or muffle it with a false, hackneyed optimism. Not only do I not try to run away from it, but more than that: I allow that voice to ascend to the last degree of allurement, until either-or, to the last brink of the precipice. There is a feeling within me, sustained by Jewish historical experience, that when a Jewish era reaches the last test, when the juncture of life or death is reached, a new Jewish spiritual exaltation or a sinking into a catastrophic decline of assimilation—then the former wins and vanquishes all obstructions. The question is only, When do we discern the moment that we are facing the last national test? When does it become evident for each part of our people throughout the world? Yes, for each one of them!

In the light of all that, how can we speak about wholeness among ourselves in order to reach national spiritual harmony. Both our literatures must move toward harmony, they must make common cause. If not—then both of them are facing danger. The same goes for the relationship between Israel and the Diaspora. The least move of Israel toward negating the Diaspora, toward disparagement or nonrecognition of the national significance of Yiddish today, when with Yiddish millons of Jews went to *Kiddush Hashem* [martyrdom] will be catastrophic for Israel. Similarly, it should be emphasized: if Yiddish and Yiddish literature will not turn their faces and full hearts to the greatest event in our history during the last two thousand years—to the rise of Israel. The least turn today of Yiddish toward sectarian obstinacy, or to slick abstractions, or to empty cosmopolitanism, as, for instance, standing, God forbid, with its back to Israel, and with its face to Israel's enemies—or even to being neutral to Israel—such an attitude would be catastrophic for Yiddish and Yiddish literature.

In this respect I have a feeling that we will attain the desired harmony. Yiddish literature will embrace the Israel event wholeheartedly. It will become permeated with the revelation of the socialist Pioneer-Jew, the tiller of deserts; the Haganah fighter, the protector of Israel—as it was permeated with the revelation of the Hirsh Lekert Jew,[1] the Hasidic Jew, the Ghetto Uprising Jew.

But in order to be wholesome and in full harmony with it too, our literature must arouse a new culture-energy everywhere, wherever Jews live, especially here in America: to awaken an interest in fashioning again an ethnic way of life, to inspire a new, full, all-embracing Jewish education, to awaken an interest in a reconstruction of our Jewish home life— especially in a united school system, in Jewish day schools and higher Jewish educational institutions. If we do not achieve a united Jewish school system, then we will not have achieved anything.

How should this be done? Are we not standing in America at the brink of a cultural abyss? Does not our literature here live in a state of desolation, of forsakenness? Is not the fact tragic for us that the great Jewish settlement in Soviet Russia has no Jewish elementary schools, not even one daily Jewish newspaper? Does not the fact hit us in the face that the Jewish labor movement, the Jewish unions, Jewish socialism, no less than the middle class, have all iniquitously deserted Yiddish, Yiddish literature, and the Jewish way of life?

Yes, surely it hits us, and therefore, because it hits us we came here, we have called this conference. Not in order to play around with empty optimism, not just to convene and then to go home. We came here in order to drink publicly, together the poignancy of the truth, of our cultural life, to give ourselves an accounting and to be shaken by this accounting. We came here to demand from ourselves Jewish cultural reconstruction, life-reconstruction, people-reconstruction; and from our literature we demand that it should today more than ever more fully and profoundly grasp its role—its mission. Our people is experiencing today both its most tragic and its most restorative era. On one shoulder death still openly lies, while on its other shoulder it is carrying the tablets of life. We are demanding from each Jewish writer wherever he is, whether in Soviet Russia, Europe, Israel, or America: Accomplish your mission to make complete and to preserve wholly the broken body, and the broken, tortured heart of our people.

(1948)

NOTE

1. Hirsh Lekert (1879–1902), Jewish revolutionary in Russia. A member of the Bund, he was executed for shooting the governor of the Vilna Province, who had been responsible for the manhandling of Jewish workers. Lekert's courageous bearing in his last days made a deep impression on the contemporary Jewish labor movement, and he was the hero of several dramas, including one by Leivick.

NOKHEM SHTIF

Nokhem Shtif, also known by the pseudonym Baal Dimyon, was a noted Yiddish critic and philologist, a fervent protagonist of Yiddish culture, and a founder of YIVO in Vilna, Poland.

Shtif was born in Rovno, Volhynia, in 1879, and died in Kiev in 1933. He received a thorough grounding in Hebrew, knew the Bible by heart, read Hebrew literature, and studied the Talmud. He graduated from the Rovno Realschule, and was admitted to a college, in 1899, in Kiev. Here he joined the Zionist organization. After the Kishinev pogrom, in 1903, he helped organize the Jewish self-defense. Later he participated in the conference that organized the Seymists—the Jewish Socialist Labor party. In 1904, after he had been expelled from college, he fled to Switzerland, where he stayed a year. In Bern, in 1905, Yiddish made an enduring impression on him thanks to Sh. Ansky (the author of *The Dybbuk*), and to the traces of Yiddish propaganda which Zhitlowsky had left in Switzerland. Shtif became an ardent Yiddishist, and began to propagandize Yiddishism. He returned to Russia, "settling" in Petersburg, where he lived from writing.

In 1920 Shtif wrote the study *Humanism in Early Yiddish Literature*— an excerpt of which is included in this anthology—showing, in his own words, the dominant ideas of that literature: "humanism, the desire to fraternize with the world and its culture, matter versus spirit, humanity versus Judaism, a program of social, and cultural reform, knowledge versus mind, speculation, productive work versus idleness."

In the last phase of his life Shtif accepted the Yiddish chair of the Kiev State Academy in the U.S.S.R.

HUMANISM IN
EARLY YIDDISH LITERATURE

The Positive Program

Early Yiddish literature was forced to undertake a great deal of destructive work until it reached its full fervor, its *positive program;* it was not so easy and smooth a process, to clear away the great garbage can, to cleanse minds of the mountains of mold and dust that had accumulated over hundreds of years. In many cases—and, as it happens, in the finer ones from a literary point of view—this program was actually attained indirectly by way of destruction; the bleak Jewish environment was automatically to open one's eyes to what is more beautiful and better. The positive program of early Yiddish literature (for it was a programmatic literature!) consists of the Haskalah ideals: *education* and *productive work* (handicraft, agriculture). At the present time we have more than enough "college" and self-educated people, and even more adult-education students, and the people are rushing with tremendous momentum to the source of knowledge; at the present time it is difficult to comprehend that great enthusiasm for education, and one can even afford to be ironical about "small-town" Maskilim[1] who reveled in Schiller's *Glocke*[2] and recited it somewhat like a kind of *Pardes.*[3] However, at that time it was not merely new, innovative, and venturesome in the devoutly fanatic environment which considered all extraneous knowledge which was not derived from the Jewish way of life as wantonness and heresy, or at best as distraction from the Torah. This was a *revolution,* a profound upheaval whose significance in Jewish life can by no means be overestimated. A person of our generation can get an idea of it when he recalls the first period of socialist revolutionary propaganda in a Jewish town: the same enthusiasm, the same brightness in one's heart, the same enamoredness, brotherhood between "comrades," the same secrecy, the same piercing, suspicious glances, the curiosity, fear, and hatred in the surrounding environment.

And the most remarkable feature of this educational enthusiasm is its profound *humanity* in regard to the idea and the sober *positiveness* in practice. In an environment which was immersed in one's own values,

277

having blind faith in itself and isolated from the entire world, writers who themselves were also mostly isolated from the world, except as far as the book was concerned, began to exalt and glorify what was human, universal, to idealize a civilized, strange world, to call on people to enter the great world, the world outside, to divest oneself from what belonged to oneself and to merge with all of mankind. Even the language, the only weapon in their struggle, their own writer's tool, even this they did not spare: the language of the country, foreign languages should become our own languages; there is no need for any barrier between Jews and the world, between man and man. From this, from their profound commitment and enthusiasm for an enlightened, free world, originates their coldness to the Yiddish language, which they themselves honed and polished, to Yiddish literature, whose foundation they had laid. And not on account of "petit bourgeois" views, as a Marxist quibble recently deduced.

And at the same time, what sober positiveness! It was not a question of "Enlightenment, daughter of heaven," of florid language and speculation but of actual human knowledge; about natural science, mathematics, languages, about a knowledge in general which should be the basis for a *realistic* world-view, for a person who proceeds consciously and armed to conquer a world, to build a more beautiful, better life. Whether we felt here the effect of Russian literature in the 1860s, when we had among us Uri Kovner,[4] a pupil of Pisarev,[5] or here their own thirst for actual knowledge, a reaction against our eternal speculations came to the fore— no matter which, it is the result which is important! And the practical result is that this actual knowledge corresponded best with the basic idea of humanity, with that which could cure us best of spirituality, straighten the mind and unite us with the world. Not in vain did that generation give birth to famous mathematicians, medical men, philologists, and but a few philosophers. Incidentally, this was the best method to break the wild Jewish arrogance: the theorist had to have respect for the doctor, for the engineer: one could not accomplish their work with a verse from a sacred book or a quibble.

Best of all, the positive and, incidentally, the progressive, element in their program appeared in their views on the Jewish *material* situation, in their striving to reform the Jewish economy. They were too sober and far-sighted to be persuaded that everything, even the Jewish spiritual way of life, could be changed by education and book knowledge. "Jews, alas, need bread, not sacred books," the enlightened author says in Mendele's *Dos Vintshfingerl* ["The Magic Ring"].[6] They saw with a clear eye how far the backward Jewish economic situation: saloon-keeping, storekeeping on a very small scale, unsubstantial occupations, and, even more, idleness, has an influence on Jewish spiritual and social life, on its political position in the country, and yearned that Jews should have *bread* together with a modern book, and with a new spiritual way of life. We already see it in Isaac Ber Levinsohn in *Hefker-Velt.*[7] "Who has here a stable occupation—he complains, and, therefore, they are put to shame among the gentile nations worse than the gypsies." With the same courage and frankness that assaulted Jewish spirituality an attack was made on Jewish occupations and even more on Jewish idleness. Jews have not heard such sharp words, perhaps, from their most truculent enemies as they had occasion to hear from Jewish writers.

Those who were put to shame were not merely matchmakers, teachers of children in a *cheder,* brokers, traveling agents, Jews with the writings of a fire-victim, with his great-grandfather's treatise under his arm, the whole band of beggars who languished and withered all their lives and died in someone else's shrouds, but Jewish shopkeepers and businessmen as well. And in an environment which was full of respect for the clergy, for the learned Jew, the idler, where the "aristocrat," the *cheder* teacher, could not make up his mind to give a child a name after a deceased relative who was a craftsman, and a Jew who was a merchant had the most respectable occupation, in such an environment they began to revile Jewish cultural connoisseurs, trade was treated as bankruptcy, as a swindle and deception; and the craftsman, the ignoramus, was exalted. Something like a moral protest, as in a doctrine by Tolstoy, lay primarily in hating beautiful, easy occupations, everything that does not smell of the perspiration of work, and touching is the idealization of callused hands. Toil, lending a hand to things, here suddenly became elevated to a high degree, and agriculture, "Ivan"—i.e., what was lowest and most humble according to Jewish ideas—became an ideal. This is, as was said, primarily a moral category, "a piece of bread that is not kneaded from a stranger's perspiration," the "honest penny."[8] But in addition a healthy economic understanding is involved here. The progressive economic process, which clearly revealed itself in Russia in the sixties of the nineteenth century; the spoiled nobility around whom Jews revolved in the "Pale," *falls,* the end of a nature economy, industry grows in the land, the rosy process had to lead to the decline of old Jewish occupations, and a large part of the middle class should have to have recourse to work. Early Yiddish literature, with its new ideas about work sanctioned, welcomed this process of transition internally, and by this facilitated it psychologically in a certain measure. At the same time it exalted the workingman with his instinctive sense; he, the ignoramus and lowly person, is capable of elevating the whole of folk-life because it still possesses a little muscle, and blood, and is not so otherworldly, he is still capable of earning, and can still gain from the new way of life, he has nothing to lose.

Handicraft, work—this is the prose and agriculture, the "plow"—this is the poetry, the romantic aspect. For one had to possess a little imagination and dream to wish to make of Jews—village peasants in Levinsohn's times and later also, when one considers the Jewish estrangement from the soil and work and in consideration of the external obstacles: from the beloved Russian government. This was the way that was to lead to the furthest end: to reconstruct the whole of Jewish life on "normal" foundations, on *human* foundations, the older Jewish writers thought, as was the case with all peoples in the land.

Because the closest, the most precious thing for them was what was human and communal and traditionally Jewish, the "national," as many would have said today, was strange to them. The idea of isolating oneself, of setting oneself apart, was odious to them, and therefore national romanticism, the later "Love of Zion," could not play the slightest role in their soil-romanticism. In the worst times of Jewish political depression, they walked around with their heads held high; not to yield, not to run away: our time will come! For their faith in man and humanity was profound and strong.

A Generation

For hundreds of years the people lay in a deep stupor. The bullying of the Polish gentry turned Jews into "Moshkes" and "Itshe Meyers,"[9] into saloonkeepers and impractical persons, economically enslaved and spiritually humiliated. Terrible Cossack pogroms (the massacres of 1648 and 1768)[10] destroyed hundreds of Jewish communities. Under the effect of the most disgraceful medieval pain and mockery, the people shrunk into itself, snuggled in like a sick child, lulled itself to sleep in heavenly matters, in mystic dreams, became enthusiastic for false Messiahs, for a Sabbataï Zevi,[11] a Jacob Frank,[12] and became extinguished, dead to the world. And then there arose a generation as though newly born, fresh and enthusiastic, with an awakened thirst for life and a belief in its own powers, that it is competent to redeem the people. Only a generation before one could merely despair in the people, and a Lithuanian young man, Solomon Maimon,[13] educated like Dick's "Khaytsikl Aleyn" [14] who lived to see the Mezritsh Magid,[15] ran away on foot from the foul-smelling corner to Berlin, to the fortress of enlightened absolutism, and tasting there of the "Tree of Knowledge," never returned to his people. Now things began to stir. At the cradle of the new age stood the French Revolution, German romanticism, the politically aroused Jewry in Europe, reform by force and one's own word of enlightenment there. And the first stirring of the new generation was: to the bright light! To human beings! Inside are mold and chains, there outside are sun and freedom. A feverish critical work began to destroy all old foundations of Jewish life, to review all consciences. This was the sharpest, most merciless self-criticism, one of the rare minutes when a whole generation flares up with a heroic feeling to make a spiritual stock-taking, to uncover the ugliest wounds, in order to seek a remedy for them, when the conscience becomes aroused to responsibility, and generations and people behold before them a distant, bright purpose and feel strong and great enough to clear mountains from their path.

The responsibility itself here increased in terrible proportions, as seldom happens, when one blames oneself that one is not so tall as Og, the king of Bashan,[16] and does not live forever. One had to liquidate the accursed heritage of the regime of the Polish gentry amid the worst circumstances: amid a regime of Cossack absolutism, in an environment of slavery and savagery, in a land of peasants that had only begun to extricate itself from a nature economy, which such culture as existed was to be found among the nobility, liberalism lay in its swaddling clothes, reveled in German romanticism and Hegelian philosophy, and the Jew was a stranger and despised. One's heart ached at the sight of Jewish anguish and humiliation, the lowly position in the surrounding environment; and it was a great temptation to find justification for the sorely tried people, to cast the great stone for Jewish shame at the heads of their pursuers and tormentors, those who locked up the depressed people in the darkest, wet cellar-hole in the large prison for all. Once such a cry burst forth, and we heard the angry protest against the injustice of the world that is being committed against the Jewish people (the *Nag*).[17] Always, however, and everywhere and at every opportunity, Jewish shame and anguish were turned against Jews themselves. We alone and no one else are the guilty ones! And our greatest sin is that we have separated ourselves from a world, and excluded ourselves from the human community, rocked ourselves to sleep in desolate, wild dreams. People began to demolish the old structure of Judaism, which obstructed a world for us. With a wonderful self-sacrifice these most devoted people of the masses revenged themselves on their own people, spat poison and gall at all Jewish life, tore down all accepted foundations of the people's life. We have already seen how they accomplished this.

Did not something exist in Jewish life that deserved to be esteemed and spared. Certainly! A time will come when the passé dispute will put an end to anger, and they, the grim revilers, will discern in the puddle "Precious sprinkles of gold, such bright sparks of fire, which one does not obtain in the great boiling seas";[18] Linetsky will recall with affection Shakhne Upir, a spring of humanity and mercy, who does not have the means to subsist for a day and yet he offers kindness and help wherever a misfortune occurs; and Mendele will describe with enthusiasm the prince, the Sabbath Jew, the profound humanity and honesty of quiet people, who are scarcely seen and heard and they live only for the sake of others. All this will come later, when it will be possible to approach Jewish life with a calm heart and an objective eye. Meanwhile, however, it is one's duty to destroy, this is the demand of the time! And Jewish writers did this with knowledge and conscience, with temperament and talent. They accomplished their goal. Later, in the second critical epoch, in the eighties, the new moon of the great national and social movement, which still exerts influence on our generation, the Jewish *masses proved* that they had outgrown spiritual Jewishness and old-fashioned benefactors, they had found their leaders. Somewhere in Petersburg sat the Jewish elite and clergy, strongly absorbed in ways to assuage the sullen nobleman, and the Jewish mass sought in emigration, in national and social organizations, new ways for its political and economic liberation and human redemption. The old community providers were, as it were, washed away together with their methods, and young students, without a sign of a beard, without half an ounce of Jewishness, possessing only a little human knowledge and education, and a heart full of human ideals and dreams, occupied the top positions and won the confidence of the people.

A remarkable fate of a literature: it wanted and had to be *more* than literature! It stood before a Chinese wall. It itself was shady [*tref*], wild, and strange, and it was supposed to be the iron ram, the breaker of walls, an elevator of the whole of Jewish life. At the present time, when we have widespread political journalism, it carries out the largest part of the rough programmatic work, which often has very little of the aesthetic about it, and literature can indulge in purely aesthetic pleasure. What our older literature accomplished with programmatic methods, with satire and exhortation, this our modern literature actually accomplishes as well, but in a different manner; not with the pointer, but with images and emotions. Without deliberate intention it develops taste in the people and, as a matter of course, understanding for what is human and eternal, it connects us with a world. At that older time, however, literature could not afford white gloves, and the Jewish artist often had to have recourse to the school-teacher's pointer. For previously an atmosphere had to be created for literature among the Jewish people, a thing we already found ready and finished in our time. Yiddish literature had to be artistry here and political journalism, the pulpit and romanticism, an *entire culture* in images, since this was the only secular and modern element we possessed in Yiddish. And if we can come at the present time to the Torah people with a "storybook" and find readers and appreciators for it—it is early Yiddish literature to which the greatest credit here is due.

It was not a traditionally Jewish literature but an anti-traditionally Jewish one, something quite illegitimate. After all, we should remember that we owe the very idea "traditionally Jewish," the outstanding Jewish charm inhering in it, to none other than Mendele, the "most traditionally Jewish" writer of that group. A contemporary nationalist would have called it an "anti-national" literature: it caused us to hate everything that is redolent of Yiddish things, of what is our own, and drove us to "guard strange vineyards," to foreign cultures and languages, customs and ways. We know, however, that this was the greatest national merit in which a literature can pride itself before a people! For the road to oneself lay then *through the outside world.* In order to become a more modern people, to assume a human appearance, we had to go to school with the outside world. In the nationalist cliché, Haskalah and Haskalah literature had long borne the bad reputation of assimilation, and assimilation has for that reason, perforce, meant every possible evil, and according to Maskilic-Marxist interpretation, been strongly bourgeois. We know, however, that that was our *Reformation,* the most profound and most honest one, which redeemed us from our domestic slavery, and from the confinement of spiritual Jewishness. May this assimilation that opened our eyes be blessed. Without it we would not have found the way to ourselves. And not merely the work of demolition, but the positive program as well. For the most important element in this program is that it has not lost its value and significance to the present day. For we again became brimful of Jewishness, but in a new "national" transformation. The national cliché rants and deafens the minds, lulls in us the awakened feeling for man and the world. The cliché extends much more widely and more densely than among the official national standard-bearers; there does not exist even the furthest revolutionary thought to which the national cliché has not adhered, and which has not made it its servile partisan. It poisons us, stuffs us again with self-love, makes an ideal of every bit of what belongs to oneself, from a ribbon to a booklet, from an informal club and a little song, and deafens in us the critical feeling and the feeling for self-criticism. Let, then, the assimilationist early Yiddish literature serve as a faithful guard and admonisher, and preserve us from self-falsification.

(Kiev, December 1919)

NOTES

1. Adherents of the Jewish Enlightenment, or Haskalah movement.

2. A famous poem written in 1799 by the German writer Friedrich Schiller (1759–1805). It presents symbolically, through the casting of a bell, the various stages of human life, proclaiming the ideals of peace and cooperation.

3. *Pardes:* mnemonic word formed by the initials of four main streams of biblical interpretation current in the thirteenth century, viz., *peshat* (literal meaning), *remez* (allegorical—often philosophical), *derash* (Aggadic), and *sod* (mystical).

4. Uri Kovner (1842–1909), Hebrew and Russian author who criticized Haskalah literature for its remoteness from everyday life.

5. Dmitry Ivanovich Pisarev (1840–68) was the leader of the Russian new radicals who called themselves "thinking realists" or "nihilists." He rejected all art except "art with a purpose."

6. A novel whose first version appeared in 1865 as a small volume, and later, from 1888–1889, was expanded into the large two-volume book by the same name.

7. Isaac Ber Levinson (1788–1860) was often called the Mendelssohn of Russia because of his pioneering efforts in behalf of the Jewish Enlightenment in the Czarist period. Levinson's satiric drama *The Lawless World (Die Hefker-Velt)* was a significant Yiddish literary achievement.

8. (Moshe Aaron) Shatskes (1825–99), *The Jewish Passover Eve* (Warsaw, 1881). Shatskes's book describes with humor and irony the troubles the Jews— particularly the men—have to endure in the four weeks between Purim and Passover.

9. Terms of contempt for Jews in Poland.

10. Cossack massacres of Jews perpetrated under the leadership of the chieftain Bogdan Chmielnicki (1593[?]–1657).

11. Sabbatai Zevi (1626–1676), famous pseudo-Messiah, creator of a large movement which convulsed Jewry.

12. Jacob Frank (1726–91), pseudo-Messiah, creator of the Frankist sect and movement.

13. Solomon Maimon (b. 1753 in Lithuania, d. 1800 in Germany), philosopher and Maskil, a friend of Moses Mendelssohn. He is famous for his autobiography.

14. Isaac Meir Dick (1807–93), a Maskil who was born and died in Vilna. He was a Hebrew scholar who became a popular Yiddish writer. *Khaytsikl Aleyn* ("Khaytsikl Alone"), 1864, is one of his classic tales, written in the style of the old-fashioned Yiddish books of edification.

286286FAITH OF SECULAR JEWS

15. Rabbi R'ber (1710–72), one of the famous Hasidic Rebbes after the Baal Shem Tov, also known as the "great Magid" (preacher) of Mezritsh.

16. A very tall king, against whom the Israelites went to war in the desert, and who was defeated by them.

17. A novel by Mendele Mokher Sforim, one of his most effective satires, written in 1873, which is an allegory of the history of the Jewish people as the world's scapegoat.

18. I. I. Linetsky (1839–1915) Yiddish novelist; *Der Vorm in Khreyn* (lit.: "The Worm in the Horse Radish"). His most popular work was his picaresque novel *The Polish Lad* (*Dos Polishe Yingel*), 1867, which was based on his own life and the persecutions he had experienced at the hands of the Hasidim.

MAURICE SAMUEL

Maurice Samuel was a Jewish scholar and writer who thought and wrote in English but was at the same time embedded in Yiddish and Hebrew literature; a life-long Zionist and an affirmer—not a negator—of the Diaspora; an American novelist and essayist, and the ambassador of Yiddish culture to the Americanized Jews.

Samuel was born in Romania in 1895, and was brought to England at the age of five. He studied at Manchester University, where Chaim Weizmann became one of his teachers and friends. In 1914 Samuel migrated to the United States, and after America entered the First World War, he served in the army in France.

At the end of the Versailles Peace Conference Samuel went to Poland, where he familiarized himself with the intellectual currents in Jewish secular and religious life, and with the flourishing Yiddish literature which Polish Jewry was then producing.

Samuel published twenty-five books. In addition, he translated a number of books from Yiddish and Hebrew. As a linguist with a sensitive ear for the peculiarities of each tongue, Samuel knew that language is not only a means of communication, but is also the reservoir of a people's experience, ethos, joys, and sorrows. That is why two of his enduring books are on the Yiddish classical writers Sholem Aleichem and Y.L. Peretz. *The World of Sholem Aleichem,* which appeared in 1943, was awarded a prize by the city of New York; *The Prince of the Ghetto* (on Y.L. Peretz), which was published in 1948, won the acclaim of American as well as Yiddish critics.

To the end of his life in 1972, Samuel remained a balanced Jewish humanist who saw gleams of light in the non-Jewish world, particularly among the Anglo-Saxons. He believed that being Jewish-centered, one is also world-centered. "My people is my instrument for cooperating with mankind, my channel to humanity. . . . Love of humanity, when not implemented by love of a people, is usually gushy and diffused sentimentalism."

287

MY THREE MOTHER-TONGUES

How fortunate and fitting it is that I should have been born myself
and not somebody else, and therefore that I was born into the Jewish
people. How fortunate and how fitting, also, that I was born into the
English language and did not have to read Shakespeare and Gibbon in
a foreign language, or, God forbid, in translation. I would have it that
English is peculiarly suited to me, it fits me so neatly and so intimately,
I could not, as I am a Jew, have done without it. ("Praise God," said the
monk, "for that he did cause rivers to flow through great cities!")

Shakespeare and Gibbon have held before me the standards of the
English language as an art. Shakespeare is as precious to me as a personal
teacher, and I hold with Samuel Johnson that he is greater in the comedies
than in the tragedies.

A fascinating and instructive pastime would be a treatise comparing
Shakespeare with Gibbon, the *Histories* with the *Decline and Fall,* the
one taking in all of life for its own sake, the other, the doctrinaire, seeing
in all of life a thesis; "I have described the triumph of barbarism and religion." Can't you just imagine the fat little man passing a church with
averted gaze and muttering, like an old-time fanatical Jew, "Shakets
teshaktsenu vesaav tesavenu . . . let it be abominated and let it be deso-
lated, for it is anathema," after which you turn in your thoughts to
Shakespeare taking his ease between rehearsals at the Mermaid Inn.
I have had many a good inward laugh on the subject, and a rush
of quotations, but I must hurry on, for an even more important subject
has been waiting, suppressed, since the first paragraph of this chapter.

Which speaks to me more intimately, the Bible in Hebrew, with which
I am long familiar, or the English King James Version? I read, "Ubavel
tsvi mamlakhot tiferet geon kazdim—and Babylon, the glory of king-
doms, the beauty of the Chaldees" excellency, shall be as when God over-
threw Sodom and Gemorrah. It shall never be inhabited, neither shall it
be dwelt in from generation to generation; neither shall the Arabian pitch
tent there; neither shall the shepherds make their fold there. But wild
beasts of the desert shall lie there; and their houses shall be full of doleful

creatures; and owls shall dwell there, and satyrs shall dance there. And the wild beasts of the islands shall cry in their desolate houses and dragons in their pleasant palaces: and her time is near to come, and her days shall not be prolonged." Then I read the English and the Hebrew alternately, as I have done countless times these many years and I wonder, am I nearer to the Prophets in the Hebrew or in the English? Does not the Hebrew—ubavel tsvi mamlakhot—ring for me with the grandeur of Elizabethan England and the religious passion of the Protestant England of that time? How can I fix the tonality of the original Hebrew as it was intended for or received by the ears of the first listeners? And when, where, for whom was it put into the present permanent form? If a super-committee of the foremost living scholars were to answer these questions in a chorus of unanimity, I still would not know.

Subsuming it in a flash, I the Englishborn* American Jew, with my heart equally in America and Israel, accept the Shakespeare–English Bible–Hebrew Bible synthesis that is me gratefully and completely. If there are odd bits of me elsewhere, that is so much to the good. And if I seem to consider the Bible as nothing but literature, that is because to do more would take me out of my depth.

If I may use an Irishism, the third elements in the synthesis of me, Yiddish, is a thing apart. I grew up with it as a child, I grew away from it as a youngster and a young man—so much so that when I arrived in America at the age of nineteen I could speak only a babu Yiddish— and found it again on the East Side of New York. It was a strange encounter, at first apparently accidental, but when I got down to systematic study the language rose inside me to welcome the prompting from the outside. It has become almost as much myself as English, but less so than Hebrew. Lecturing, on occasion, in Yiddish I have had to go begging for many words and locutions; in English everything comes flying toward me at the slightest inward nod. But then again I have not read Yiddish with anything like the fullness of English—though Lord knows how much of English literature is a blank to me.

What sets Yiddish apart for me is a sort of despair. It is so difficult to translate, and the difficulty receives circular reinforcement from the absence of a solid body of Yiddish literature translated into English—or for that matter, any other modern language. It is a self-perpetuating

---

* Technically Roumanian-born and brought to England at the age of five. Of the Roumanian language the only traces in me are some words I picked up in the Roumanian subsection of the Manchester ghetto.

alienation from what we call "the great world." It gives me quite a turn, as we used to say in England, to think that the Yiddish poetry of Chaim Nachman Bialik (he was equally great in Hebrew and in Yiddish) and of Aaron Zeitlin and Jacob Glatstein and Chaim Grade will probably never be known beyond the faithful circle of Yiddish readers. Each of them "struck one clear chord to reach the ears of God," but He has not seen fit to let its echo come to the ears of others than the faithful. The meagre translations that exist, though sometimes better than passable, are an infinitesimal fragment of the whole corpus.

The same melancholy pervades me when I brood over the Yiddish prose writers. Sholem Aleichem is a resounding exception and I am satisfied to be remembered as his herald in English. Two other Yiddish writers seem to have broken the spell—Sholem Asch and Bashevis Singer; on examination it will be revealed that they are not Yiddish writers— that is, insofar as they have found a large English audience—but writers in Yiddish. Though they treat of Jewish subjects there is no Yiddishness in them. This is especially true of Sholem Asch. In his successful books he kept an eye on the outside world and translatability—which is why I found him so easy to translate. I never "translated" Sholem Aleichem; I wrote round him. I did the same with Y. L. Peretz, who is almost Sholem Aleichem's equal, but he never caught on. One man haunts me with special insistence as an inheritor of unfulfilled renown; Zalman Shnaiur, who, like Bialik, wrote with equal freedom and grace in Hebrew and in Yiddish. I should have done with *Shklover Yidn, The Jews of Shklov,* what I did with *The World of Sholom Aleichem.* Now it is too late, unless a younger generation of translators is prepared to take the gamble.

The faithful will be around for quite a time; their numbers may even increase. By "the faithful" I mean those readers and speakers of Yiddish who have fastened to the language as I did, not the happy-go-lucky pickers-up of phrases here and there, or those who remember only what they overheard from parents and grandparents and remember that little badly. How did the scores or hundreds of Yiddish words and phrases—often distorted and debased or given new shadings—find their way into American English? I believe vaudeville in big cities, with their high proportion of Jewish spectators, explains much of it. These last were always good for a laugh when a familiar Yiddish word was thrown in: the sudden, scattered laughter was infectious ("What did he say?"), an explanation from the performer usually followed and the fashion spread. In the borsht circuit, where nearly the entire audience nurtures a vestigial Yiddish, the appeal to gregariousness, security, separateness, insideness, being in the know is irresistible. Between them, the two overlapping types of audience launched the words on a public always susceptible to novelty, the latest thing and the exotic. What happened to Yiddish in the sequel is beyond the Divine compassion.

The horror of it may be mitigated by an awareness that this gallimaufry of disjecta membra of the Yiddish language is not the Yiddish language, as most Jews with a smidgin of Yiddish believe. Their belief has a touching quality of obstinacy and pride—"Sure I know Yiddish: chutzpah, beigel, gelfilte fish, boychik, nudnik, mazel tov, kosher, feh, shtik, shema yisroel!"—reflecting a new-found affection. Some of the words have permanent value, and will rise out of the vulgar and vernacular into general acceptance; others will sink into outmoded slang and disappear. It is an interesting collection but a thing of anguish to the faithful.

Like the Bible, the Yiddish language loses its meaning if not seen under its meta-literary aspect. Both were the product not of art for art's sake, but of art for God's sake. Yes, Yiddish too. You cannot read Yiddish intelligently as a whole without feeling God, the Sabbath, the High Holidays, the Exile, the Return at the center, all created by the Bible. If you are a veltlecher, a secularist, and unbeliever, you get at least an echo of them.

It is the Exile, or Diaspora, so vividly evoked on the Mountain of Curses, that predominates in Yiddish life and literature, even when, perhaps particularly when, over against it there rises the gaiety and playfulness of Yiddish life. The seal of a horror which the Mountain of Curses could not overtop has been set upon Yiddish. We shall find ease and welcome in America, and we shall answer with love; but freedom, even in Israel, cannot, should not erase the memory of the Holocaust. Jeremiah lamenting, "Behold, and see if there be any sorrow like unto my sorrow" may be accused of arrogance, for there had and have been exiles, exiles unnumbered, though no such repetition of exiles as Jewish diaspora history. But beyond description and understanding is the Holocaust, for none but we can grasp the conception of it; that the Jewish people wherever it can be found all over the world shall be sought out and exterminated. This is not merely Hitler's Nazism. In 1901 Eugen Dühring, a German philosopher of high standing, wrote, "On the threshold of the new century it is no longer relevant to speak of the usual half-methods or merely palliative means to be used against the Hebrew evil among the peoples. As far as I am concerned the only adequate answer to the Jewish question lies in the wiping out of the whole questionable species."

Even thus, we must not fall into an arrogance of sorrow. Since no one will want to understand, we must carry this memory with us unspoken, only hinted at. We must also remember that Yiddish is a mirror of the Diaspora in its totality, with all its possibilities. Thus it must be remembered in Israel too. There and in the Diaspora a cultivated—I will not even say scholarly—Jew cannot do without at least a fair grounding in Yiddish, just as the pious Talmud Jew took and takes it for granted that he should be able to read and understand the Aramaic of the *Zohar,* the Kaddish, the Kol Nidre, the *ho lachmo anyo,* and a ketubah (wedding contract). Thus, to sum it up, the educated American Jewish Jew must be grounded in the English of Shakespeare and the King James Version, the Hebrew Bible and Yiddish. At a pinch he can substitute for Shakespeare quite a number of geniuses all the way from Chaucer to W. H. Auden, but the King James translation and the Hebrew Bible (and, yes, the Siddur) are indispensable.

(1972)

SOURCES

Chaim Zhitlowsky: "What Is Jewish Secular Culture?" from *Oifn Sheydveg* (Paris, August 1939), pp. 152–59, translated from Yiddish by the editor of the present volume; "The National Poetic Rebirth of the Jewish Religion," from *Gezamelte Shriften* (1912), 4:243–61, translated from Yiddish by Percy Matenko and the editor.

Morris Raphael Cohen: "The Piety of an Agnostic" and "Religion," from *A Dreamer's Journey* (Glencoe, Ill.: Free Press, 1949), pp. 229–36 and 211–18.

Horace M. Kallen: "Is There a Jewish View of Life?" and "What Price 'Jewish Living'?" from *Of Them Which Say They Are Jews,* edited by Judah Pilch (New York: Bloch Publishing Co., 1954), pp. 104–6 and 113–18.

Liebman Hersch: "My Jewishness," from *Mein Yiddishkeit* (Geneva, 1944), translated from Yiddish and abridged by Percy Matenko and the editor.

Shmuel Niger: "What I Believe as a Jew," from *Yisroel: Folk un Land* (Chicago: L. M. Stein Publishing Co., 1952), pp. 7–24, translated from Yiddish and abridged by the editor.

Yudel Mark: "Jewishness and Secularism" (abridged version of "Yidish-keit un Veltlekhkayt"), from *Shul-Pinkes* (Chicago: Sholem Aleichem Folk Institute, 1948), pp. 9–50, translated from Yiddish by the editor.

Tsivyon: "Jewishness and Faith," from *Far Fuftsik Yor Geklibene Shriftn* (New York: Elias Laub Publishing Co., 1948), pp. 24–27, translated from Yiddish and abridged by Percy Matenko and the editor.

Albert Einstein: "Just What Is a Jew?" from *Der Yidisher Gedank in der Nayer Tsait,* compiled and edited by Abraham Menes (New York: Congress for Jewish Culture, 1957), pp. 375–78, translated from Yiddish by Percy Matenko and the editor; "Jewish Ideals" and "Is There a Jewish World Outlook?" from *Albert Einstein: Mein Weltbild,* edited by Carl Seelig (Zurich: Ullstein Buch Nr. 65, Europa Verlag, 1965), pp. 89–91, translated from German by Percy Matenko and the editor.

I. L. Peretz: Selections from *Peretz,* translated and edited by Sol Liptzin (New York: YIVO Institute, 1947), pp. 354–78 and 342–50.

Ahad HaAm: "Imitation and Assimilation," from *Selected Essays by Ahad HaAm,* translated from Hebrew by Leon Simon (Philadelphia: Jewish Publication Society, 1944), pp. 117–24; "Judaism and Jewish Nationalism," from *Essays, Letters, Memoirs,* translated from Hebrew by Leon Simon (Oxford: East & West Library, 1946), pp. 265–67.

Simon Dubnow: "The Doctrine of Jewish Nationalism" and "The Secret of Survival and the Law of Survival," from *Nationalism and History,* edited by Koppel S. Pinson (Philadelphia: Jewish Publication Society, 1958), pp. 86–99 and 325–35.

Israel Zinberg: "Two Philosophies in Jewish Life," from *Cultural Historical Studies* (New York: M. Shklarsky Publisher, 1949), pp. 70–86, translated from Yiddish by the editor.

Z. V. Latsky-Bertoldy: "On Jewish Heresy," from *Erd-Geist* (Kiev, 1918), pp. 19–37, translated from Yiddish by the editor.

Abraham Golomb: "From Secular to Integral Jewishness," from *Tsu die Heikhn fun Yidishn Geist* (Paris, 1971), pp. 174–81, translated from Yiddish and abridged by Percy Matenko and the editor.

Hayim Greenberg: "The Eternity of Israel" and "The Future of American Jewry," from *An Inner Eye,* edited by Shlomo Katz (New York: Jewish Frontier Association, 1964), 2:304–11 and 2:69–76.

Maurice Samuel: "The Long Way Round," from *Congress Weekly,* June 14, 1954; "My Three Mother-Tongues," from *Midstream,* March 1972.

H. Leivick: "Yiddish Literature: Guardian of Our People's Wholeness" (address given before World Congress for Jewish Culture session on literature, New York City, 1948), from *Essays and Speeches* (New York: World Congress for Jewish Culture, 1963), pp. 158–63, translated from Yiddish by the editor.

Nokhem Shtif: "Humanism in Early Yiddish Literature," (Berlin: Klal Publishing House, 1922), pp. 50–60. Abridged and translated from Yiddish by Percy Matenko and the editor.

INDEX

297